To,
Jim
Happy Christmas (2016)
Lots of love,
Catherine & Ian
x

# *A Brush with Brown*

OVERLEAF *Croome Court, detail, before the building of the Chinese bridge (watercolour).*

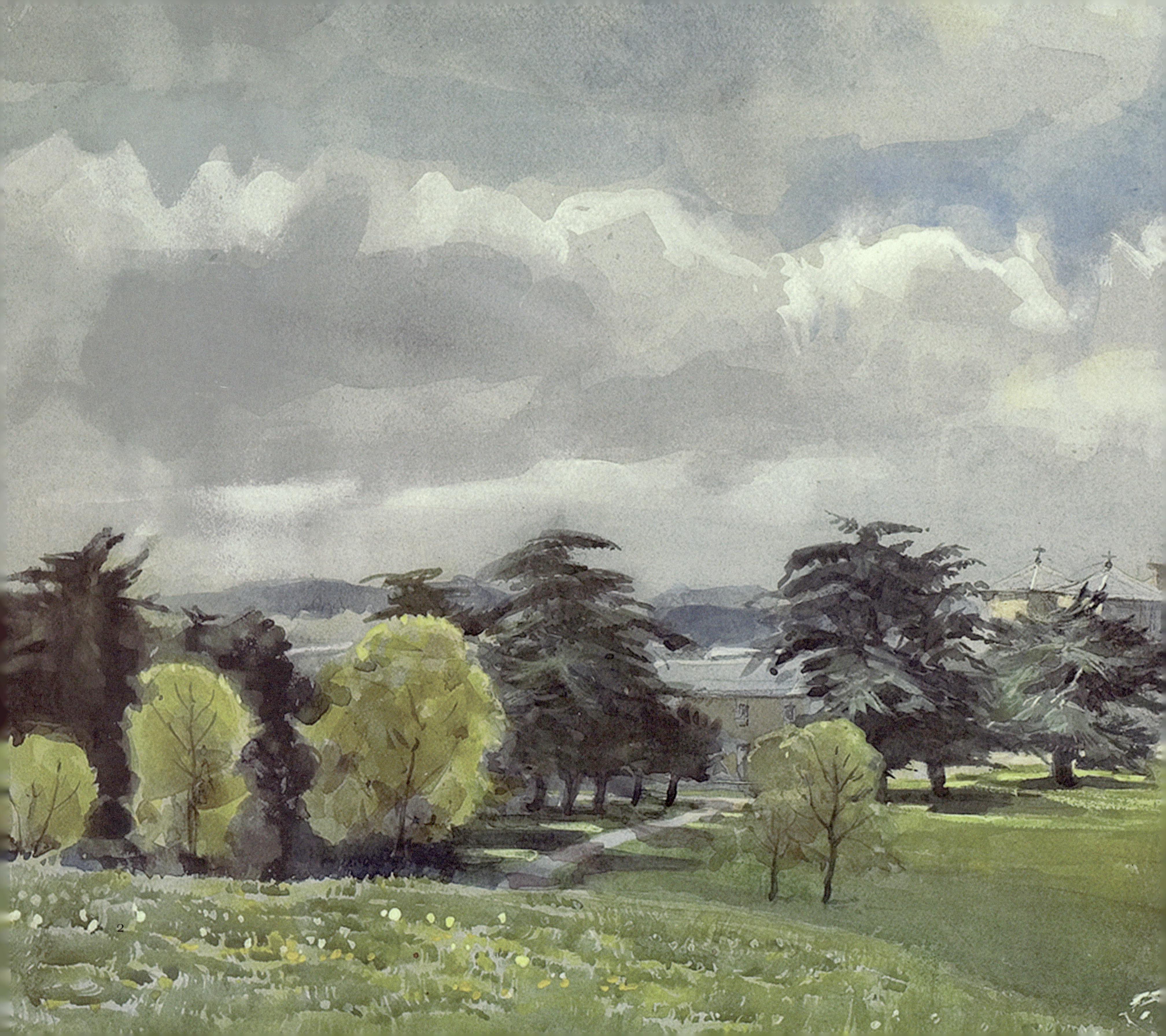

# *A Brush with Brown*

## THE LANDSCAPES OF 'CAPABILITY' BROWN

Tim Scott Bolton

FOREWORD BY H.R.H. THE PRINCE OF WALES

THE DOVECOTE PRESS

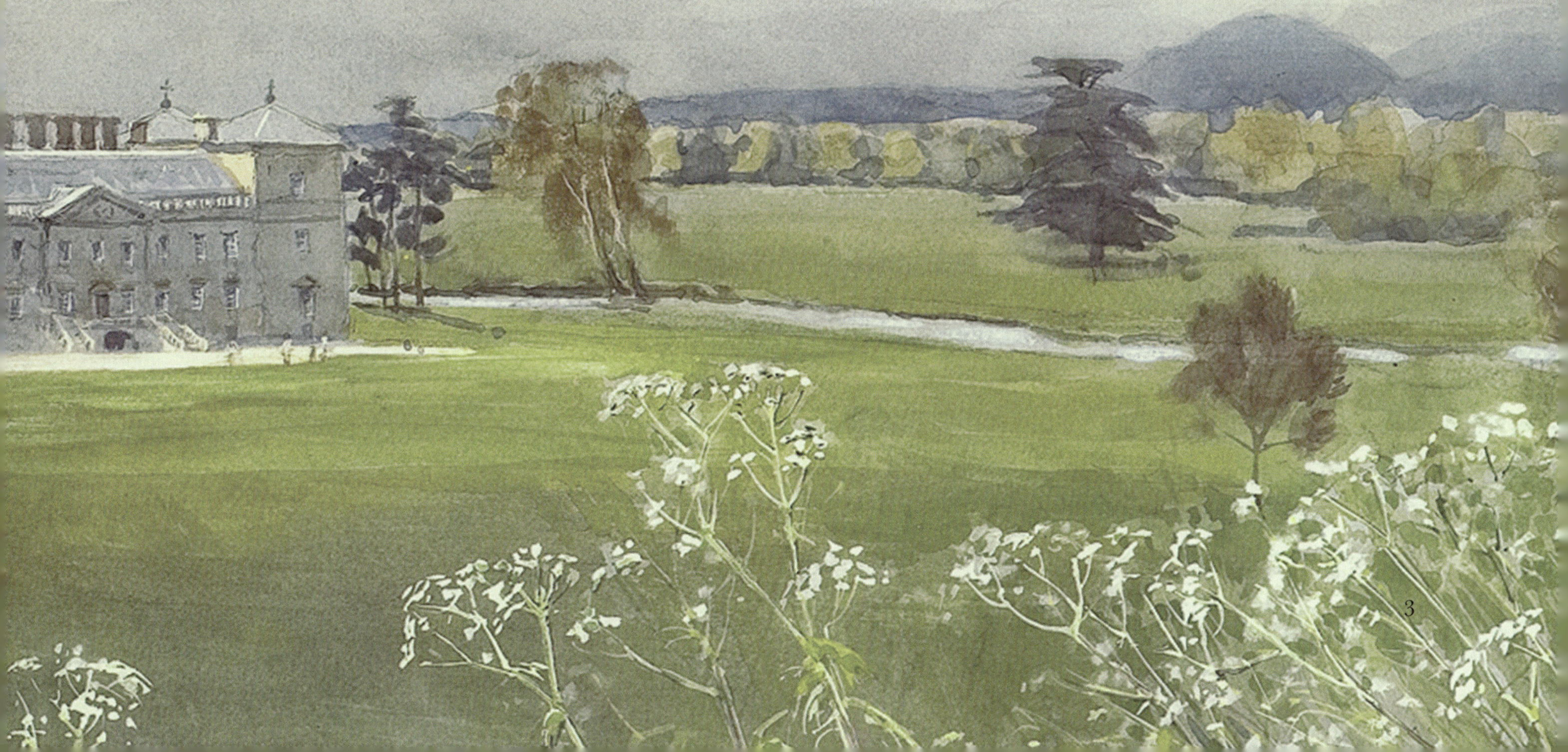

*for Tricia*

First published in 2016 by The Dovecote Press Ltd
Stanbridge, Wimborne Minster, Dorset BH21 4JD

ISBN 978-0-9929151-3-1



Designed by Humphrey Stone

Typeset in Baskerville

Printed by GraphyCems on 150 gsm Munken Pure and bound
by them in Navarra, Spain.

All papers used by The Dovecote Press are natural, recyclable products
made from wood grown in sustainable, well-managed forests.

A CIP catalogue record for this book is available
from the British Library



1 3 5 7 9 8 6 4 2

# CONTENTS

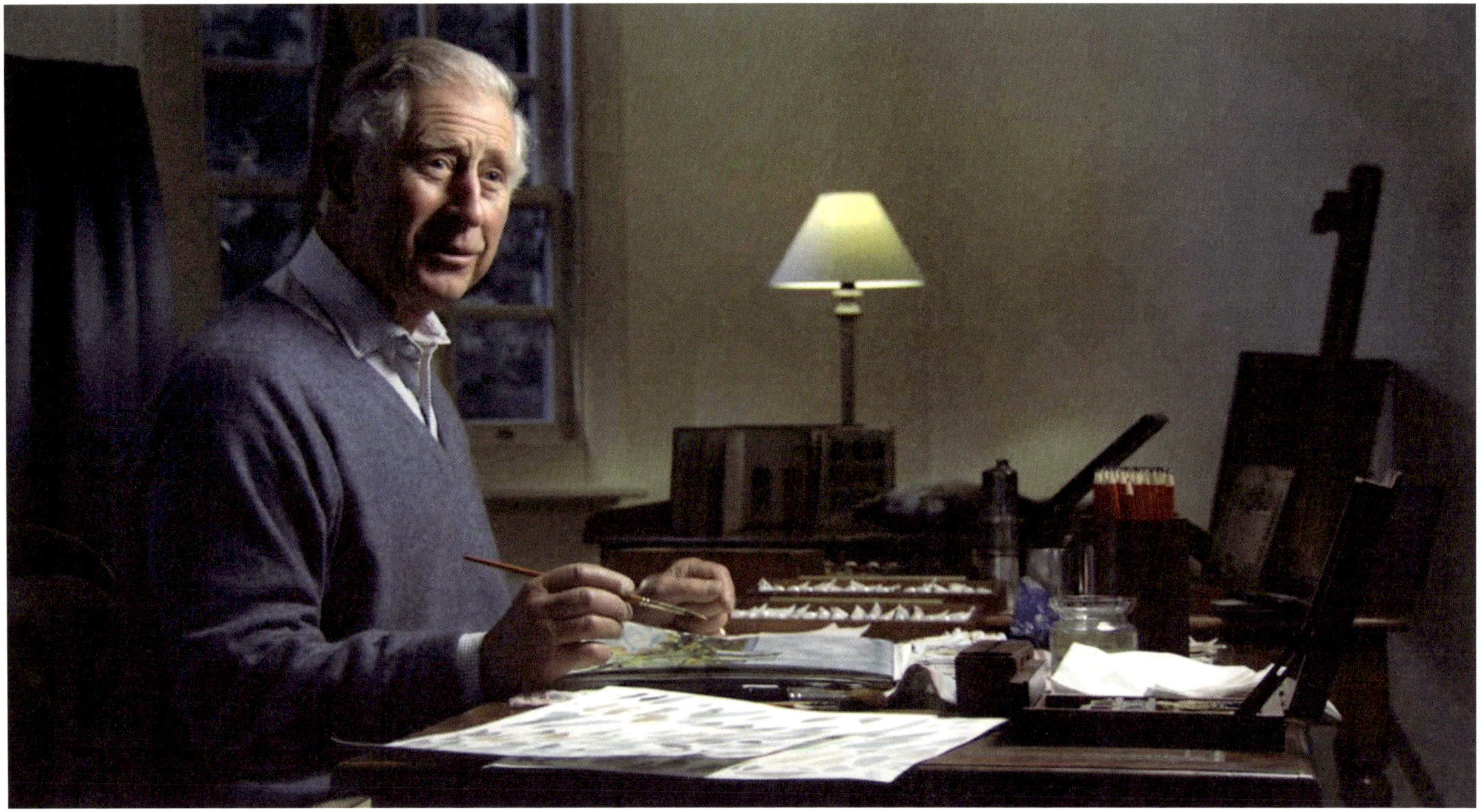

*H. R. H. The Prince of Wales during the filming of 'Royal Paintbox' (a Margy Kinmonth Film © www.FoxtrotFilms.com).*

CLARENCE HOUSE

'All gardening is landscape painting' declared Pope in 1734 at the start of the great English landscape revolution, and 'Capability' Brown set out, twenty years later when the movement was at its height and he the chief architect, with the intention of creating a painter's paradise. Hence, on the tri-centennial of his birth in Northumberland in 1716, it is the most natural thing that Tim Scott Bolton should have chosen to paint some forty views of his sublime and now perfectly mature landscapes and publish them in tribute to his colossal achievement.

Painters are naturally drawn to Brown's landscapes. His patrons saw the idealized landscapes he conjured as physical realisations of 17th century paintings of the world of classical antiquity. His work was the apogee of the movement which started in an age which described itself as 'Augustan'; the age of Pope and Kent and Burlington. It is almost impossible to imagine, even looking at all those wonderful Kip engravings, the colossal rigid formality of the surroundings of the great manors and estates of England in the mid-18th century as Brown approached them. But where Kent jumped the garden gate, Brown was to banish the hand of man for tens of square miles and create a seemingly 'natural' bucolic paradise of pasture, woodland and great singled-out and clumped park trees. He found this 'Virgilian' perfection already nascent in the folds of the English countryside, waiting to be discovered. In fact, his detractors argued, his artifice created landscapes which 'differ very little from common fields, so closely is Nature copied in most of them'.

Lancelot Brown's relationship with my own ancestors was not entirely without its complications. Spurned by the circles of King George II, despite being at the height of his powers and fashion in the 1760s whilst working on Blenheim and Chatsworth, it was King George III who, as a man with a fascination for agriculture and farming, and as someone who would have completely understood the Elysian beauty of Transylvanian farming and landscape, brought Brown into the fold of Royal patronage. In July 1764, he made Brown Chief Master Gardener at Hampton Court. Brown went on completely to re-structure Buckingham House in his inimitable way, the foundations of which survive today as the gardens of Buckingham Palace.

Brown has remained the most famous of all landscape garden designers, his peerless and powerfully influential gardens exhibit his masterly handling of ingredients. He made the new style and conjured from the old a beauty, intrinsically there, 'of fields and woods, herds of cattle and swarms of bees'. As a very amateur painter, I can only feel profound admiration for Tim Scott Bolton's wonderful celebration in this book of many things that I cherish, as well as his talent in bravura in its execution.

Charles

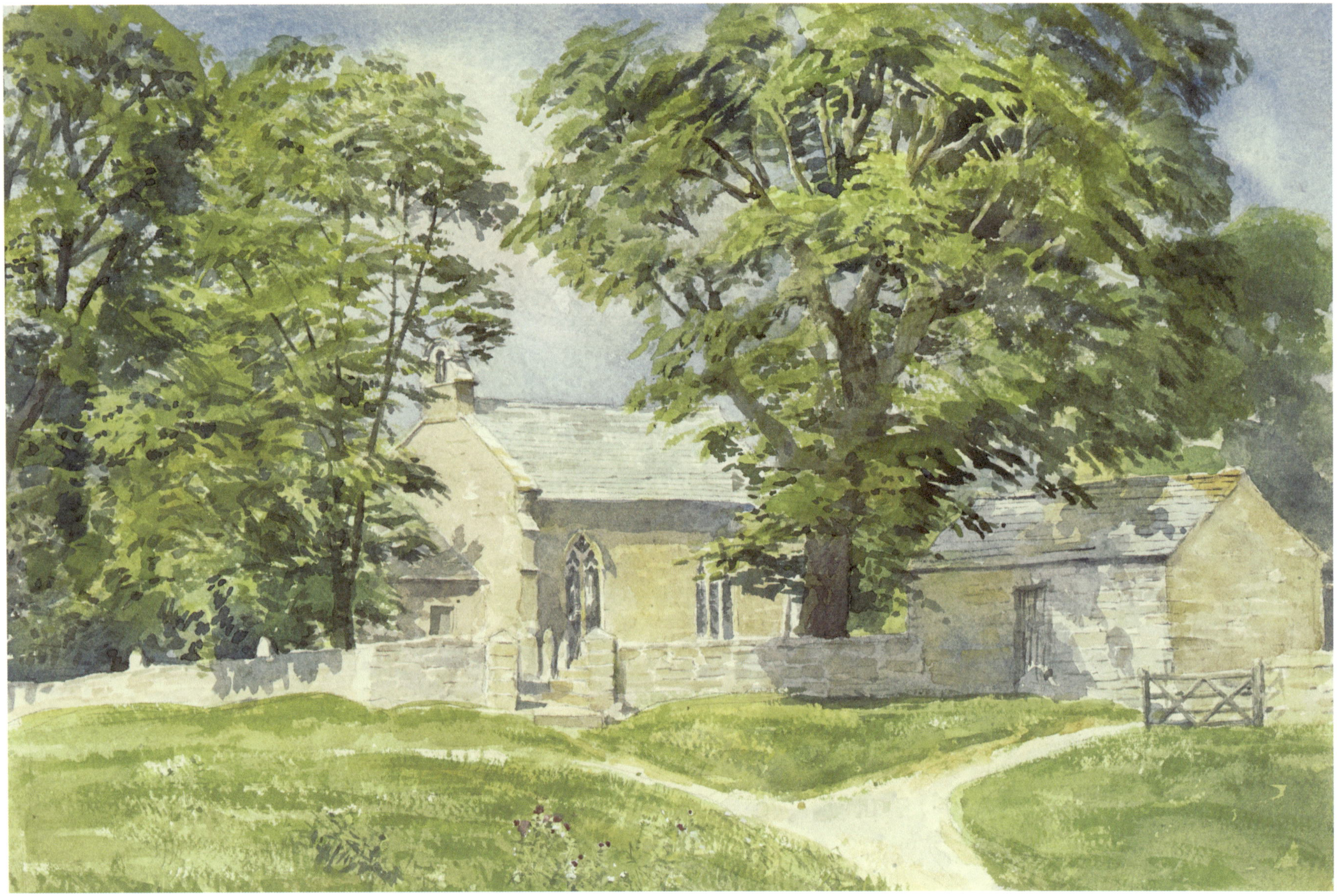

*Kirkharle, St Wilfrid's Church, where Lancelot Brown was baptised (watercolour).*

# INTRODUCTION

*At Blenheim, Croome and Caversham we trace*
*Salvator's wildness, Claude's enlivening grace,*
*Cascades and Lakes as fine as Risdale drew*
*While natures vary'd in each charming view.*
*To paint his works would Poussin's Powers require,*
*Milton's sublimity and Dryden's fire.*
*Born to grace Nature, and her works complete*
*With all that's beautiful, sublime and great!*
*For him each Muse enwreathes the Laurel Crown,*
*And consecrates to Fame immortal Brown.*

ANON

## *Lancelot Brown's Life*

I am writing this in the lazy heat of an Indian noon shaded by one of several chhatris among the domes and castellations of a maharaja's palace. I look down on a broad river in whose muddy waters a crocodile idles by, hardly stirring, and can't help speculating what Lancelot 'Capability' Brown would have done with all this.

Much is here that would have existed in eighteenth-century England. Formal gardens surround the palace. Castellated walls keep the outer landscape at bay. There is a plentiful supply of labour still digging ditches and moving earth around by hand, or with the help of an ox and cart. There is a noisy and unsightly village too close to the big house, which in this Indian case includes a temple from where a cacophony of drums and horns continues long into the night. Brown would almost certainly have suggested the villagers and their houses be moved, as was the case at Milton Abbey and Bowood, among others.

In fact twenty-first century India would be somewhere an eighteenth century English observer would recognize – with its earthy smells, the calm rhythm of agriculture largely done by man and animal, the crowded villages with sometimes the great house whose life is totally unrelated to that of the people outside. Of course, now it is the tourist who sits in this gilded cage, but once it would have been the maharaja who, under different circumstances, might have been Lancelot Brown's client.

### KIRKHARLE 1716–1739

I was introduced to the idea of embarking on this book by Kitty and John Anderson, who happen to own the Kirkharle estate where Lancelot Brown was born in 1716. He was christened in St Wilfrid's Church, which is built of warm mellow stone and remains unchanged to this day – hence my wish to paint it. Kirkharle lies in the Wansbeck valley of Northumberland and Brown's ancestry was of local yeomen farming stock. His father was steward to Sir Thomas Loraine and both died when Lancelot was still a boy. Thomas Loraine's heir, William, was an enlightened and progressive landlord who allowed Brown's widow and family of three daughters and three sons to remain housed on the estate. He might also have helped educate the Brown boys at the nearby schoolhouse at Cambo, paternalistically encouraging them in other ways – such as allowing access to Kirkharle's library.

It was here that the young Brown would probably first have come across such books as Stephen Switzer's *The Nobleman, Gentleman and Gardener's Recreation*, and Batty Langley's *New Principles of Gardening* of 1728 which suggested planting aesthetically pleasing walks and groves. This new pioneering approach to the naturalistic and picturesque in landscape gardening licensed landlords to profitably use their land for grazing livestock and growing timber in areas previously clipped and pruned at great cost.

At the age of 16 Lancelot was employed by Sir William in a number of improvements that were being undertaken on the estate. It was a form of apprenticeship for his later success, providing a thorough grounding in land reclamation, drainage, husbandry and horticulture.

### THE OPEN ROAD AND STOWE 1739–1751

In 1739, at the age of 23, Brown left Kirkharle armed only with his limited experience, a good deal of optimism and two introductions from the Loraines. Thanks to them he was engaged to create a lake and other landscaping at Kiddington Hall in Oxfordshire.

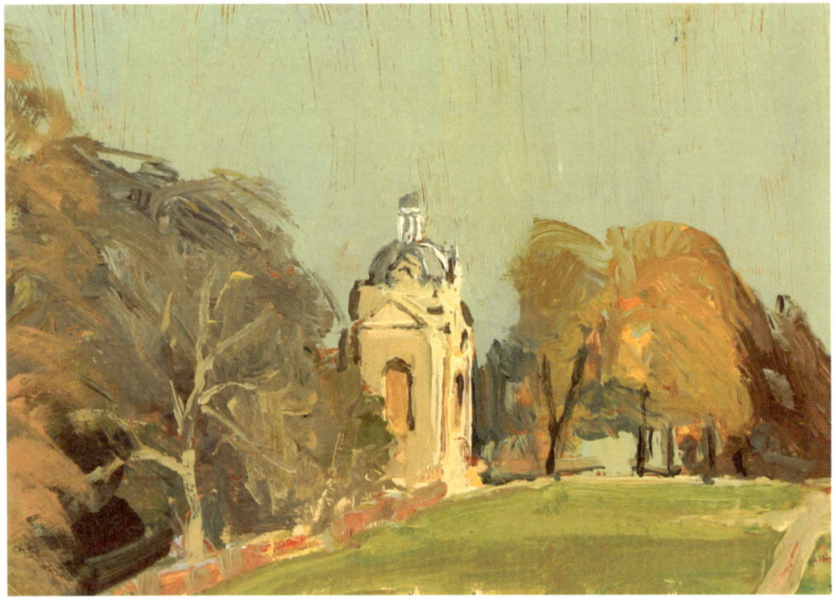

*Stowe, Boycott Pavilions where Bridget and Lancelot Brown lived (oil).*

Not much is known of this period in 'Capability's' life. He spent time in Boston, Lincolnshire, for it was there he became acquainted with the Wayet family, courting and eventually becoming betrothed to their daughter Bridget. He also gained additional experience in land drainage and management of water through the Wayet's involvement in the drainage of the fens.

Lancelot and Bridget were finally married at Stowe in 1744, by which time Brown was Viscount Cobham's Clerk of Works and beginning to earn a reputation as a talented and skilled landscape gardener, particularly where water was involved.

Viscount Cobham was not above lending Brown to friends and relatives, hence his work at Wakefield Lawn and Nuneham Paddocks. In 1749, following the death of the Viscount, his nephew and heir, Richard Grenville, brought his own staff to Stowe and there was no place for Brown. He and Bridget continued to live at Stowe for another two years, before finally moving south to London.

### HAMMERSMITH 1751–1764

On leaving Stowe, Lancelot had enough work in prospect at Kirtlington, Wakefield Lawn, Belhus, Warwick Castle and Charlecote and others to become an independent landscape surveyor. It was probably George Lucy of Charlecote who offered the 33-year-old Brown a house to rent in Hammersmith, then a hamlet adjoining the village of Fulham with a handful of elegant houses on the Mall by the Thames. The river was a lifeline to many thriving local businesses, such as sailmakers and boatbuilders. The rich fertile soil made it popular with market gardeners and nurserymen, who all sent their produce downstream by boat to the great city of London.

Two nurserymen in particular were of use to Brown, providing him with useful contacts and supplying him with trees and shrubs – sometimes in their tens of thousands. They were John Williamson in Kensington Gore and Grey's Nursery in Fulham, the latter supplying many of the cedar of Lebanon which grace the majority of the properties designed by Brown. This tree became one of the hallmarks of a Brown landscape, and some great gnarled specimens he planted survive to this day, often dwarfing the house nearby.

It was probably John Williamson who introduced him to the Bartram's box scheme, whereby selected seeds and plants were carefully packed in moss and shipped from Pennsylvania by the botanist John Bartram. Not unlike the organic vegetable box schemes now, Bartram selected what was supplied. These were received by enthusiastic collectors, many of whom were Lancelot's clients, all of them eager to plant the extraordinary variety of shrubs and trees being imported from Britain's North American colony, such as maples, robinias, ailanthus, tulip trees and red oak.

Soon after settling in Hammersmith, Brown met Henry Holland (the Elder), who lived nearby. Holland wore two hats, working as a mason on mansions for various architects, and designing and building a number of houses around Fulham. When Lancelot received instructions from Lord Coventry to comprehensively redesign his estate at Croome, he turned to Holland to build the main mansion. The Browns and Hollands became close friends. Later his son, also Henry, married Lancelot's daughter, Bridget (confusingly the same name as her mother), further unifying the two families.

Success breeds success. After he had satisfactorily obtained his first commissions other work poured in, beginning with Warwick Castle.

Although Brown is chiefly known for his landscapes, he was also concerned with considerable building projects. At the time, few architects of any stature were practising. The great Palladian designers such as Vanbrugh and Kent had either died or retired and the new generation, the likes of Chambers and Adam, were only emerging. It was thought important that the buildings and landscape surrounding the country house should be a cohesive whole, so what better than to commission one man to do both?

It appears that the arrangements made were totally flexible; sometimes just a plan was drawn and occasionally, on execution, the genius of the design was claimed by the owner! On other occasions Brown would be responsible for all design and for overseeing the work. The landowner might provide such things as horses and carts or some of the labour. It must have been complicated to draw up accurate estimates with all these variables, but with experience his skill

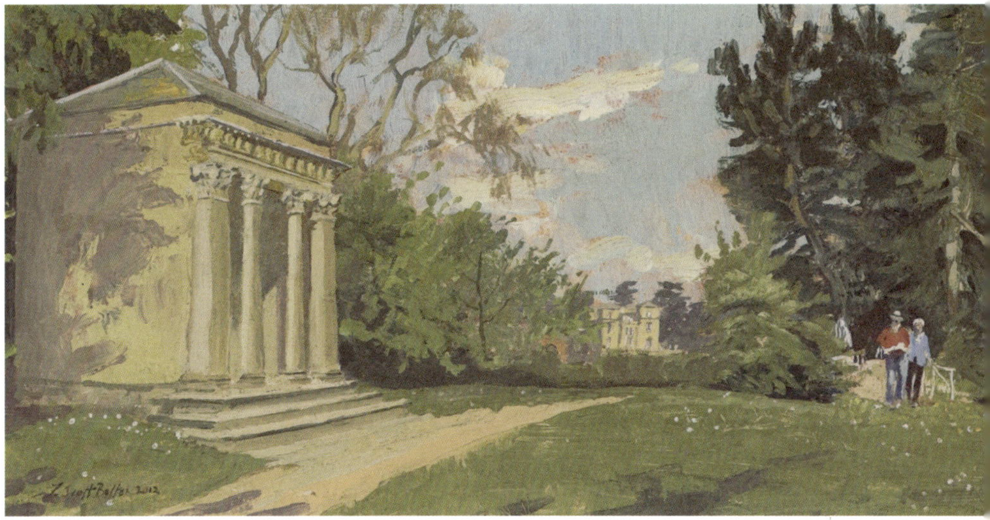

*Croome Court, the Island Temple surrounded by the lake (oil).*

at working out costs became keenly honed. The amounts charged by Brown varied from a few hundred pounds to a substantial £21,500 at Blenheim.

The date I have put against each property was the one on which Brown first visited the site to study its 'capabilities'. This is not necessarily when most of the work was done, indeed some jobs took many years. Burghley, for instance, took most of his working life. He returned there regularly, becoming a close friend of Lord Exeter, an intimacy mirrored at other properties.

Brown was very 'hands on' and spent much of the year on the road, both looking at new work and supervising existing jobs. This was complex and at the mercy of the weather. One of his talents must have been in employing the right subordinates, for he had a pool of trusted foremen to oversee various jobs on-site. He was an asthmatic and not robust, periodically suffering bouts of ill-health.

From the contemporary portrait of Lancelot Brown by Nathaniel Dance one sees a face not only humorous but shrewd. It conveys a strong man with a prominent nose and dark eyebrows and eyes. His clothing and wig are subdued, suggesting someone who was trustworthy and not flamboyant. He was notorious for dreadful puns, but despite them was respected and genuinely liked by his clients. It is

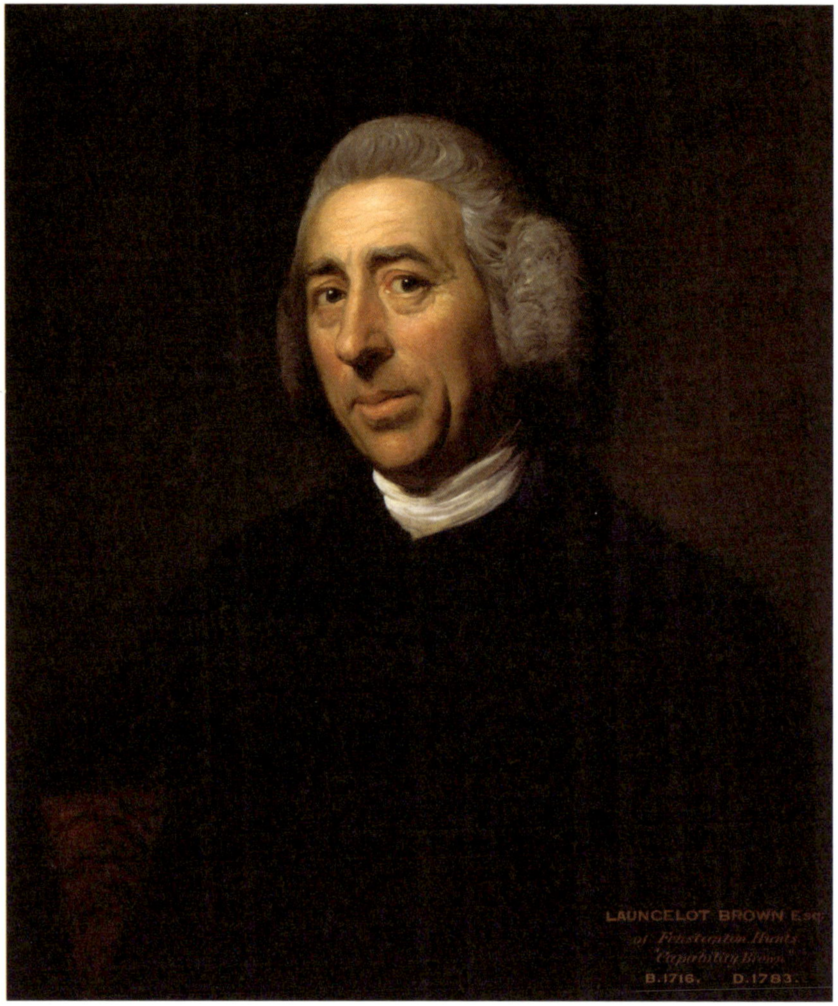


*Lancelot Brown, one of two copies of the portrait by Nathaniel Dance, courtesy, National Portrait Gallery.*

a tribute to Brown's talent that there were not more disputes: one notable exception was with Sir John Griffin Griffin at Audley End, which I've written about later.

The principal new works started in the early 1750s were Petworth, Kirtlington and Burghley, all of which I have included. Others, such as Belhus, Moor Park and Beechwood, have been altered or destroyed and therefore have been omitted.

A number of ducal commissions were undertaken in the late 1750s and early 1760s. These include Alnwick (Duke of Northumberland), Chatsworth, (Duke of Devonshire), Ashridge (Duke of Bridgwater), Harewood, for the mere Mr Edward Lascelles, and Castle Ashby for the Earl of Northampton.

## ROYAL GARDENER HAMPTON COURT 1764–1783

In 1764 Lancelot Brown was appointed 'Master Gardener' and 'Surveyor to His Majesty's Gardens and Waters at Hampton Court'. Later that year he was also appointed Gardener at St James's. The duties were not onerous and the salary reasonably generous, £2000 a year plus a house; in this case Wilderness House near the great maze at Hampton Court. It was here that Brown happily lived with his family for the rest of his life.

Brown's appointment brought prestige as well as security. It was his golden age and henceforth he never lacked commissions. George III took a keen interest in gardening matters and suggested Brown should 'improve' the layout at Hampton Court, which daringly he declined because he recognised the importance of the existing gardens. Brown has been accused by his detractors of destroying many fine formal gardens, perhaps with some justifica-

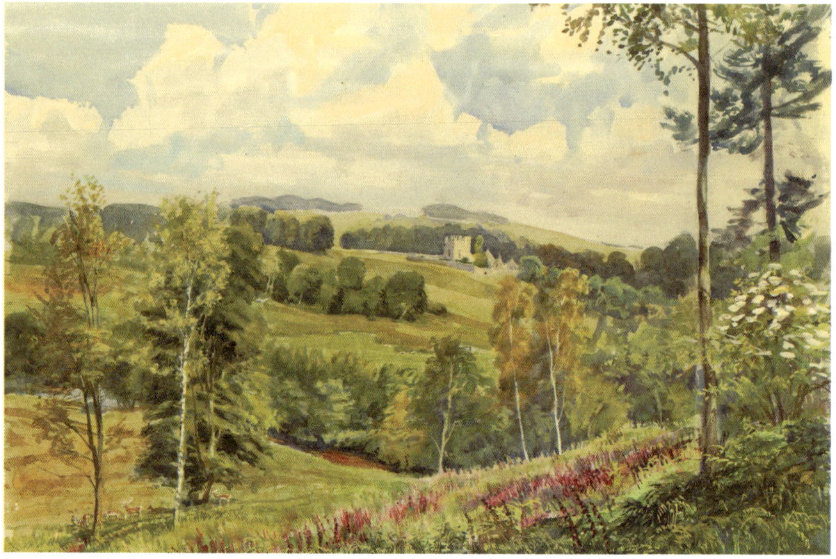

*Hulne Park on the Alnwick estate (gouache).*

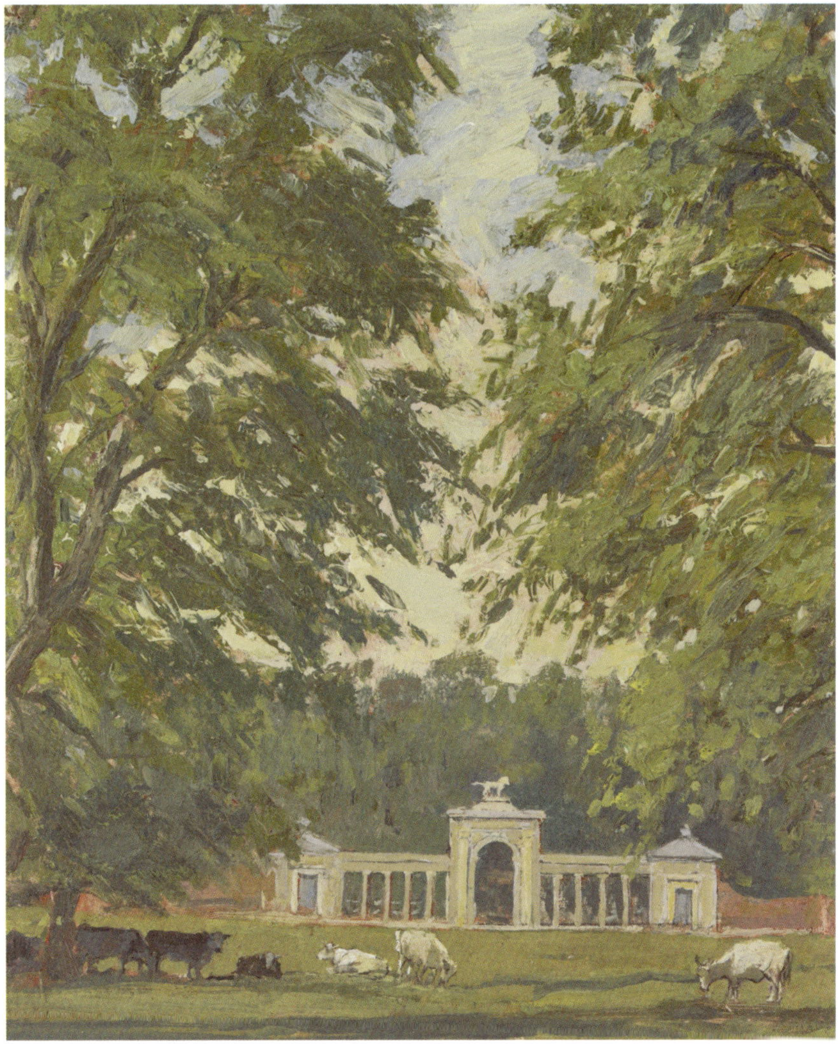

*Syon. The lion gate designed by Robert Adam (oil).*

tion, but he also spared many former features when he considered them worth retaining in his new design.

Lancelot Brown was slowly accumulating a considerable fortune. His £2000 stipend and other earnings probably annually brought in about £6000. He perhaps felt that money in Drummond's Bank (where he banked for much of his career) should be translated into something more substantial, and in the eighteenth century this meant the acquisition of land. Land understandably holds a special status that no other commodity can rival. It brings with it respect and often more tangible honours with entry into the hallowed ranks of the squirearchy and nobility.

While Brown was working at Castle Ashby in 1766 he learnt that his client, Lord Northampton, was in negotiation to sell his estate at Fenstanton to Brown's banker, Henry Drummond. It seemed probable that his lordship was in financial difficulty and needed to raise money. Brown wrote to Northampton saying he would be willing to buy the property if the sale fell through. This eventually happened and Lancelot became the proud owner of the two villages of Fenny Stanton (now Fenstanton) and Hilton, 1000 acres and the Lordship of the Manor.

In the short term the acquisition proved a poisoned chalice. In 1770 the position of High Sheriff of Huntingdonshire was thrust on Brown's unwilling shoulders by the Earl of Sandwich, an honour he could ill afford the time to do. Lancelot Brown, his elder son, was in the Earl's employment and as First Lord of the Admiralty the Earl also helped another son, John, enter the Royal Navy, so Brown was

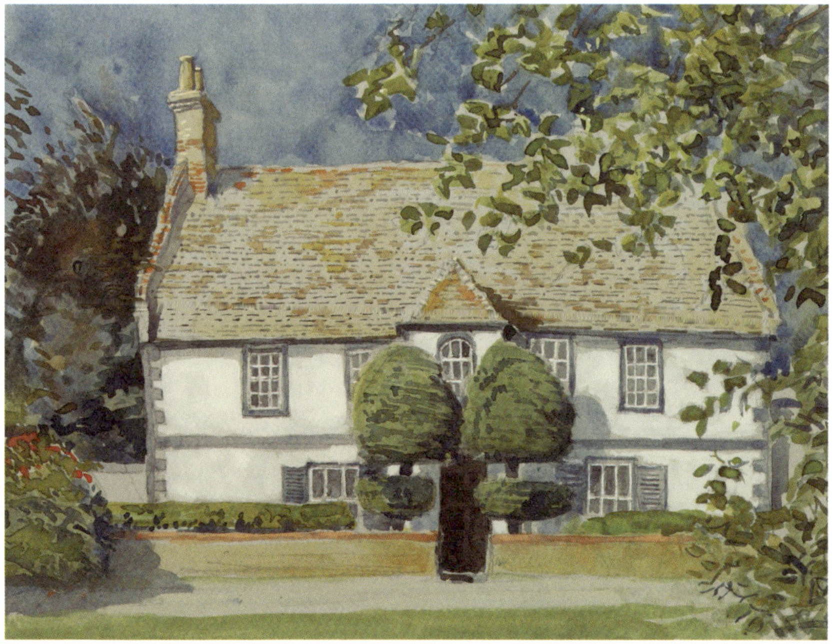

*Fenstanton Manor (watercolour).*

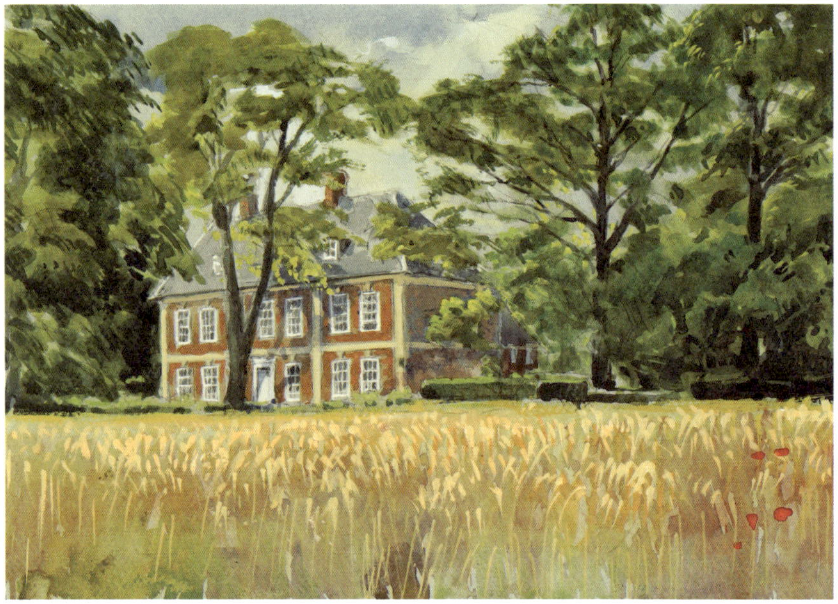

*Fenstanton Manor Farm. Both these houses were on the estate that Brown purchased (watercolour).*

as good as obliged to take on the duties of High Sheriff. As it turned out he was relieved of some of the work because he had the prudence to call his elder son by his own name, Lancelot. The son often deputised for the father, and many were none the wiser!

I too had an onorous duty in Fenstanton in that I had promised to give a talk on Brown to the local garden society. Disconcertingly, in the front row sat Jane Brown, whose book *Lancelot 'Capability' Brown, The Omnipotent Magician* was the fount of most of my knowledge. In talking to her and other local people it appeared that the estate was rarely visited by Brown and there was some doubt as to which house he might have stayed at. The two most distinguished houses had both been tenanted and, as either might have been contenders for his residence, I painted a small picture of each. The landscape is flat but has a watery charm with its rows of willows and big East Anglian skies. Although some plans were drawn up for the estate little work was done here and Lancelot Brown's only permanent residence is six feet somewhere in the graveyard. A gravestone proclaims 'Lancelot Brown (Capability), Lord of the Manor of Fenstanton, 1767–1783 lies buried near this spot'. Within the church is a substantial monument to his and Bridget's children.

Brown's links to Drummonds Bank brought a succession of commissions. The bank cultivated lordly clients, but a number of craftsman and artists were also customers, including James Gibbs, Johann Zoffany and Thomas Chippendale. Brown joined this elite group and in turn Drummond sought Brown's 'capabilities' at the family estate at Stanmore. Unlike Brown's account books, which are incomplete, the records of bank transactions give a good picture of the payments made to him by his clients and the scope of the work. Many payments received by Brown were passed straight on to others who, in most instances undertook building work. An example is Claremont, bought by Lord Clive (of India), where Brown was commissioned in 1769 not only to fashion the park but rebuild the house. The initial plans were drawn up by Brown but once approved he passed on the house building to Henry Holland (later his son-in-law). The total sum expended at Claremont was £27,612.16s.11p, a king's ransom which Nabob Clive could well afford.

The rejection of Sir William Chamber's proposals at Claremont in favour of Brown kindled a long-standing and simmering jealousy. The knighted establishment architect with all the appropriate classical training resented the unqualified new boy muscling in. James Paine penned similar objections in his *Plans of Noblemen and Gentlemen's Houses*: 'so we have seen a genius of this kind, who, after having been from his youth confined against his nature, to the Serpentine walks of horticulture, emerge, at once, a complete architect, and produce such things, as none but those who were born with such amazing capability, could possibly have done'. Indeed, at Croome Court Brown did boldly launch into a major building project without the experience of his peers.

From 1765 Brown's activities permeated all corners of England, from Burton Pynsent and Petworth in the south to Alnwick and Wallington in the north. The latter must have been an especially poignant return to the home of his youth. Of his brothers, John had settled at Kirkharle, acting as agent to the Loraines, and George was at Wallington working for the Blacketts. In 1770 Lancelot returned

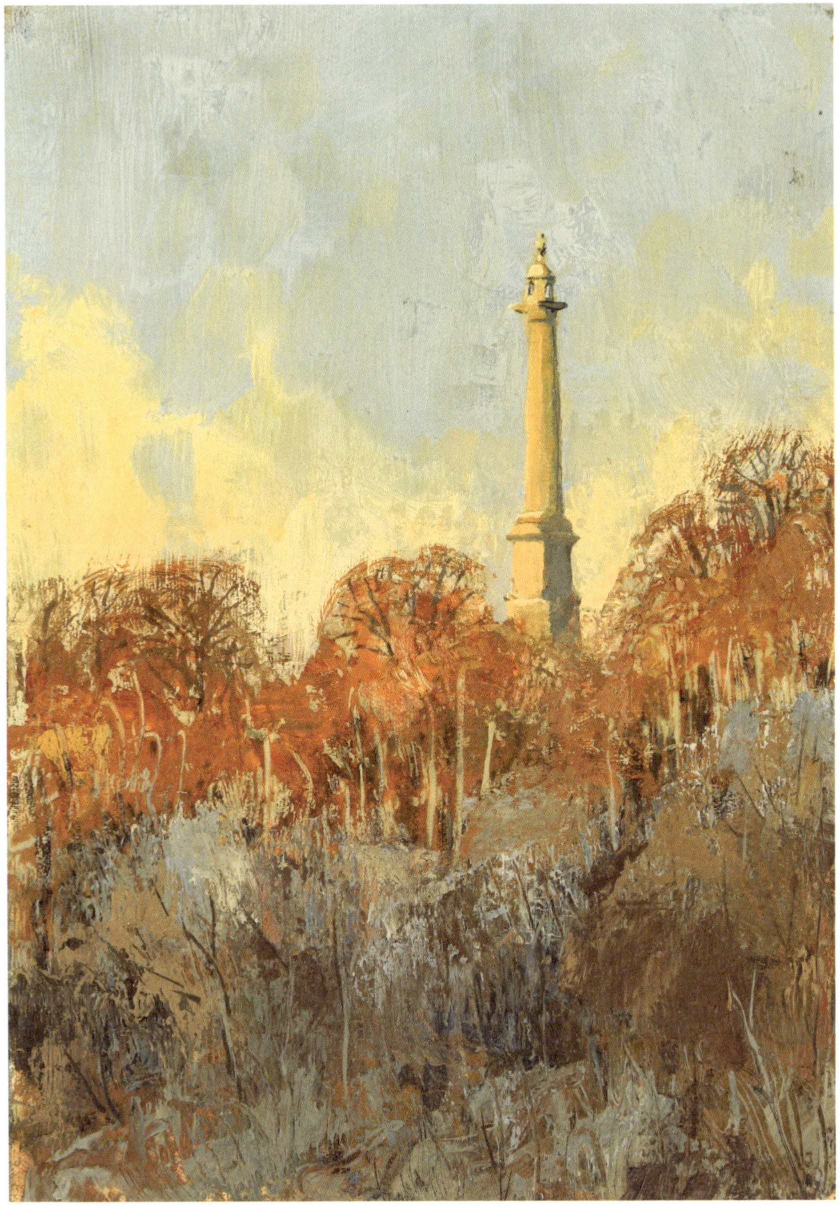

*Burton Pynsent (oil).*

as a celebrated landscape designer, commissioned by Sir Walter Calverley Blackett for alterations to the garden at Wallington and the digging of a second lake at his nearby estate at Rothley, which survives largely as Brown designed it.

'Capability' Brown almost single-handedly created the concept of an independent landscape designer and his success in his time was unsurpassed. His reputation extended throughout Europe, launching a fashion for the Jardin Anglais. One admirer was Catherine the Great, who commissioned a 1000 piece dinner service from Josiah Wedgwood, many of whose plates were illustrated with landscapes created by Brown. These include Alnwick, Audley End, Blenheim, Burghley, Chatsworth, Claremont, Roche Abbey, Syon, Sherborne Castle, Stowe and Wimpole – all of which I have painted for this book.

Like the deadly sins or days of the week, I can identify seven reasons why Brown succeeded.

Fashion. He was born in an age of change and the ideas he pursued had already been pioneered to some extent by such people as Vanbrugh and Kent. Brown further refined the development of the naturalistic landscape known as 'The English Garden'.

Technical Skill. He was an efficient and imaginative engineer who had gained wide experience, initially at Kirkharle, perhaps in the fens, and finally at Stowe where he served as clerk of works in a time of great activity and met some of the leading architects of the period.

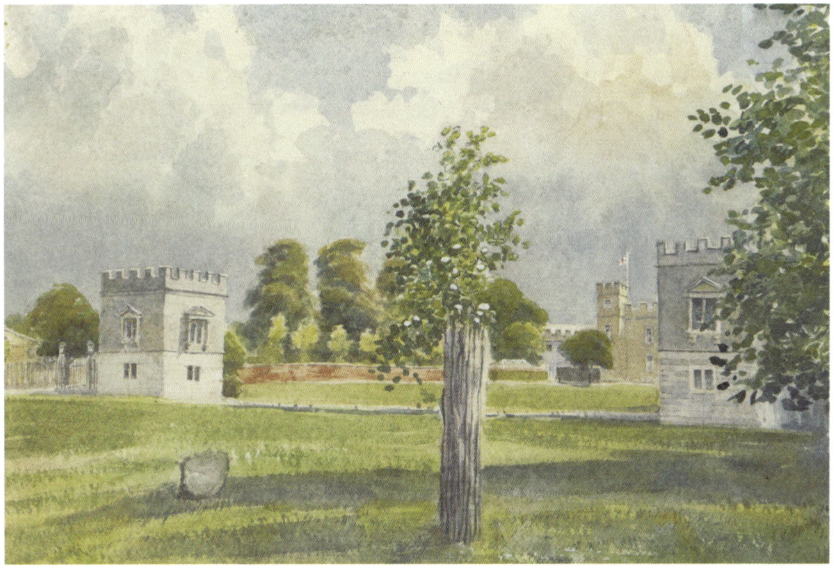

*Syon House, the 'Pepperpot' lodges (watercolour).*

He was an especially skilled water engineer with a keen knowledge of soil types, critical in the success of land drainage and lake building.

Delegation. Although a competent architect and builder, he preferred to concentrate on landscape. Once the ink was dry on a contract he often delegated major building work, usually teaming up with his son-in-law, Henry Holland. He also took great care to appoint efficient clerks of works to oversee the daily fulfilment of his plans. He did visit sites, but inevitably spasmodically, and must have been a sound judge of character in those he employed.

Eye. He obviously had a speedy and accurate eye in assessing the 'capabilities' of a landscape. He became celebrated for his ability to ride round a property and draw up plans from what might have seemed a cursory 'recce'. Where necessary he made accurate surveys with a theodolite.

Sociability. He was a man who inspired confidence and his geniality ensured he was welcome at any table. He was also extremely hard-working, conscientious and absolutely honest. In other words, people liked having him around.

Botanist. Experience brought knowledge about planting and the types of trees, shrubs and flowers that would thrive at a particular site. He had close bonds with a number of reputable nurserymen, who advised him about any new imported plants which landowners might be eager to procure.

Horticulturalist. The kitchen garden was the powerhouse of the great country estate. Brown built or altered many walled kitchen gardens, enabling gardeners to produce early and late fruits and grow exotics such as pineapple. None of these gardens exist in their original form today. Many were altered by the Victorians but most fell into disrepair after the First World War because of a shortage of labour, new science in storing fruit and cheap imports. No longer was it economic for the country house to be self-sufficient, as were most great estates in the eighteenth century.

Brown's landscapes are not bloated and self-important but a quiet statement of the naturalism that has become the hallmark of the English countryside. His was a subtle eye, and a restrained sophisticated artistry. He had the quality of genius, uniting remarkable craftsmanship with a profound conceptual awareness. As with a great piano sonata there is a sense of something mysterious and beautiful in his work, but one cannot quite put a finger on why this is. The sign of a job well done.

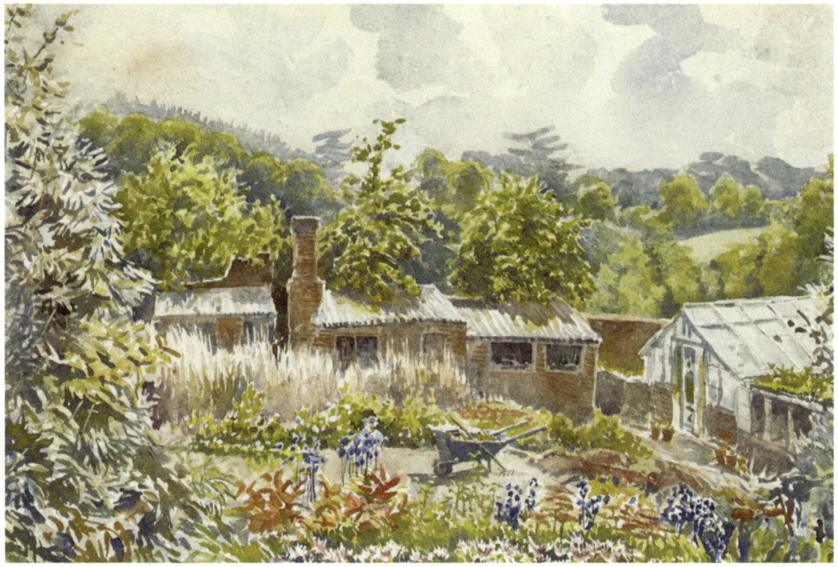

*Longleat, the walled garden. One of the many walled kitchen gardens Brown was involved in, nearly all now dilapidated or in other use (watercolour).*

On the 6 February 1783 Lancelot Brown was returning from a visit to his old friend Lord Coventry to Henry Holland's house in Hertford Street when he had a fit and collapsed and died. The probable cause of death was the severe fall.

Fickle fashion turned against Brown in the next generation and his reassessment as one of our greatest landscape architects was only realised in the mid-twentieth century. This book is a celebration of his achievement.

## *On Painting*

When it was suggested I paint a series of pictures of Lancelot Brown's landscapes for an exhibition I had only a vague idea of the extent of his career, but the seed fell on fertile soil. In my work as a landscape painter I find it easier to concentrate on a project and then collect a body of work for an exhibition. In the past the themes have varied from Scottish rivers or the Wiltshire countryside at home to more exotic places such as India, the Middle East or more recently Romania. When I have an exhibition and all the pictures are dispersed I always feel a certain emptiness. In this case the painting of the pictures has taken two years, and *A Brush with Brown* will perhaps compensate for this sense of loss when many of my pictorial friends say goodbye!

Landscapes by classical artists of the seventeenth century such as Jacob van Ruisdael, Salvatore Rosa, Nicholas Poussin, and especially Claude Lorrain, formed part of the picture collection at many of the great houses. These Elysian views, with clumps of trees and temples reflected in calm waters, inspired the naturalistic movement in garden design. Is it not appropriate that I, as a painter, should now gain inspiration from Brown's landscapes?

The landscape painter has largely been a second class citizen in the art world. Turner and Constable did succeed in having their large landscapes in oils accepted in the Royal Academy, but generally the fashion was for narrative pictures, often historic, based on the studio. Watercolours were not considered 'painting' in the loftiest sense of the word and were not taken seriously by the great institutions. It is one of the tragedies of English art that the watercolour painters of the late eighteenth and early nineteenth centuries were not recognized as internationally important, for arguably it is only in this field that Britain has led the way in a painting revolution.

Watercolourists came into their own with the Grand Tour. Artists often accompanied aristocratic parties on their travels and because of the difficulty of taking oils, watercolours were used. For instance Cozens accompanied William Beckford to Rome, in an entourage which included two musicians and a physician. Turner did thousands of small sketches when travelling, both in pencil and watercolour, and some are considered among his finest work – although to him they were an aide-memoire for his more finished and ambitious oils.

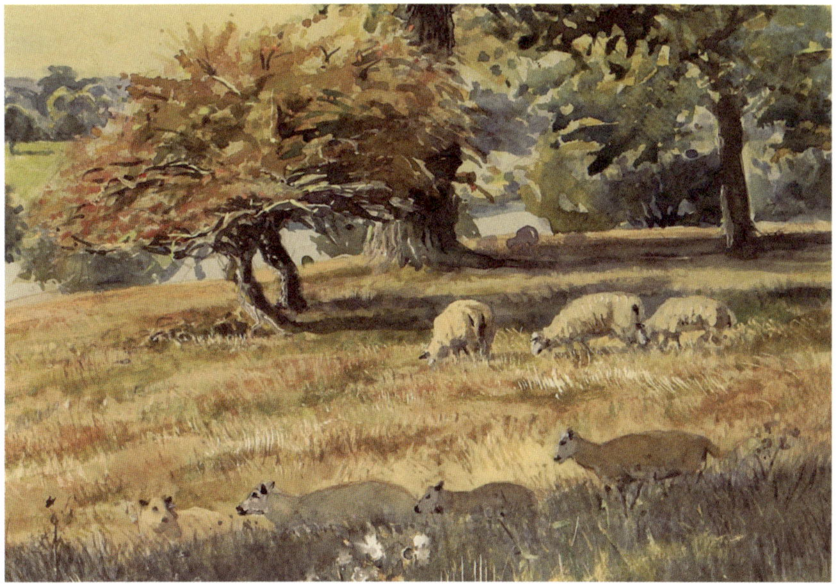

*Heveningham Hall. Detail showing how areas can be pictures within a picture. Looking at a painting in this way gives the idea that images are made up of many parts which have to unify to create the whole. In working I always start with the whole concept and then find myself creating almost self-contained pictures within this (watercolour).*

I admire Edward Lear, both as a person and as a topographical artist. He was haunted by his inability to achieve success in the Academy with his large oil paintings, but it is his watercolours done *en plein air* that are now considered his greatest achievement. He travelled extensively, and I too share the restless urge to paint that he felt when in some exotic land. When there is a fine view at hand and the fleeting light is at its most glorious, I am deeply unhappy without a paintbrush in my hand.

Lancelot Brown was lucky to have been born in an aesthetic age, the eighteenth century, the Age of Enlightenment. Today we live in utilitarian times and I fear all I see is ugliness in much that is new. Even the iconic buildings proclaim their own greatness and ignore their relationship to their neighbours. By contrast, in the eighteenth century there was an aesthetic concern for the whole. Even the vernacular architecture in poor village housing had a visual unity at one with the surrounding landscape. Of course this does not

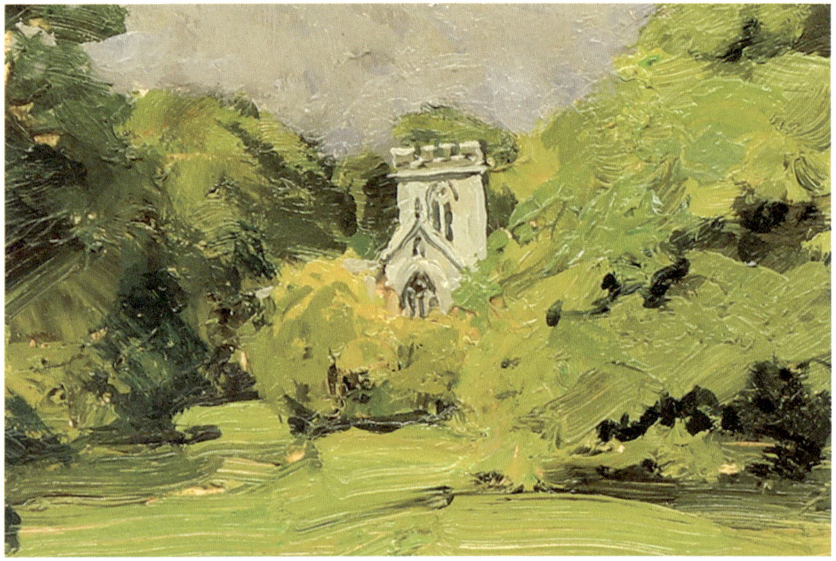

*Sledmere Hall (detail). Magnifying a small area in great detail gives an impression of the brushstrokes and creates an abstract image which I find exciting (oil).*

address the obvious physical advantages of living in the twenty-first century, but beauty is often the victim.

To me landscape painting is also about capturing a moment. Not only does the sun move and the countryside change with cloud and shadow, but the season must be accurately reflected. By working swiftly I try to capture an immediacy and a truth about the view at the time of painting.

Art can be considered a visual language and the actual physical act of painting are the sentences that make up this language. I find I build up a library of strokes and marks, enabling me to swiftly create the illusion of the scene. A painter should allow their own unique style to evolve and this will reflect to some extent their own character. This does not preclude being endlessly influenced by others, but is this not the case in most aspects of our lives?

Painting could be described as 'a falsehood seeking a truth'. If when painting the artist does not seek some truth, whether it be human emotion or just the portrayal of a landscape, there is little value in what is being painted.

'Painting is silent poetry, poetry painting that speaks', so wrote Simonides of Ceos. Edward Lear liked to be described as 'the painter of Topographical Poetry'. Similarly, I try to find the underlying rhythm of the fields, hills, rivers, and even village streets, in any landscape.

In painting the landscape poetry which 'Capability' Brown created I felt lucky to be there 250 years after many of the parks were planted. They are at their full maturity, something that could only have been imagined at their inception. Often the buildings have been altered or demolished and many of his landscapes have been developed for housing or 'rationalised' for modern farming. I have only sought out places where Brown's work exists as far as possible as he perceived it.

Each property has its own unique characteristic and Brown adapted his plans according to the circumstances, including his client's wishes. I too have tried to paint in the most appropriate way to reflect best what I saw, using oil, gouache and watercolour. With many of the pictures that follow I have explained more fully my method of painting and techniques.

TIM SCOTT BOLTON
*Wiltshire 2016*

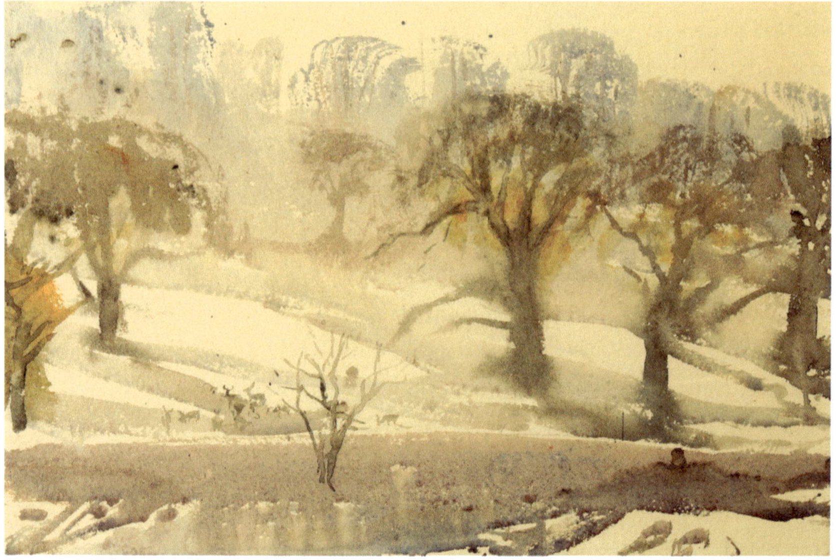

*Sherborne Castle. A swift sketch on a cold winter's morning (watercolour).*

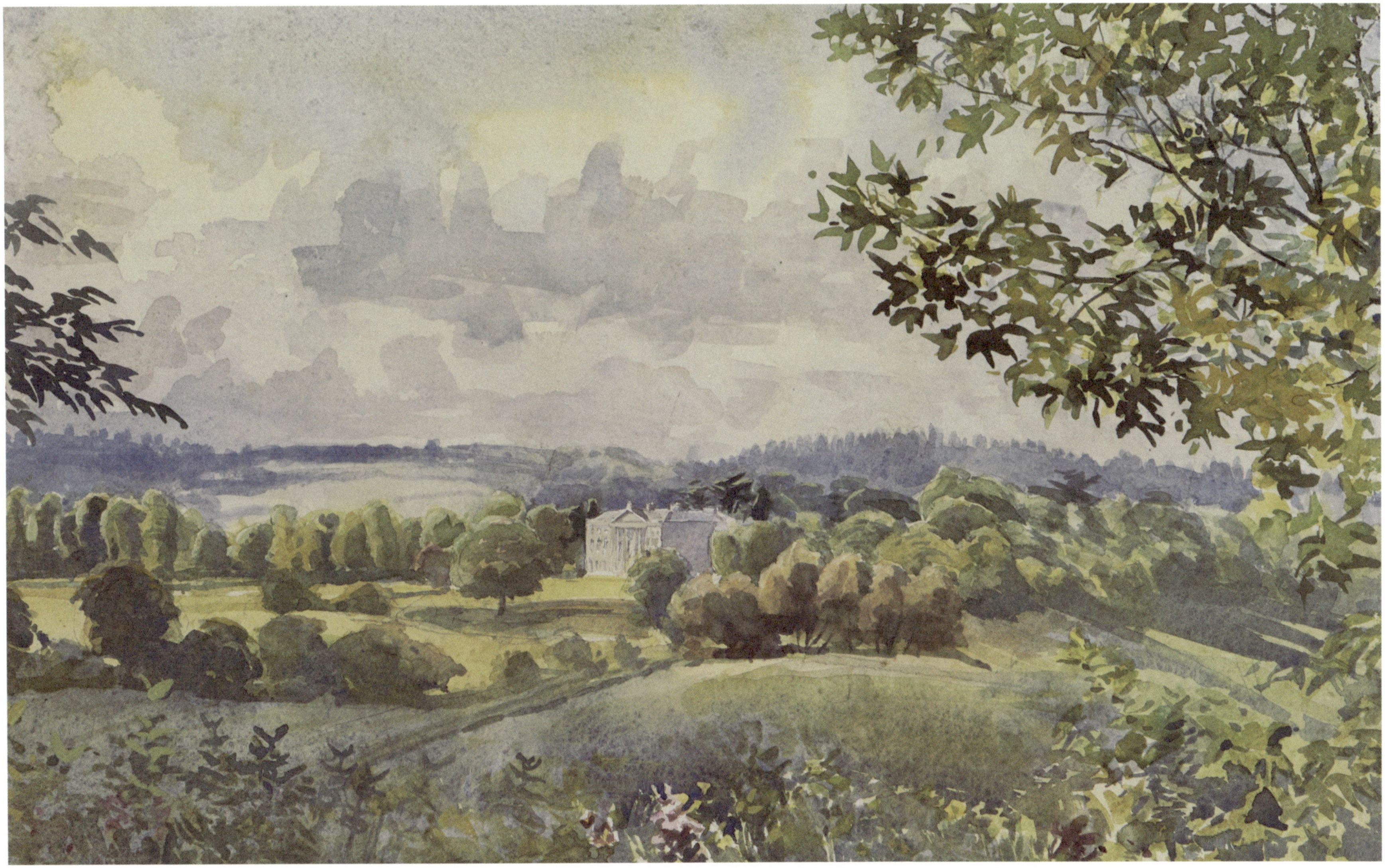

*New Wardour Castle. The poetry of the English countryside ( watercolour).*

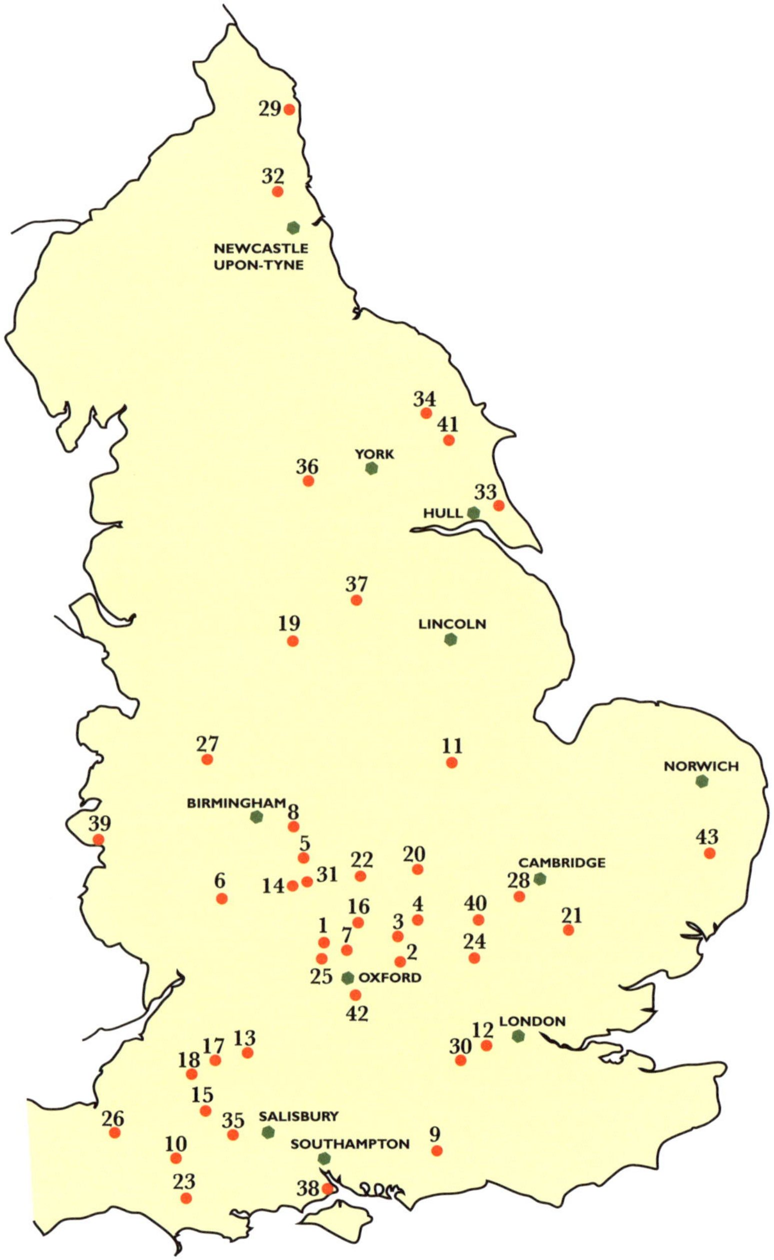


1. Kiddington Hall
2. Wotton House
3. Stowe
4. Wakefield Lodge
5. Warwick Castle
6. Croome Court
7. Kirtlington Park
8. Packington Hall
9. Petworth House
10. Sherborne Castle
11. Burghley House
12. Syon House
13. Bowood House
14. Charlecote Park
15. Longleat
16. Astrop Park
17. Corsham Court
18. Prior Park
19. Chatsworth House
20. Castle Ashby
21. Audley End House
22. Fawsley Hall
23. Milton Abbey
24. Luton Hoo
25. Blenheim Palace
26. Burton Pynsent
27. Weston Park
28. Wimpole Hall
29. Alnwick Castle
30. Claremont
31. Compton Verney House
32. Wallington Hall & Rothley Park
33. Burton Constable Hall
34. Scampston Hall
35. Wardour Castle
36. Harewood House
37. Roche Abbey
38. Cadland House
39. Berrington Hall
40. Southill Park
41. Sledmere House
42. Nuneham House
43. Heveningham Hall

# THE HOUSES

# &

# LANDSCAPES

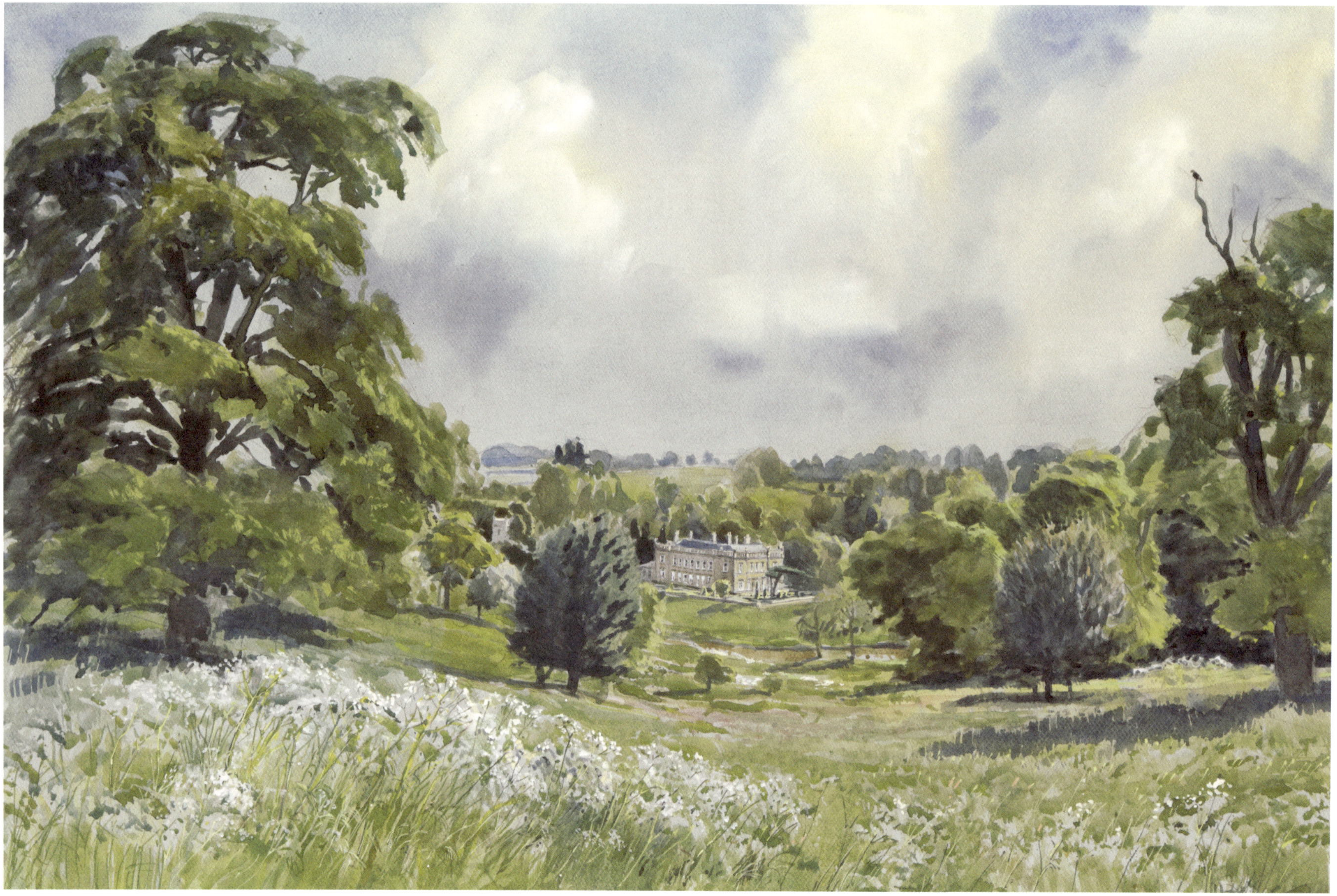

*Kiddington Hall. The park with the end of the small lake in the spring (watercolour).*

# KIDDINGTON HALL

## Oxfordshire 1740

After Lancelot Brown left Northumberland in 1739 and rode south he finally followed up an introduction to Lady Loraine's father, Richard Smith, then approaching his ninetieth year. Smith had once been High Sheriff of Buckinghamshire and had a wide network of contacts. It was probably he who gave Lancelot his entrée to Sir Charles Browne at Kiddington. It could not have been a more auspicious beginning to the young landscape designer's career. Browne's wife Mary was related to William Pitt, later 1st Earl of Chatham, who in due course was to become one of 'Capability's' greatest supporters.

Kiddington lies in the Cherwell Valley in Oxfordshire. It was Brown's first independent commission and involved the formation of lawns and a lake in front of the existing classical house. The lake's source was the nascent River Glyme, which gains stature before reaching the great park at Blenheim, a few miles to the south. It is conjecture how much of the surviving planting was done by Brown, but there are fine stands of oak of considerable age on a hillside opposite the house on the other side of the lake – and it is here where I chose to paint.

I was also attracted by the profusion of cow parsley growing in great swathes in this wonderfully natural setting. Compositionally, everything was pleasing to the eye. There was a glimpse of water, wildflowers, a well-proportioned classical house sitting easily in the landscape and the comfort of seeing the old parish church peeping out from the trees; the quintessence of an English scene.

I got up early on a fine day to catch the long shadows and the freshness of the morning before the day became lazy and hot. Dew gave the grass a twinkle. All was peaceful and serene. The time of day is so important in painting, and the luxury of going back to the same scene for short periods must be taken advantage of wherever possible. If your time is limited, try and delineate and quickly paint the main areas of light and shade before they have a chance to change with the moving sun. Of course, the other luxury is painting in a climate where the weather conditions are predictable. But much of the joy of painting in this country, as so many artists have found, are the ever-changing skies and the constant shifts of character they bring to the landscape.

# WOTTON HOUSE

## Buckinghamshire 1740

In this quiet corner of Buckinghamshire, down spring-flowered lanes, I found, unannounced, this jewel. Coming to Wotton and its house and pavilions and the many-laked pleasure grounds excited me for its unexpected beauty and tranquillity.

The house and its two pavilions owe their survival to Mrs Elaine Brunner, the remarkable daughter of George V's valet and a Swiss dressmaker, who went there in 1957, a fortnight before it was due to be demolished, in search of some columns to go round her swimming pool. The house is now regarded as one of Sir John Soane's masterpieces, but in 1957 the copper had been stripped from the roof, the fireplaces removed, and the floors were waterlogged. Elaine Brunner arranged to buy the house from Buckinghamshire County Council for £6,000, payable in six annual instalments, telephoning her husband Patrick with the news and reputedly saying, 'Darling, I have just bought a house, and I just know you're going to love it.' Thereafter she made it her life's work to restore the house and grounds, living long enough to see the re-instatement of Brown's Crescent Bridge shortly before her death in 1998. Wootton is now lived in by her daughter April and her husband David Gladstone.

The Grenville family had lived at Wotton Underwood since the early Middle Ages. In 1704 Richard Grenville left the existing manor house for a new house on a different site. It was built to a plan almost identical to the Duke of Buckingham's house at the end of the Mall, now the much transformed Buckingham Palace.

His son, another Richard, married Hester Temple, sister of Lord Cobham, the owner of Stowe. 'Capability' Brown might well have done some work at Wotton in 1740 prior to his appointment as head gardener at Stowe, but it is more probable that he was subsequently 'lent out' to the Grenvilles while at Stowe.

Sir John Soane's extraordinary interiors at Wotton date from 1820, when the house was gutted by fire.

Few houses can claim so many associations with British prime ministers. It was at Wotton that William Pitt the Elder courted and proposed to his future wife, Hester Grenville, one of Richard's sisters. He wrote of 'the beauty of its deep shades of oak, softening lawns and tranquil waters, like a lively smile lighting up a thoughtful countenance.' Richard's son George Grenville was Prime Minister between 1763 and 1765, as was his nephew William Pitt the Younger during the Napoleonic Wars. More recently one of Wotton's two pavilions has been bought by Cherie and Tony Blair.

The Grenville family papers have been bought by the Huntington Library in California and have yet to be catalogued, but the landscape would suggest that Brown had a substantial part in its development. Brown returned to Wotton in 1757 when it was the home of George Grenville and his wife Elizabeth. It is probably then that he dammed the infant River Ray to create two lakes linked by an artificial winding canal. Walks through shrubberies giving glimpses of pavilions and the lakes, a bridge with a cascade running through its arches, ha-has and cattle in the park, clumps of trees and clearings in woods with urns and statues – all combine to conjure the naturalism of a classical picture.

The walk around the lakes is about three miles, so as to save time

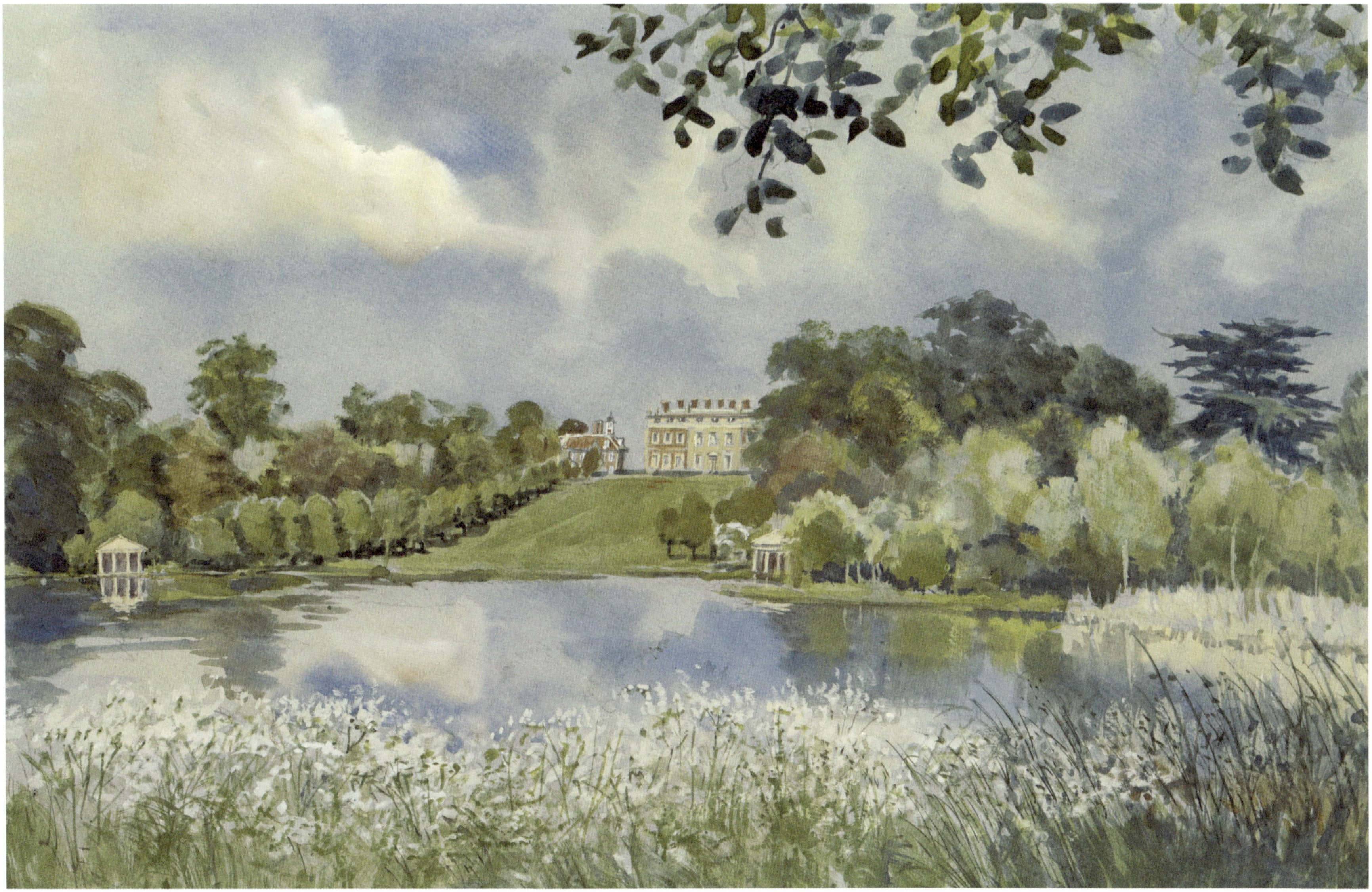

*Wotton House in cow parsley time (watercolour).*

I found a view which encapsulated much of the nature of the place. Many hours can be spent in prospecting and many a picture is lost by want of time, so my usual philosophy is to paint the first view that really pleases me.

# STOWE

## Buckinghamshire 1741

Lancelot Brown's rise from Northumberland obscurity to household name can be directly attributed to his appointment as head gardener at Stowe in 1741. Initially, he was on probation for six months at a wage of £12.10 shillings per half-year.

Richard Temple, later created 1st Viscount Cobham, inherited Stowe in 1697. The viscount was a formidable employer. On retirement from the army, buttressed by his wife's brewing fortune, he began gardening with the zeal he had shown for soldiering as one of Marlborough's generals. Charles Bridgeman was commissioned to create double avenues, straight canals and jagged bastions – all of which were laid out in a severe military style that defied the natural countryside beyond. He also removed the village of Stowe, leaving only the little medieval church of St Mary's. Bridgeman was followed by William Kent, who softened his predecessor's work with a more gentle approach, and created the Elysian Field, with its Temples of Ancient Virtue and British Worthies, as well as the Temple of Concord and Victory, and the Palladian Bridge.

Brown's promotion was swift. The then steward hanged himself in the wake of a dispute with Cobham. His replacement absconded with the Michaelmas rent money, with the result that Brown became Clerk of Works, a secure position at a considerably larger wage. He was soon handling whole contracts, an invaluable experience for his later career. His secure position allowed him to marry his betrothed, Miss Bridget Wayet, at St Mary's – which still stands concealed by trees near his lordship's great mansion. The latter was a known agnostic and bon viveur. Perhaps he preferred to gaze out over a pagan landscape dotted with temples dedicated to pleasure and Greek gods than at a House of God representing abstinence and sobriety? We can only guess what the young Mrs Brown, a good Christian, thought

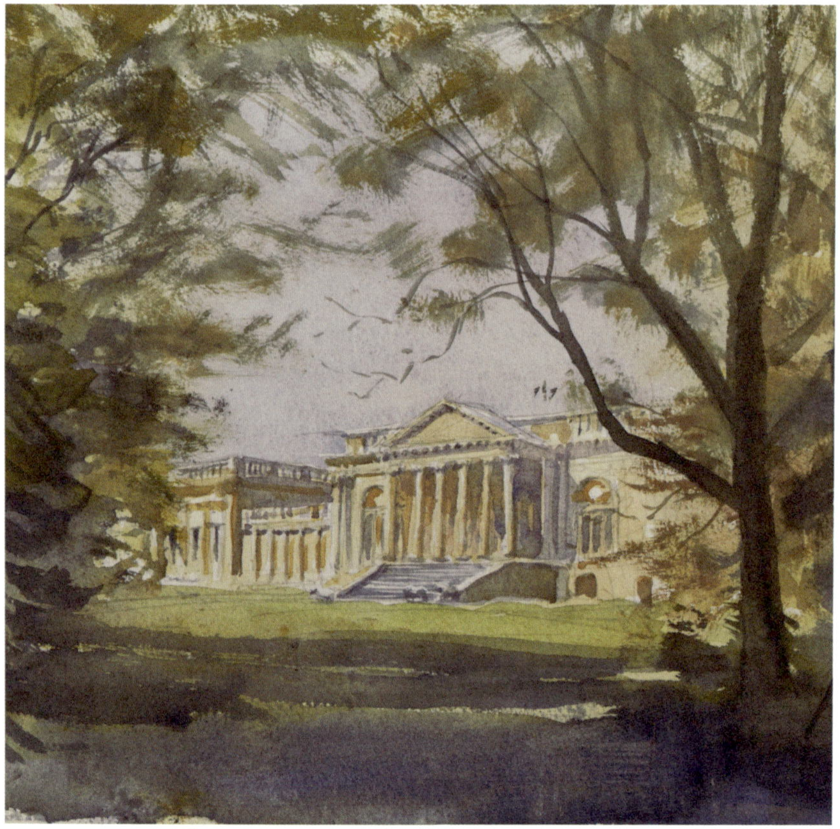

*Stowe. South front of the house from the church (watercolour).*

as she passed through the Elysian Fields and confronted a voluptuous Venus disporting herself on a pagan altar in the Rotunda, or read the words 'since all things are uncertain indulge thyself' in the sleeping parlour of Dido's Cave.

The Browns first home was the western Boycott Pavilion, an elegant house of some architectural pretension. One person who Brown will have welcomed into its parlour was James Gibbs, architect of the Radcliffe Camera and St Martin-in-the-Fields. The two men worked together on various projects at Stowe. Gibbs was generous with his time. He enjoyed encouraging and teaching others, instilling in Stowe's young Clerk of Works a good understanding in the art of siting and designing buildings. Both the quirky Gothic Temple and the Queen's Temple were built to Gibbs's designs, and there is little doubt that Brown oversaw their construction.

The new fashion in landscape design which was espoused and developed by Brown is summed up in Alexander Pope's almost prophetic few lines:

*To build, to plant, whatever you intend,*
*To rear the column, or the arch to bend,*
*To swell the terras, or sink the grot;*
*In all, let nature never be forgot.*
*But treat the goddess like a modest fair,*
*Nor overdress, nor leave her wholly bare;*
*Let not each beauty ev'ry where be spy'd,*
*Where half the skill is decently to hide.*
*He gains all points, who pleasingly confounds,*
*Surprises, varies and conceals the Bounds.*

How many men have been successful in their careers without luck and contacts? Brown had ample of both, but he had two other crucial qualities – an endless optimism and the bedrock of genius. Perhaps the most important of his contacts was that forged with William Pitt (the Elder). Close to Cobham both politically and personally, Pitt was a regular guest at Stowe. A keen gardener, he soon made a habit of seeking out Brown's company. The two formed a lifelong bond and Pitt's labyrinthine network of family and social contacts were of enormous help to Brown when he left Stowe as an independent landscape designer following Cobham's death in 1749.

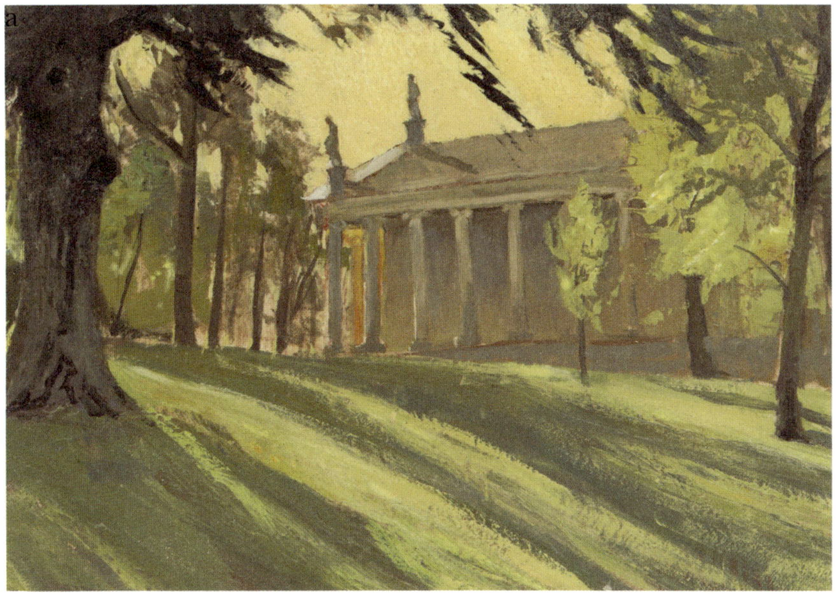

*Stowe. Temple of Concorde and Victory. This stands at the head of the Grecian Valley which was largely executed by Brown (oil).*

Sanderson Miller was another frequent visitor to Stowe and soon a close friendship developed between the two men. Miller, too, had a wide circle of aristocratic connections, who looked to him as their mentor in architectural matters. His estate at Radway, near Stowe, was peppered with his follies, and Brown was much impressed with his ideas when he visited there in 1750.

Today, a great school occupies Vanbrugh's mansion. To me, at least, it seems that public schools now more resemble pleasure grounds, as Stowe has always been, than the austere penal colonies of Tom Brown's school days. The National Trust maintain the gardens and grounds, and are responsible for the restoration and maintenance of the many temples.

It always helps a painter if he has visited a site before. I have been to Stowe a number of times but could not resist again painting the great view over the serpentine lake, with the Palladian Bridge and

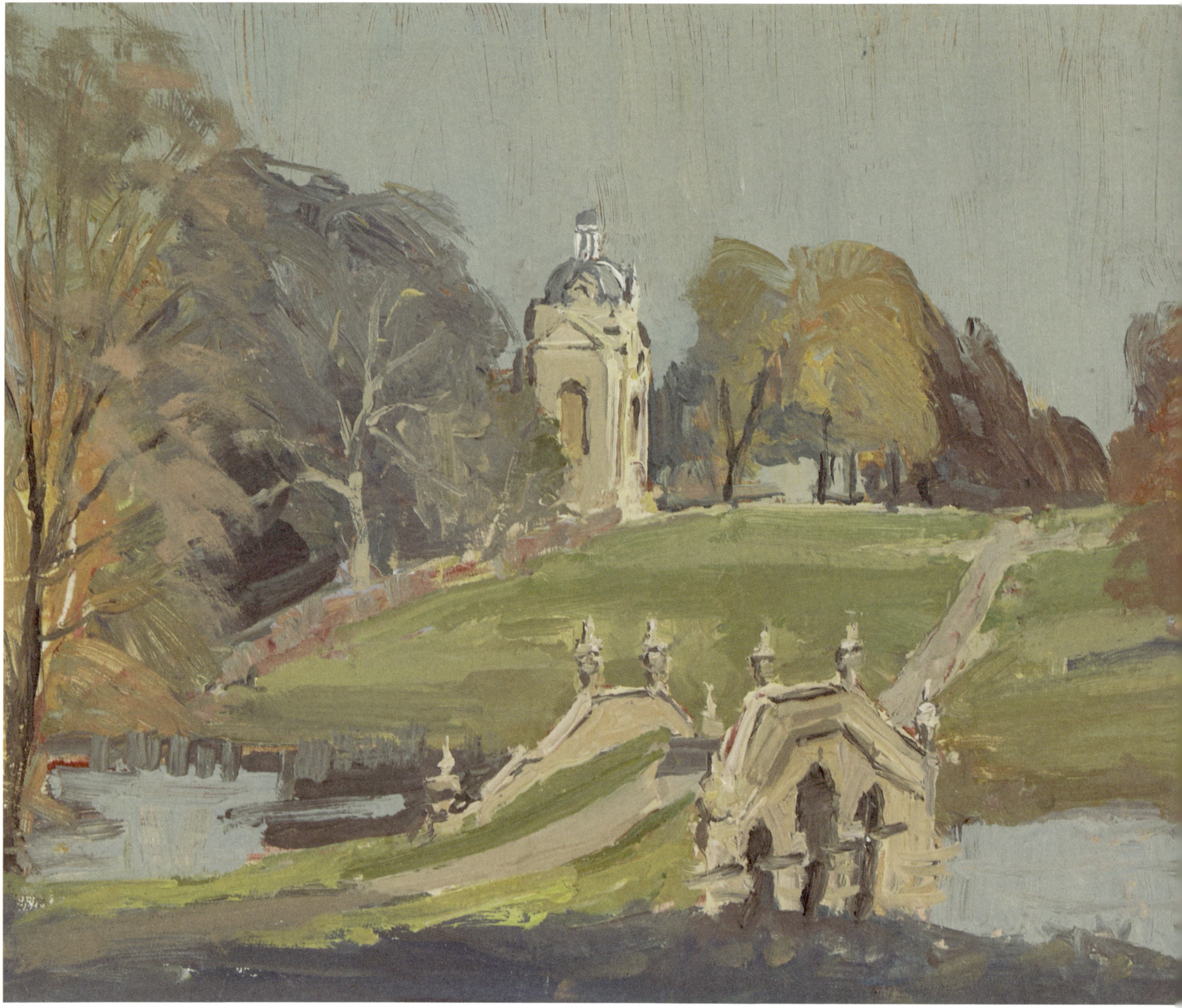

Mr and Mrs Brown's first home, the Boycott Pavilions, beyond. The mood of the day was bright and the autumn maples were red, the complementary colour to the green grass around. High key in painting means that the overall picture is light in tone. The illusion of sunlight is achieved not only by flooding the canvas with warm hues of red and green but sharply contrasting the shadows so that they are dark in tone and cool in temperature. The brighter the sunshine, the greater the contrast between light and shade.

*Stowe. The Boycott Pavilions (oil).*

# WAKEFIELD LODGE

## Northamptonshire 1740

WAKEFIELD LAWN, as it was then known, was the home of Charles Fitzroy, 2nd Duke of Grafton, who in 1740 commissioned William Kent to turn the existing hunting lodge into a classical house. Horace Walpole, the inveterate gossip and critic, thought the result 'too heavy'. However it does have a certain Vanbrughian gravitas, standing beside it's more restrained classical stable block. The block once boasted 16 heated stables – indeed it was conjectured that the Duke's horses were bedded in more luxury than the guests in his house.

Before the house and grounds were completed, William Kent died from 'mortification in his bowels and feet'. In 1748 Brown was engaged to complete the work on the house and design the grounds. Although just over the county boundary in Northamptonshire, Wakefield adjoins Stowe. This was the year before Brown left Stowe and he was still being 'lent out' by Viscount Cobham to friends and neighbours.

The landscape is largely as conceived by Brown. A park, with a few clumps of oak, slopes down to the main lake which snakes along the valley below, well watered with springs and forming a headwater of the Great Ouse. Beyond, the land rises to what was once an extensive 'lawn' but is now largely arable. However, bands of trees break up the view and in the distance the prospect is closed off with more extensive planting. Some ancient oaks, probably survivors from an earlier park, are dotted about some distance to the west of the house.

Immaculate records were kept of the progress of the work by the Duke's conscientious foreman, John Wade. Bundles of brushwood faggots were used in the foundations of the 700 ft long dam built to create the lake and shape its edges. A new road was laid out, trees planted. The labourers worked a six day week, for which the men were paid ninepence a day and the women sixpence: nothing changes!

Until the late eighteenth century the Wakefield Lawn Races were held on the estate. Appropriately, the sporting connections are continued. The estate is now owned by Julian Richmond-Watson, elected as senior steward to the Jockey Club in 2003, and the stables now house racehorses.

I arrived at Wakefield Lodge on an unremittingly wet day. Such weather has its own dulcet beauty, with its soft tonal areas giving a feeling of serenity. But how to paint and remain dry? Fortunately William Kent's generous portico with its balustraded terrace solved this problem; what could be more appropriate than the view from where Brown and the Duke must have discussed and pondered over the design of the landscape? A small herd of water buffalo, an animal I last painted by a lazy Indian river, lay in a cluster, contentedly chewing the cud and enjoying the rain.

The painter often develops and changes his picture in the course of the painting, rather like a sculptor who when exploring a theme manipulates a small lump of clay into a maquette, continually remodelling it until satisfied. This is not possible with watercolour painting because each mark is for ever, but with a palette knife and lots of turpentine (or in my case Zest-it) areas of an oil painting can

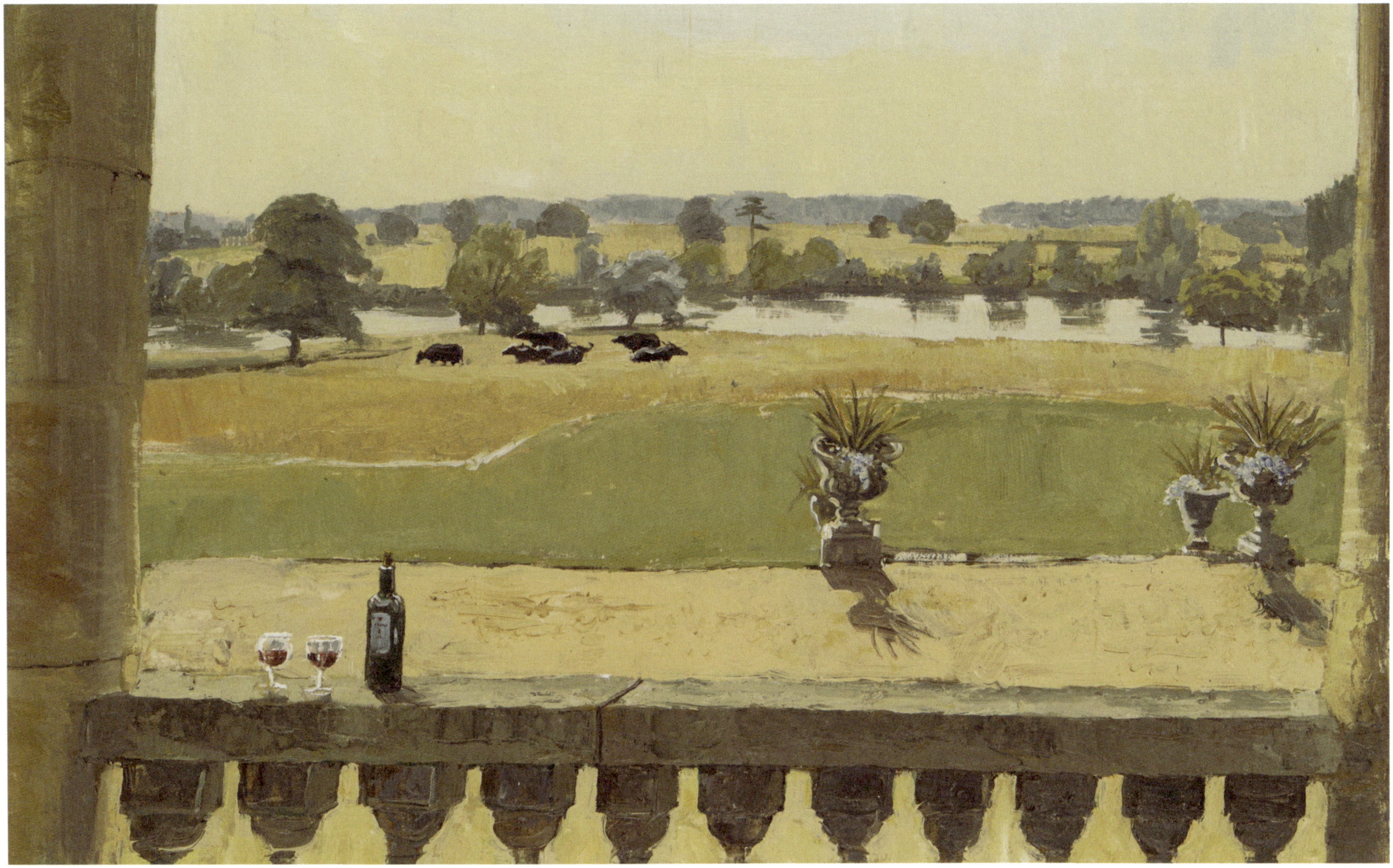

*Wakefield Lodge. View from William Kent's portico (oil).*

be shifted until the eye says 'yes that's okay'. In this case I left out the balustrade, but then felt a strong foreground would give the picture depth. This then caused another problem, a long horizontal line cutting across the foreground with no break. The day was so miserable I cheered myself up by including a couple of glasses and a wine bottle, which broke up this unremitting line and suggested a day of benign warmth and a drink on the terrace.

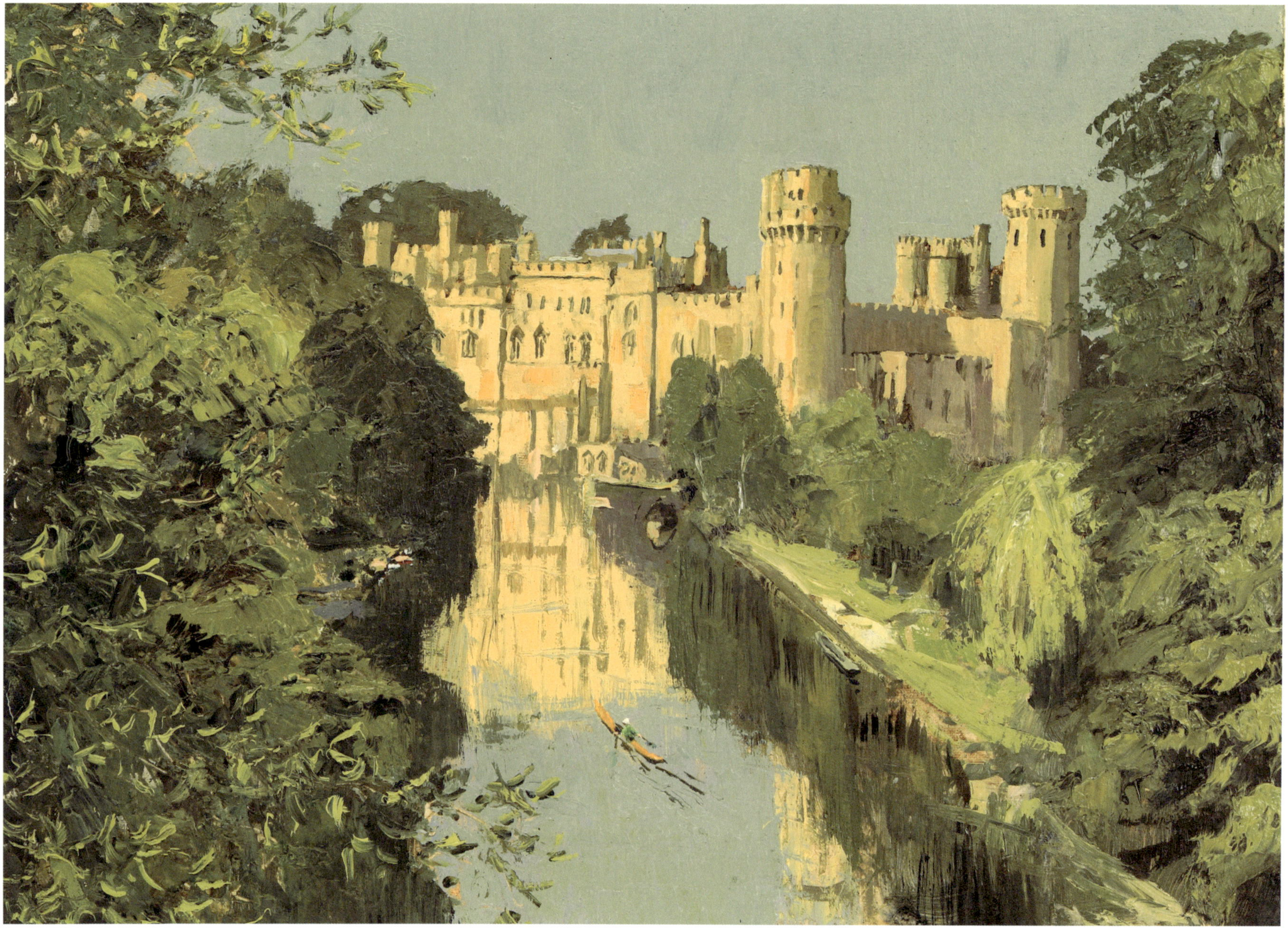

*Warwick Castle from the Town Bridge, which was built after Brown's time (oil).*

# WARWICK CASTLE

## Warwickshire 1740

Brown was employed regularly at Warwick Castle from the late 1740s for the diminutive Francis, Lord Brooke, later 1st Earl of Warwick, but exactly when work began we do not know.

However that inveterate commentator on the lives of others, Horace Walpole, wrote in 1751, 'The view pleased me more than I can express; the River Avon tumbles down a cascade at the foot of it. It is well laid out by one Brown who has set up on a few ideas of Kent and Mr Southcote. One sees what the prevalence of taste does; little Brooke who would have chuckled to have been born in an age of clipt hedges and cockleshell avenues, has submitted to let his garden and park be natural.'

It was a difficult site, sandwiched between the town of Warwick and the River Avon, which passes immediately below the great south wall of the castle. Brown designed a series of loops in the main drive to give the illusion of length. The mount, parterres and the old bailey were made into lawns and gentle slopes and, as was later achieved at Alnwick, the intended effect was the transformation from rugged castle made for defence to tranquil country house in a park. Paradoxically in existing parks, already tranquil, Sanderson Miller and his friends were creating rocky knolls and sham castles.

The old Banbury Road Bridge was once close to the mill with its cascade, the great pale stone walls of the castle looming high above. The bridge was removed after Brown's time to a position several hundred yards downstream. I chose this as my viewpoint since it gives a fine prospect of the castle and surrounding grounds.

A later contract between the Earl and 'Capability' was for alterations within the castle. This involved enlarging many of the smaller medieval rooms to satisfy the expectations of an eighteenth century grandee. It was, one would think, a perilous operation that required burrowing into the thick castle walls. How successful this was is doubtful – if one is to believe Thomas Gray's unflattering comment that Lord Brooke now had 'a little burrough in the massy walls of the place for his little self and his children, which is hung with paper and printed linnen, and carved chimney pieces in the exact manner of Berkeley Square or Argyle-buildings.'

From kingmakers to society hosts, the Earls of Warwick finally ran out of cash and energy. In 1978 the castle was sold to the Merlin Entertainments Group, who also own Madame Tussauds and Alton Towers. The gory dungeons and the gracious state rooms are now inhabited not by ghosts of the past but waxen figures passively reliving history.

My painting was done from a pochade box which I strapped to the bridge with a dog lead so there was no danger of tipping everything into the river. I like to sort out most of the main colours on the palette before I start my painting on tinted board. In mixing these with my palette knife I introduced some raw umber. This gave a unifying effect to all the colours within the picture and inbued the sky, trees and walls with a certain richness. The rain came and all I had to do was to close the lid of the box and all was protected.

# CROOME COURT

## Worcestershire 1750

Croome Court was inherited by the 6th Earl of Coventry as a plain brick house near a medieval church and village. Perhaps to our less ambitious taste it would seem charming, but the Earl wished for a new house on his ancestral lands and to develop an extensive park around it. Why did he choose the comparitively inexperienced Lancelot Brown for so ambitious a project? In this, it seems, that his friendship with Sanderson Miller was crucial. Lord Coventry wanted his new house to look like that of his friends the Lytteltons, at nearby Hagley Hall, which had largely been designed by Miller. When the latter was consulted by Coventry, he recommended Brown as he was not keen to be tied down to such a large project himself. Hagley has four square towers, one at each corner, probably inspired by Inigo Jones's Wilton House. Miller gave some help, but Croome Court is principally the work of 'Capability' Brown.

The relationship between Miller and Brown, as with Robert Adam, who also worked at Croome, seems to have been completely devoid of professional jealousy. Such was Brown's gift for friendship that throughout his career he cooperated easily with both men. Another friendship was born when working at Croome, for as well as a grateful client the Earl became a lifelong friend. A posthumous memorial, erected in 1797 by Lord Coventry to his 'old friend', Lancelot Brown, commemorates his achievement at Croome:

*To the Memory of Lancelot Brown*
*who by the powers of his inimitable*
*and creative genius formed*
*this garden scene out of a morass*

Croome was built in a boggy valley, which must have gladdened Brown's heart. He proposed extending the existing short lake to make it look like a meandering river, whilst simultaneously improving the valley by draining it. He had gained much experience as a water engineer in his early working life at Kirkharle, and probably on the fens in Lincolnshire when courting Bridget Wayet. Here, at Croome, in this his most extensive and ambitious scheme so far, he put his skill to full use.

It was a formidable undertaking, and represents one of Brown's most comprehensive commissions. In the midst of the work the Earl married Maria Gunning, one of the great beauties of the period, adding to the need for haste. Once the house had been started, the village was resited and the church demolished and rebuilt in a neo-Gothic style on a hill to the north, with fine views over the Court, park and its temples to the distant Malvern Hills.

The sad fate of the English country house in the early twentieth century was shared by Croome Court. The decline of the country estate, dependent on agriculture for its survival, began with the repeal of the corn laws in the nineteenth century, thereafter ownership of land was no longer an economic power house. Without other forms of income the way of life represented by the rural estate gradually declined. Taxation and two world wars finally brought the 'Downton Abbey' era to a close.

The eyes of the public were opened to the plight of Britain's great houses by the 1975 exhibition 'The Destruction of the Country House'. At one time in the 1950s a major house was being demolished

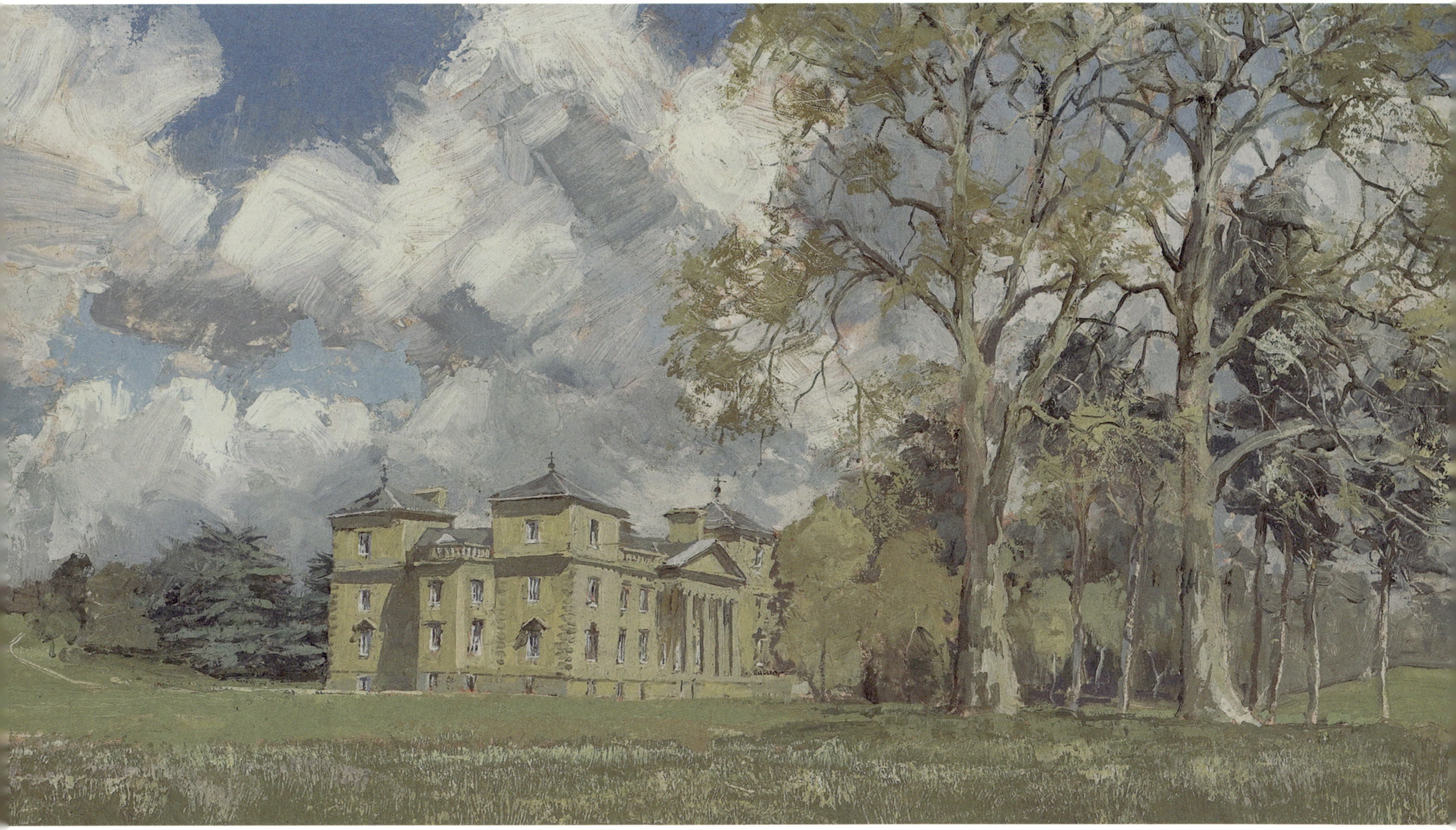

*Croome Court from the lake (oil).*

weekly. Fortunately, Croome did not share their fate, but the immediate estate was broken up and the house sold separately to a property developer who built houses in the park and converted the stable blocks and other outbuildings to residential units. The house itself – which housed the Dutch Royal Family during the Second World War – was left empty. In 2007 it was acquired by the Croome Heritage Trust and leased to the National Trust for restoration.

I first came to Croome on a sunny May weekend in 2012 when the National Trust invited selected artists to paint the house and park for an exhibition at Sotheby's the following year. It was part of a major fundraising campaign for an ambitious restoration scheme of the whole property. Painters are generally solitary beings and therefore it was a pleasure to paint with two artists I admire, Andrew Festing and John Wonnacott. Perhaps the companionship of painting with others inspires better work, and I was well pleased with my few days at Croome.

One important building that Brown designed that I did not paint on my first visit was the elegant and secluded Rotunda, tucked away on a little hill to the west of the house and surrounded by fine old cedar of Lebanon. The great cumulonimbus clouds reared into the heavens and fleeting touches of sunlight sped across the wide landscape. Not a day for outside painting; so I manoeuvred my moving studio (Renault Espace with seats removed) down a rutted track past a pen containing a scrum of sheep to a magnificent position overlooking the Rotunda. There I painted, happily immune from wind and rain, while a CD of Verdi's 'Othello' vied with the thunder.

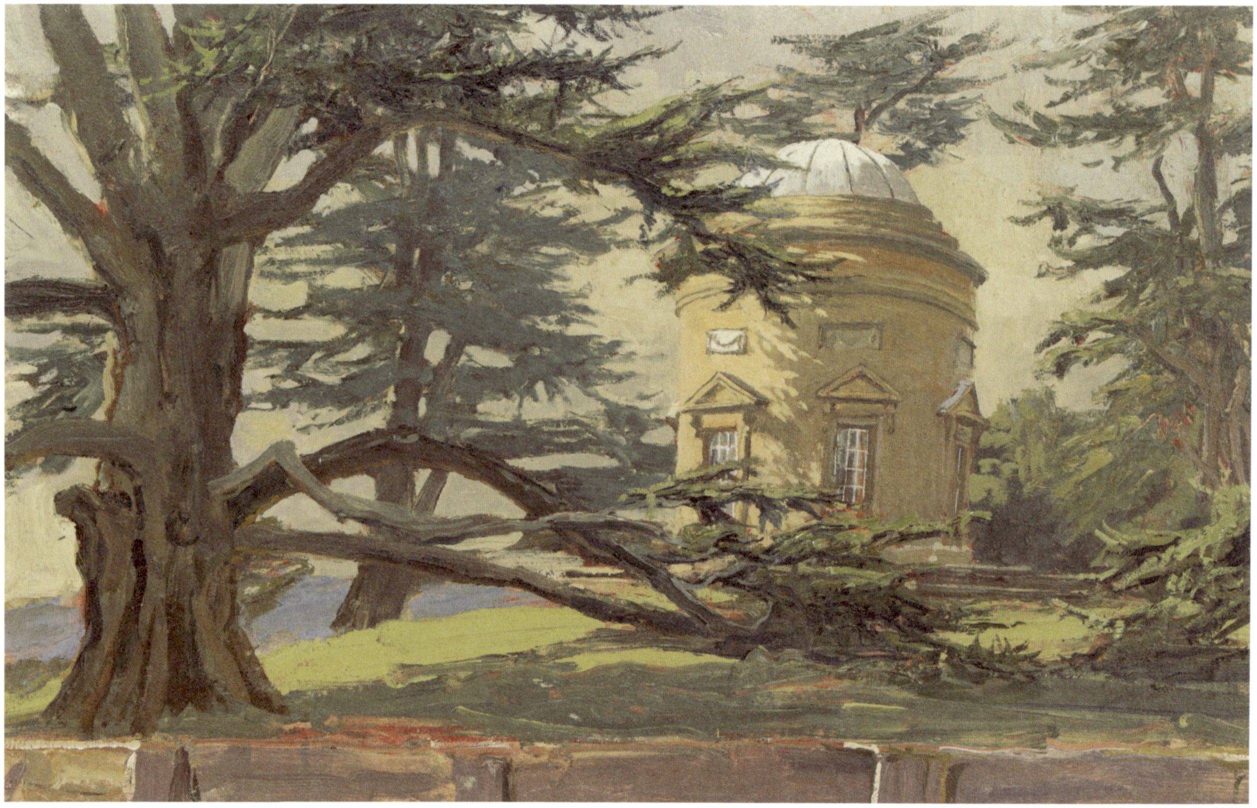

*Croome Court. The Rotunda lies in a grove of ancient cedar (oil).*

# KIRTLINGTON PARK

## Oxfordshire 1750

REVISITING Kirtlington Park in Oxfordshire was a sentimental journey for me. In the 1960s I had a girlfriend who was a polo journalist and many a chukka and the accompanying treading in were spent in its spacious grounds all those years ago.

The house, designed on generous Palladian lines by William Smith of Warwick, was built in the 1740s for Sir James Dashwood, brother of the notorious hedonist Sir Francis Dashwood of West Wycombe and Hellfire Club fame. The corpulent baronet's vast new house was described by Horace Walpole as 'situated so high that it seems to stand for the county as well as himself.' The views out over the Chilterns are glorious. The house has since been sold and is now much in use for weddings, but the 3000 acre park still belongs to the Budgett family, who built the polo ground in the 1920s.

Brown first undertook work at Kirtlington in 1750 when he was still living at Stowe. Kirtlington was a 20 mile ride away, and he worked there intermittently for 12 years, making it difficult to be certain how much of the park still bears his hallmark. His ha-ha still survives, as do some of the belt of Scotch pines he planted along the edge of the park.

I went there on a fine September day and after some deliberation decided to do an oil painting on a long thin board measuring roughly 14" x 38" (or a proportion of 1:2.7). This I felt suited the flat landscape, for I wanted my painting to embrace a wide view of the park. Generally if you use a board of unusual proportion it will make you rethink your composition. It is all too easy to take your usual canvas or paper with a proportion of say 1:1.5 and roll out your usual formula in achieving a 'satisfactory' picture. Try, for instance, placing the horizon very low (lots of sky) or very high (lots of foreground) in drawing your picture rather than it being somewhere vaguely in the middle. By doing something different you will stimulate your imagination and probably produce a more challenging and interesting picture.

OVERLEAF *Kirtlington Park (oil).*

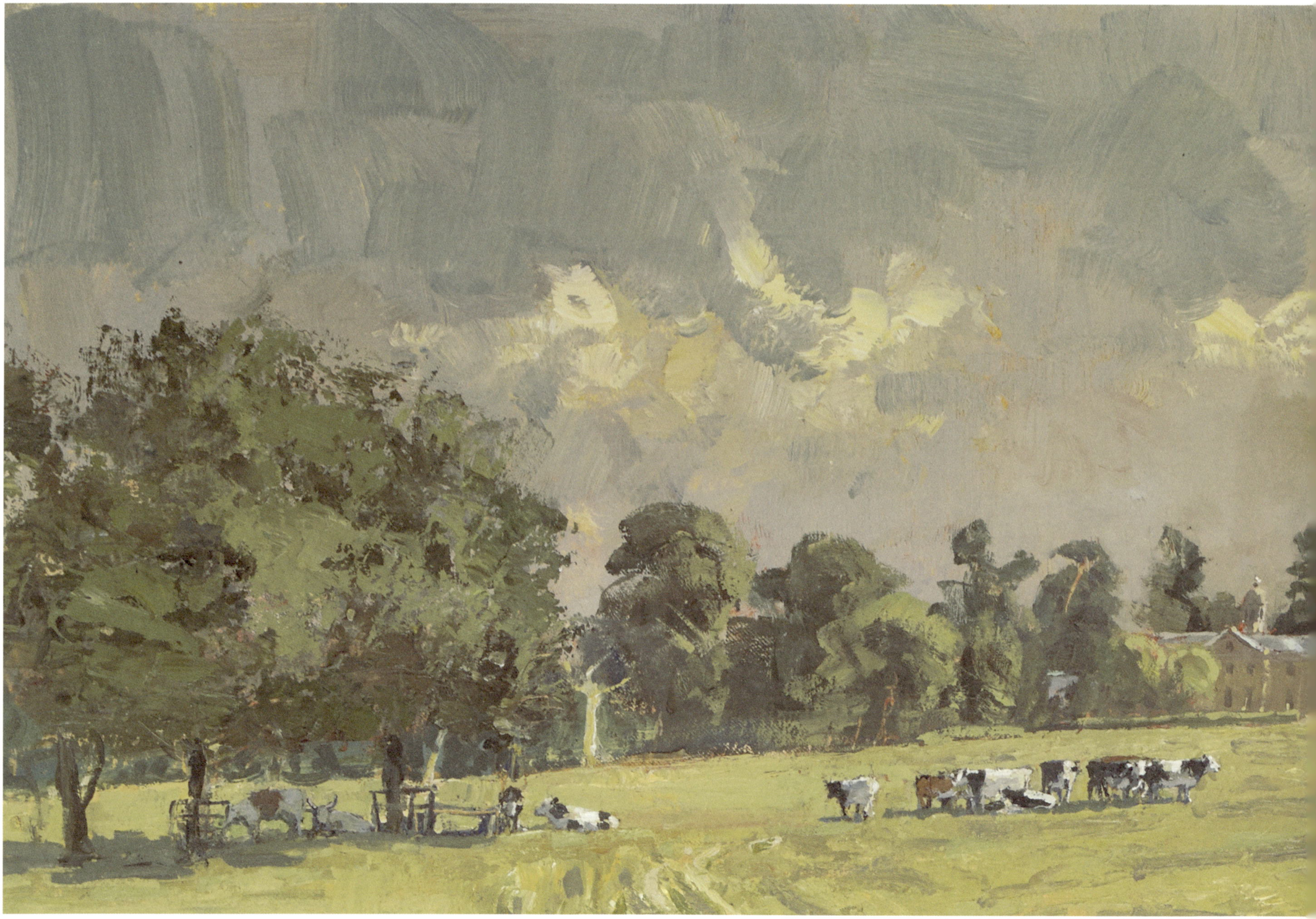

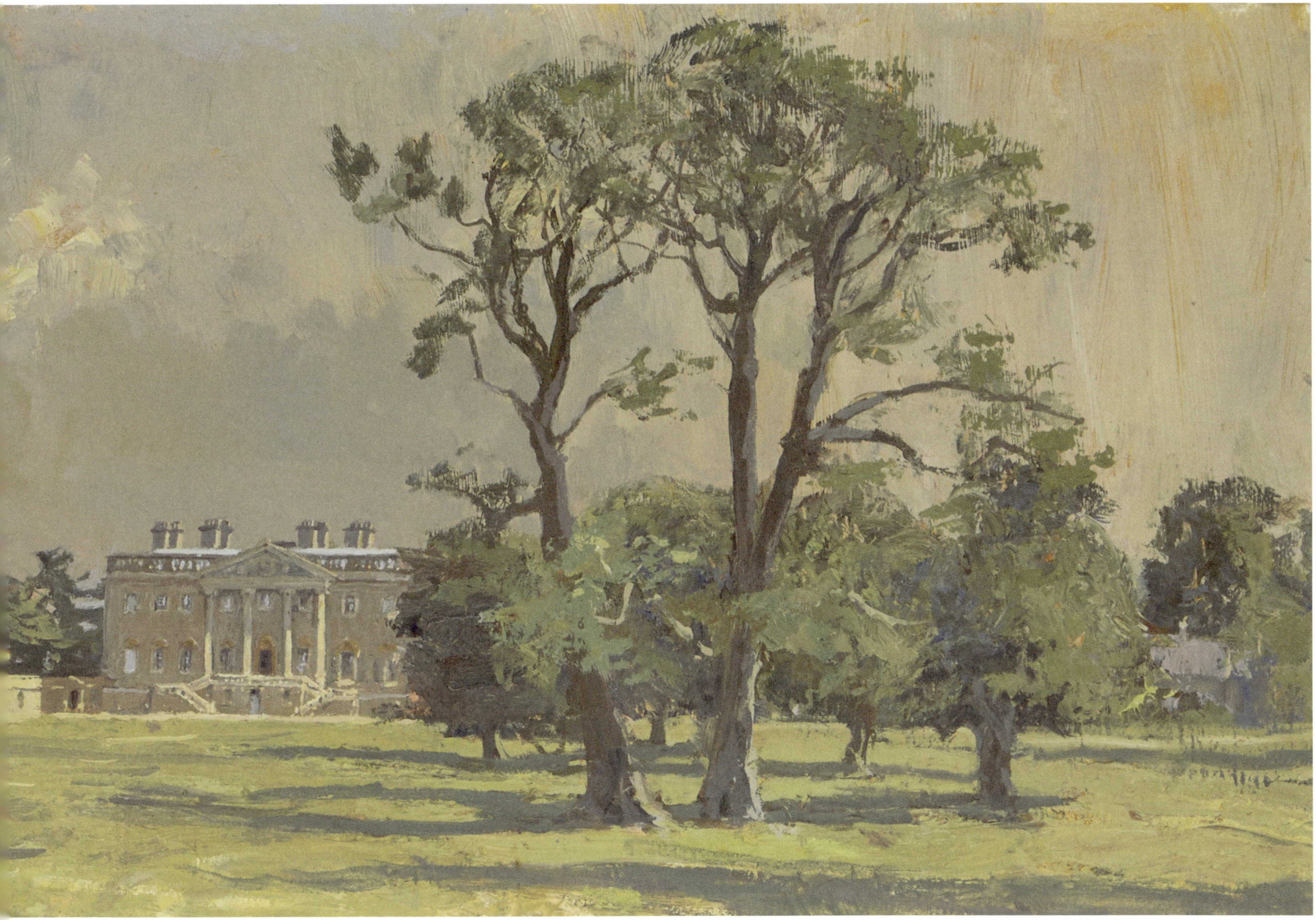

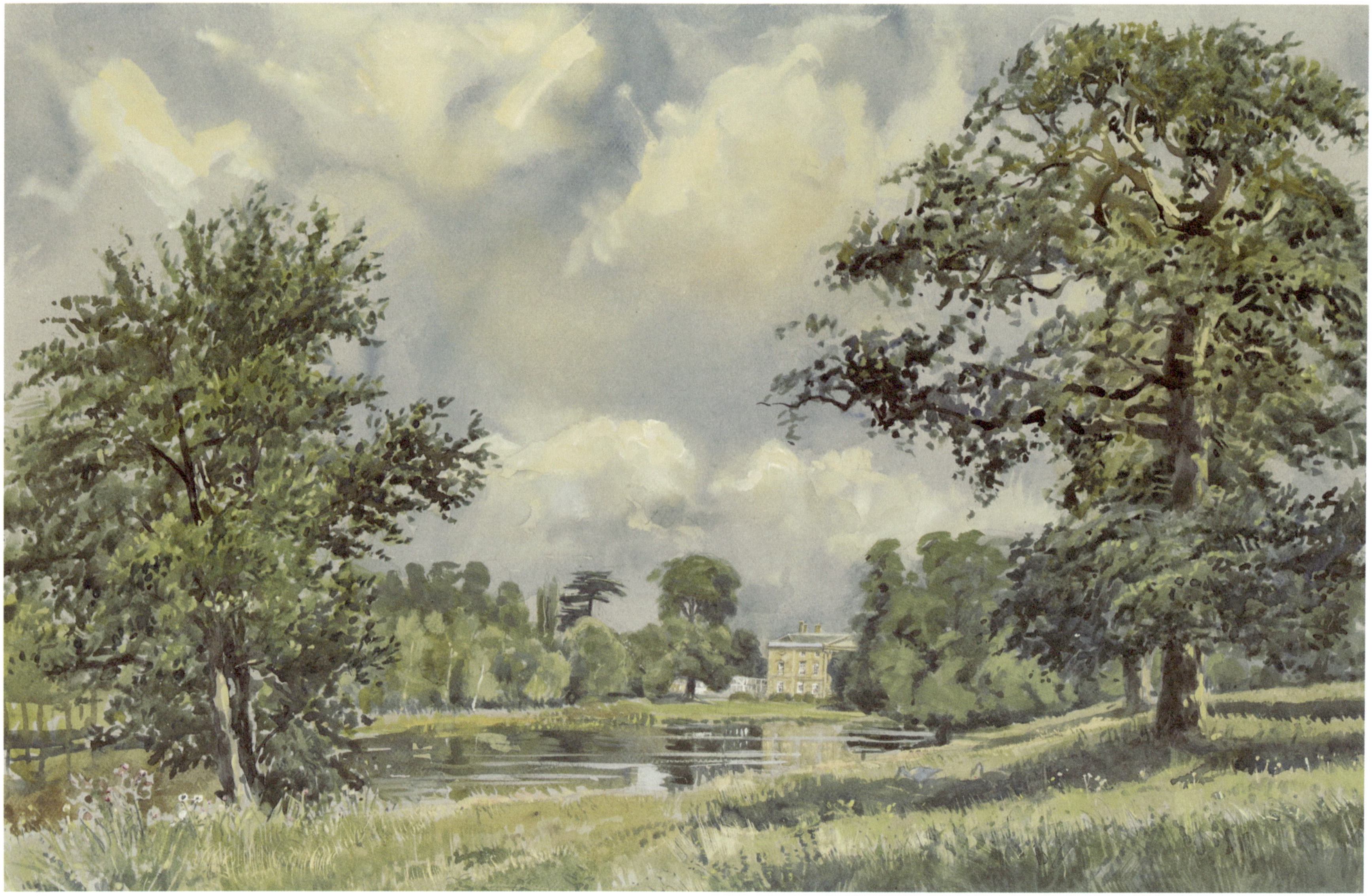

*Packington Hall (watercolour).*

# PACKINGTON HALL

## Warwickshire 1750

The Finch family, later to become the Earls of Aylesford, bought the Warwickshire estate at Packington in 1560. When Lancelot Brown originally drew up plans for the 2nd Earl in 1740 it was for a landscape to surround a classical mansion built by Sir Clement Fisher, later replaced in the 1770s by the present house, designed by Matthew Brettingham. Brown's principal task was to create the lakes, plant trees in the park and redesign the entrance drive. The impressive stable block might have also been influenced by him and bears a striking similarity to the design of Croome Court and Hagley Hall, with square towers at each of the four corners.

The suburban sprawls of Birmingham and Coventry reach out towards each other, but between the two lies the contrasting Elysium of the Packington Estate, 5000 acres of buffer. Now it is green belt, but previously much fine countryside was conserved solely because their owners looked beyond the short term option of maximum development.

Petworth has its white fallow deer, but here they are small and very dark, perhaps peculiar to Packington's park.

Some way from the house lies the most unusual church of St James, built by Joseph Bonomi with very red brick, four stone cupolas at each corner, and described by Pevsner as 'the most important, impressive English Church of the late 18th century'.

The fields were turning yellow and dotted about were puffs of white – the thistle seed heads so attractive to both the artist and finches, but no farmer's friend. I like it when the unremitting greenness of early summer turns to yellows and russets. On this late August day the faint tinges of autumn were just evident. Brown was a genius at the inviting glimpse. In this case the great house revealed itself in part. As I moved down the lake, and different aspects of the landscape were revealed, I realised how the vision of the artist and that of a great landscape designer are one and the same.

# PETWORTH HOUSE

## Sussex 1752

George London, who designed formal gardens to grace the 6th Duke of Somerset's new house at Petworth, must despair as he looks down from heaven. Of all his great gardens so fashionable at the end of the seventeenth century, excepting Hampton Court, few remain. Some 50 years later, Brown came to Petworth at the behest of Charles Wyndham, the 2nd Earl of Egremont, and made a vast map dated 1752. The overall layout of the park today reflects his original plan.

The formal gardens to the west of the house and the avenues were replaced by a great expanse of lawn. The hillside terraces were levelled into rolling slopes which gently lead the eye towards the new serpentine lake at the bottom of the valley. The lake itself was lined with clay, and 'puddled' watertight by driving a flock of sheep back and forth. Sunken fences behind snaking walls protect the private and kitchen gardens to the south of the house and the pleasure grounds to the north from the deer park. Brown's shelter planting still skirts the park along the Guildford Road. The Petworth to Tillington Road was moved and 14 miles of park wall were constructed. Clumps of trees were planted in the wider landscape within the park.

In the pleasure grounds a Doric temple was moved to its present position by Brown and an attractive rotunda was constructed by Matthew Brettingham. The total contract with Brown was for £5,500. The pleasure grounds were planted with not only native species of trees but Mediterranean imports such as bay and aloe and à la mode American imports such as brightly coloured maple, Virginia sumac and cotinus (Smoke Bushes). The nurseryman John Williamson of Fulham was charged with supplying trees and shrubs.

In 1763 Petworth was inherited by the 12-year-old 3rd Earl, later to become one of the great agricultural pioneers of the period. He established a herd of Sussex cattle and introduced pigs to the park, taking a great interest in their breeding. Because Brown's unfenced park came up to the state rooms, on one occasion a sow and its litter jumped through a window, causing chaos. Hospitable and generous, the Earl was also profligate with his affections. His only legitimate child died in infancy and he reputedly fathered 43 children by 15 mistresses. They all lived in the house with their respective mothers and rows were frequent.

The 3rd Earl was also a great patron of the painter J. M. W. Turner, who lived in Petworth for a while. My visit coincided with a Turner exhibition drawn largely from the remarkable Petworth Collection of his work. It was difficult not to be influenced by Turner's unique interpretation of the landscapes I was about to paint. The white deer roaming the park are descendants of those in Turner's 'The Lake, Petworth: Sunset, Fighting Bucks.' Similar deer grazed near me as I worked, muffled against the chill of a January day.

I chose Arbour Hill as a viewpoint to paint a panoramic view of the house and lake. Here some ancient chestnut and oak – rare survivors of the great 1987 storm – grew in a clump. Ancient trees have a rhythmic nature, their sinuous limbs writhing into the air. Compositionally, this can help the picture. With a tree it is more

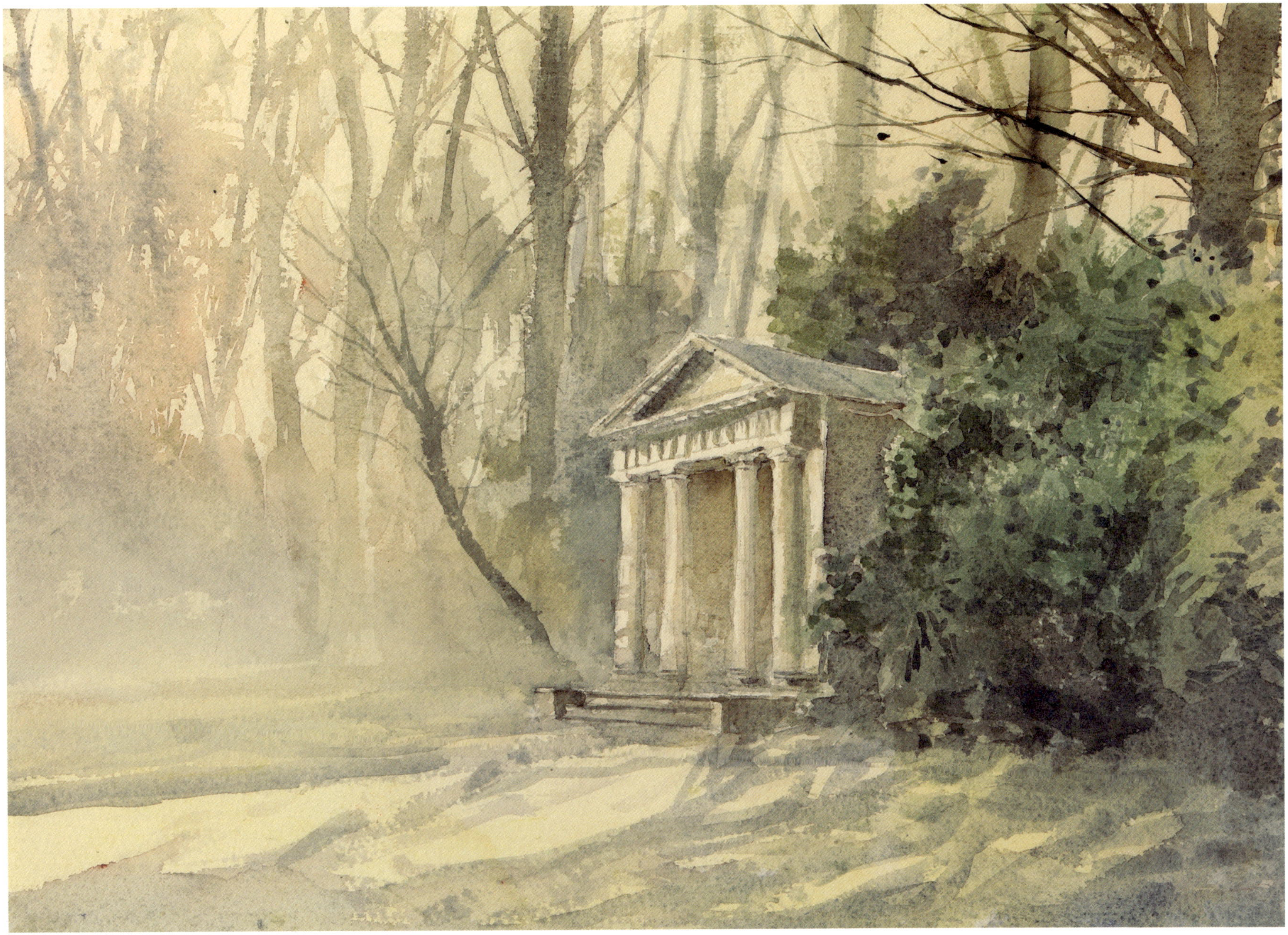

*Petworth House. The Doric Temple was moved by Brown from the upper terrace to its present position (watercolour).*

important to reproduce its natural flow than to slavishly try to copy each branch. For example, a chestnut has a twisted growth, whilst the long straight branches of an ash tend to curve down in regular sweeps. A group of trees set to one side might lead the eye back to the centre of the picture, as in the painting on the right, where the long silhouette of the great house, misty in the morning light, lies beyond its lake. Clumps of trees in the middle distance counter-balance the composition.

Drawing is important to sort out the compositional problems before embarking on a painting. Only the artist's eye can judge the balance of the picture and it is much easier to do so when a sketch has been made. I usually do this on my watercolour paper by using very light lines. When teaching, I suggest a number of different drawings are done to explore different compositions of the same subject.

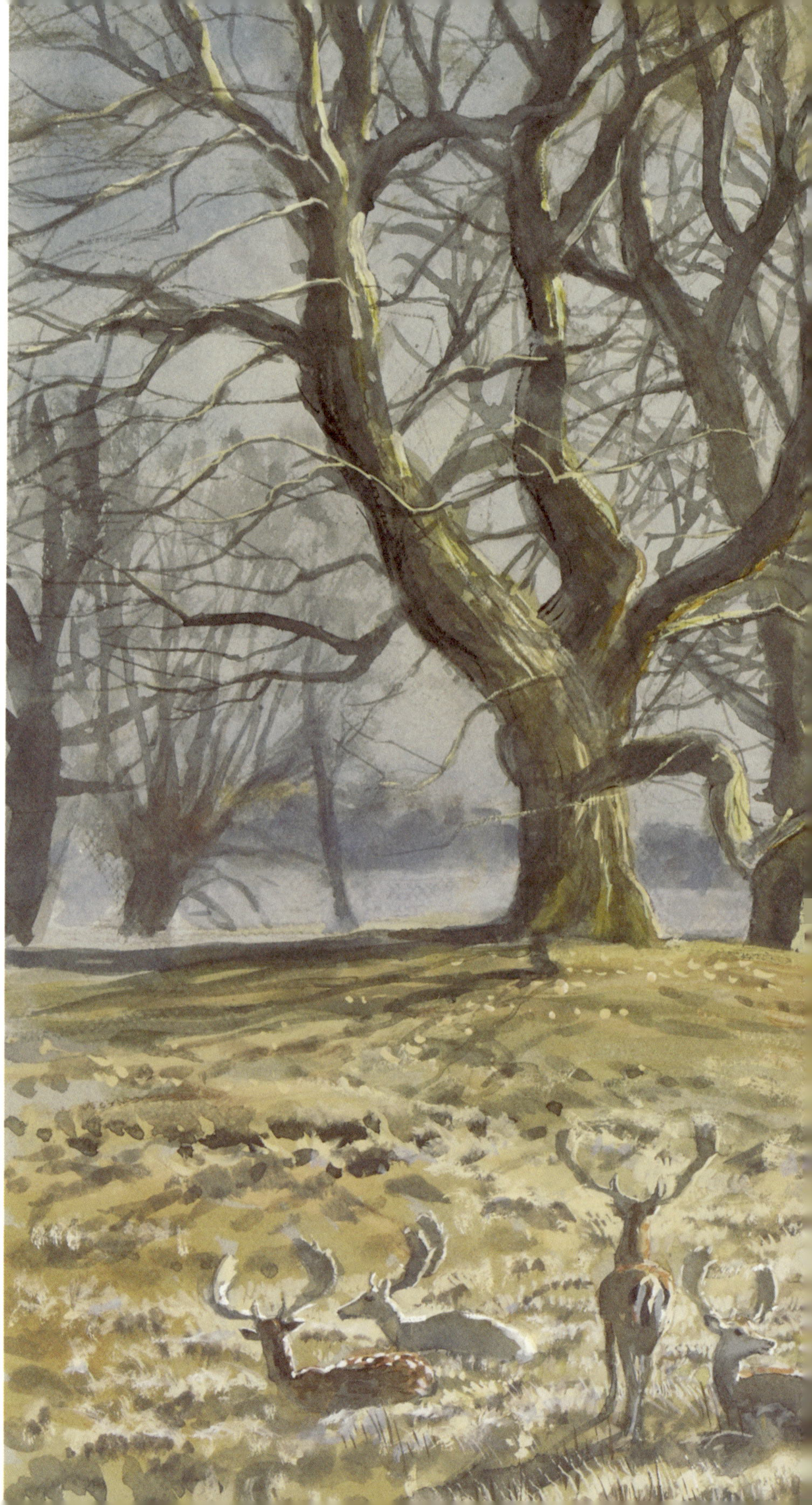

*Petworth House from Arbour Hill (watercolour).*

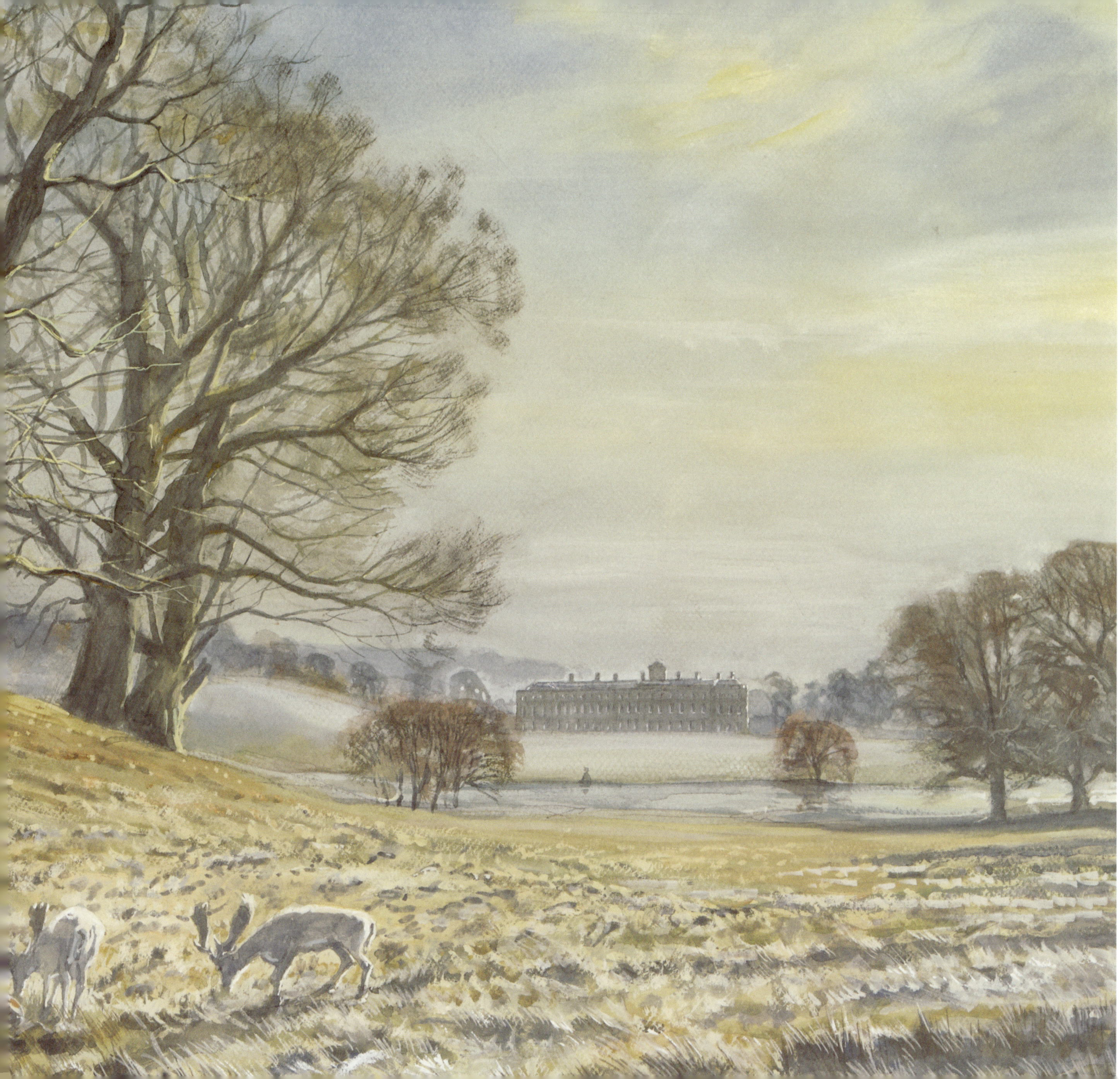

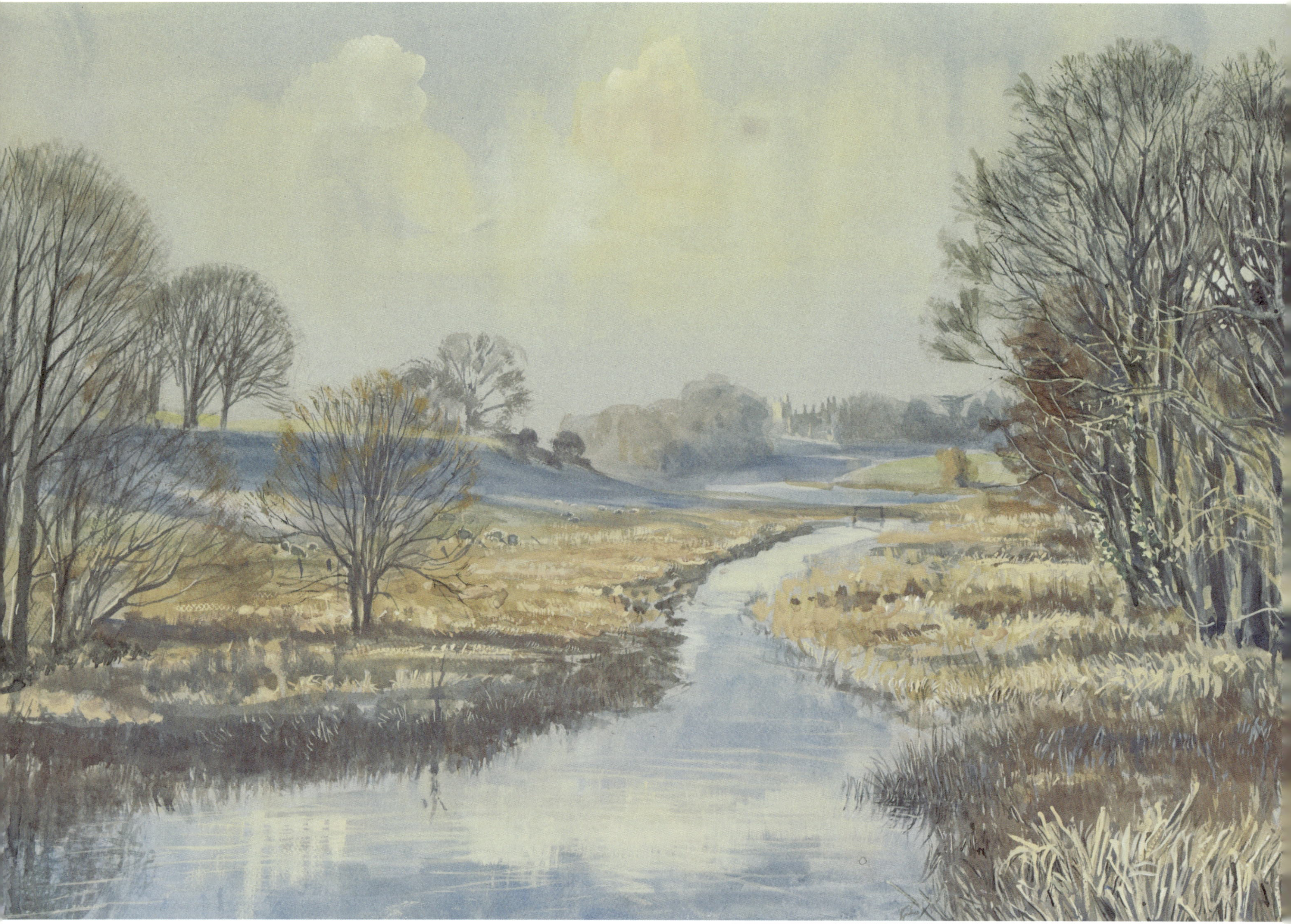

# SHERBORNE CASTLE

## Dorset 1753

THE WARM welcome extended to Brown by the Digby family was echoed when I visited Sherborne Castle on a sparkling December day. Edward Wingfield Digby gave me an extended tour. There are two castles at Sherborne; the original site was fortified by Roger, Bishop of Salisbury, in the twelfth century. In 1592 the castle was bestowed on Sir Walter Raleigh by Elizabeth I and he built the existing 'New' Castle. Shortly after Raleigh's execution in 1618, the Digbys purchased Sherborne and extended the property, and so it remains today, a flamboyant and picturesque house with prominent chimneys and towers rising into the sky. Having endured two sieges during the Civil War, the old castle was beaten down by gunfire and undermined by Oliver Cromwell, who called it a 'malicious mischievous castle – much like its owners.'

Alexander Pope visited and, as at Stowe, was moved to poetic depiction:

> Venerable broken walls, the natural cascade, with never-ceasing murmurs and the views of the glimmering waters, here there was a rustic seat of stone, flagged and rough with two urns in the same rude taste upon pedestals on each side.

He has a seat named after him, built by Henry Holland, which looks over Lancelot's lake and the castle. Just above this is Sir Walter Raleigh's seat, where supposedly a servant doused him with water when he was smoking a pipe of tobacco, it being assumed he was on fire!

OPPOSITE *Sherborne Castle in the distance from the Pinfold Bridge (watercolour).*

In 1753 Capability Brown was employed by Edward, 6th Lord Digby, to create a 50 acre lake which swept away the earlier formal gardens. Any further work was halted by Edward's death four years later. After another 20 years, in 1776, Edward's younger brother, Henry, 7th Lord Digby, asked 'Capability' to embark on a series of further changes, resulting in a landscape that remains largely unchanged, and for which the ruined castle forms a picturesque backdrop.

The original pre-Brown plans are in the archives, and show a stable block to the east of the castle. This was removed to reveal the views over the new lake, as well as upstream along the valley of the River Yeo to hanging woods and a hill called Jerusalem. Fine new stables were built on the north-west between the town and new castle. The walk through the gardens on the north side along the lake is magnificent. There are views to both east and west, which include some venerable cedars, probably planted by Brown, which dominate the mound near the old castle. To the south, from the raised lawn of the castle, there was an uninterrupted view over the ha-ha to the deer park with ancient oak dotted about a wild hillside. The melanistic fallow deer danced off as we approached.

Whilst I was there I handled a document in the castle muniments room that was written and signed Lancelot Brown in his assured and fluent hand, giving me a profound moment of satisfaction. In the 1777 game book is a note saying that 'Mr Brown came from Lord Milton's while we were at dinner and was very agreeable'. Two days later 'Capt R. Digby went with regret to Minterne before breakfast

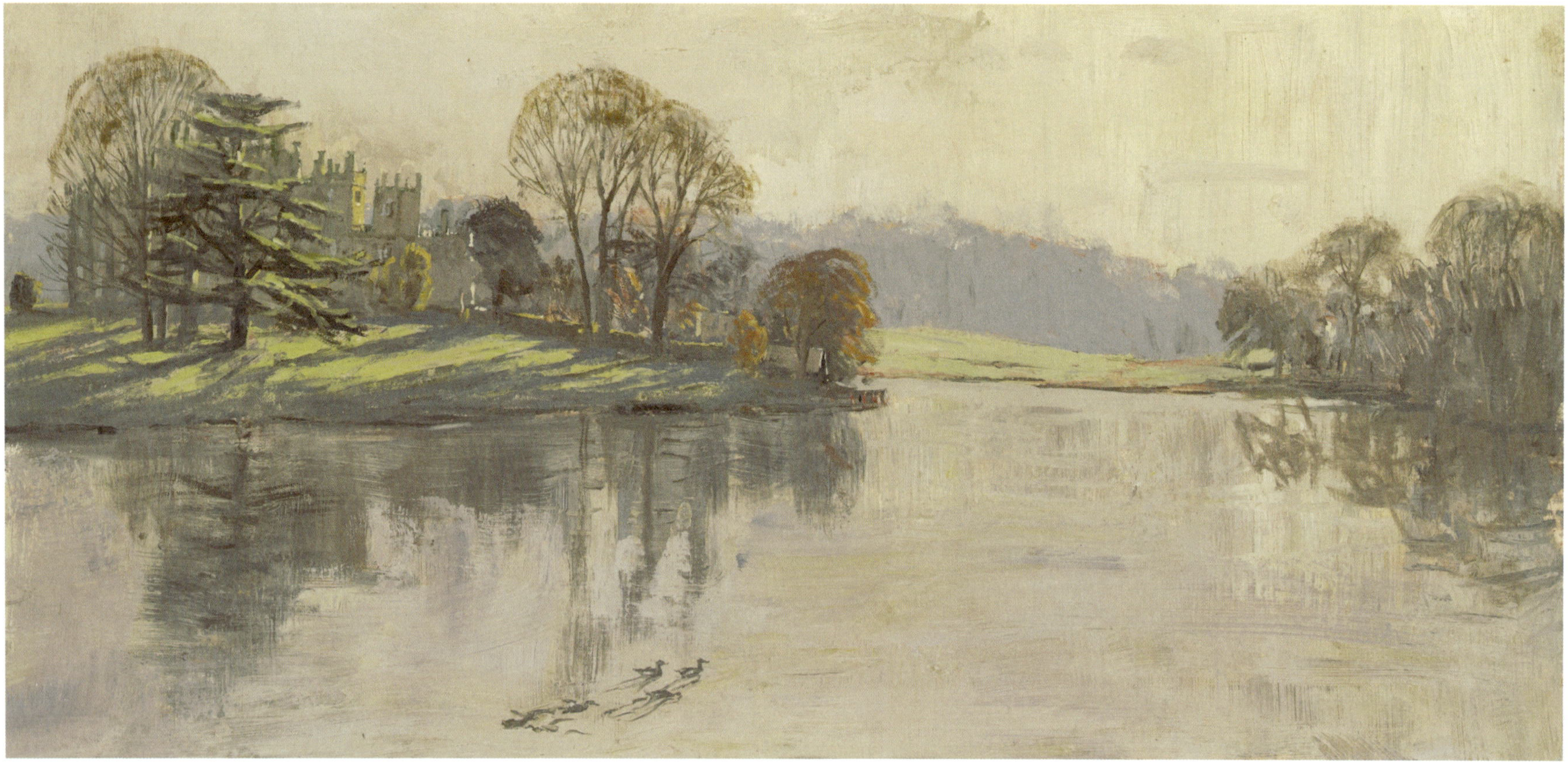

*The 'New' Sherborne Castle built by Sir Walter Raleigh (oil).*

sorry to lose any of Mr Brown's company.' This gives a cameo of a very agreeable man.

It was early afternoon when, in the warm December sun, I squinted my eyes looking south and painted a small oil. The mound where the new castle stood was striped with long shadows from the beech and cedar trees, and through and above their boughs the romantic silhouette of Walter Raleigh's castle emerged.

Another day I came back and situated myself on the delicate classical Pinfold Bridge, now disused but once on the approach road from London. The view embraced the long lake with the house in the far distance. The wild park loomed above, with the craggy ancient oaks casting long shadows across the frosty landscape. I was told to keep a sharp eye for otters, which I gather have returned, much to the annoyance of the fishermen who prize the coarse fish in the lake.

# BURGHLEY HOUSE

## Lincolnshire 1754

ONE OF the favourite poems of my youth was Tennyson's 'My Lord of Burleigh', of which this extract conveys a little of the splendour of one of our greatest Elizabethan 'palaces':

*Till a gate she discerns*
*With armorial bearings stately.*
*And beneath the gate she turns*
*Sees a mansion more majestic*
*Than all those she saw before;*

The country houses in the early dawn of the English Renaissance are like monumental pieces of sculpture. Every detail is lyrical with ornament but still unites as a single work of art, perfectly reflecting the romanticism and exuberance of the age. Burghley owes its existence to William Cecil, 1st Lord Burghley, Elizabeth I's Lord High Treasurer and 'the greatest, gravest and most esteemed councillor that ever your Majesty had.' It was he who designed and built the house, taking 32 years to do so.

In 1700 the then 5th Earl of Exeter, Burghley's direct descendant by his first wife, employed the well-known garden designers George London and Henry Wise to construct a series of elaborate gardens, containing 'canals, rising flights of terraces, ornamental fishponds, a maze, vineyards and other conceits'. Remarkably, their great Queen Anne Avenue of 1,200 double-banked limes still survives to this day.

Fifty years later, in 1754, Brownlow Cecil, the 9th Earl, called in Brown to alter the house and re-landscape the park, simultaneously sweeping away the ornate formal gardens. The earl was a straightforward man with a 'bluff, blunt featured rosy cheeked face', but with the 'unquestioned self assurance of a landowning potentate'. The two men became close friends, embarking on an amiable collaboration. The lively and knowing portrait of Lancelot Brown by Nathanial Dance was commissioned by the Earl. It still hangs in the house, and coming across it gave me a moment of surprise – as if unexpectedly meeting an old and familiar friend. He also signed Brown's petition for a royal appointment in 1758. The affection was mutual. In a letter written towards the end of his life, Brown wrote of Burghley, 'This is a great place, where I have had twenty-five

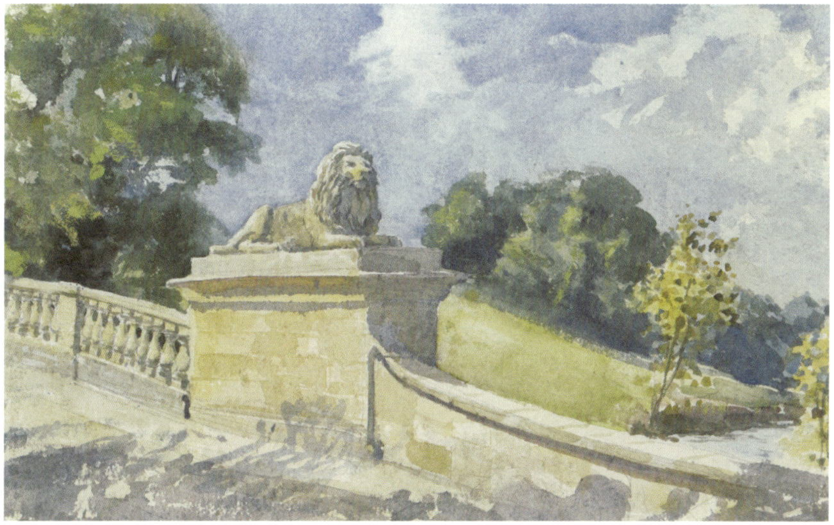

*Burghley House. Coade stone lion (watercolour).*

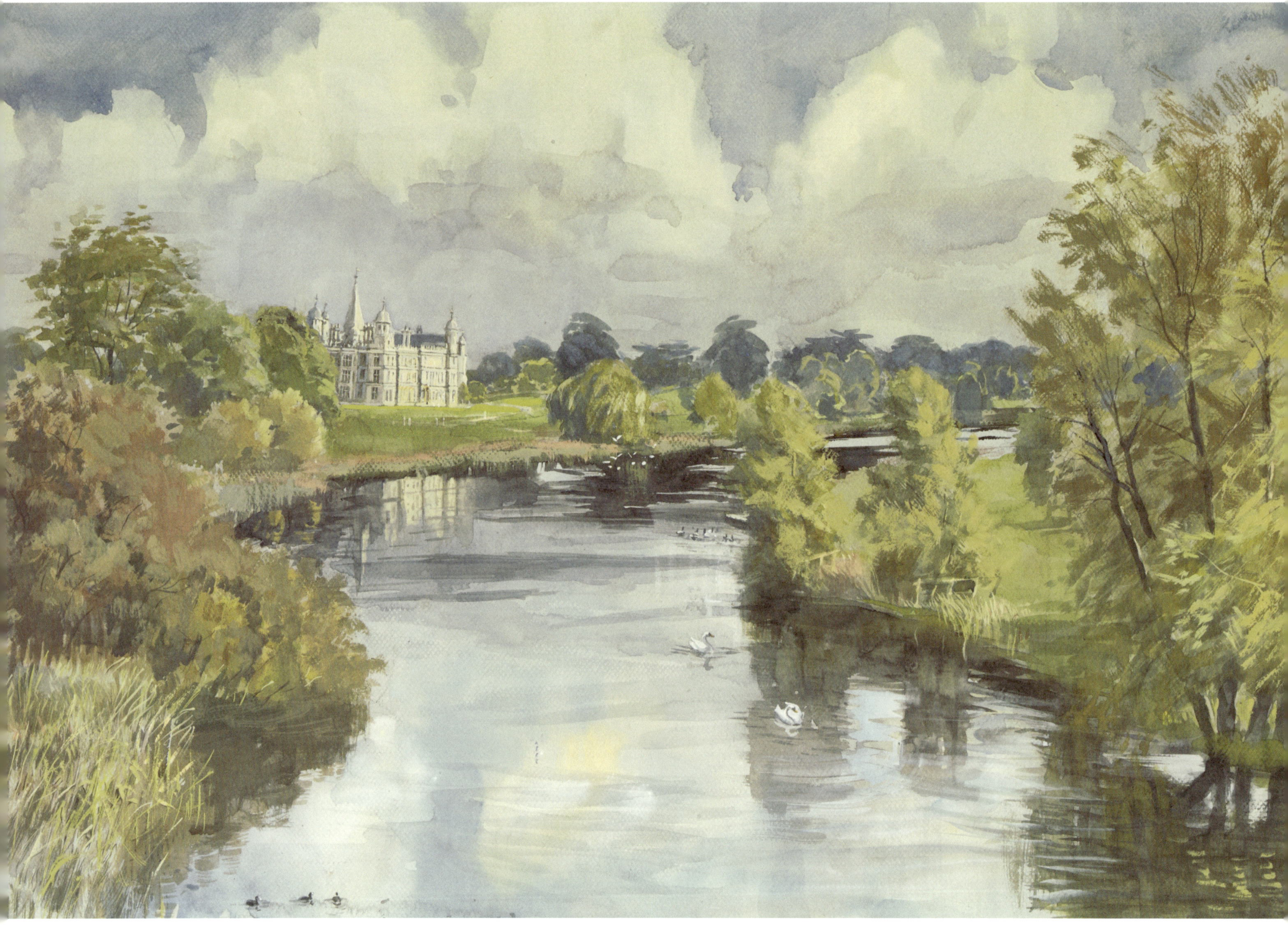

years pleasure in restoring the monument of a great minister to a great Queen'.

Brown's work at Burghley was considerable. Two wings were demolished, windows altered, the stables moved so they couldn't be seen from the principal rooms. Instead, the view now encompassed a large serpentine lake, which stretched along the south of the house and was crossed by a stone bridge ornamented with Coade stone lions bought by Brown from Eleanor Coade for £114. One consequence of the drainage work was that the once damp house became dry for the first time since being built.

As a young land agent in 1971, and living nearby, I had become familiar with Burghley and its famous horse trials, so returning to paint it re-awoke many fond memories. For a painter a windy day is an unwelcome distraction. On the late September afternoon when I went back, I spent much of my time stopping my board rattling round on its easel. Standing back to scrutinise my work, a gust tipped everything over. My viewpoint was from the Lion Bridge looking down the lake with the great house to the left. One of the frustrations of painting is waiting for washes to dry – wet into wet means that if you want to introduce more water or pigment into an existing wash you must do so immediately. Otherwise it is important to wait for the previous wash to dry thoroughly before applying another glaze. Putting more paint or water into a drying wash is a recipe for disaster and leads to ugly areas with uneven hard edges, known as cauliflowers. If you have another picture in mind from the same spot why not start it while waiting, as I did with this fine benign lion just behind me?

OPPOSITE *Burghley House, with the lake from the Lion Bridge (watercolour).*

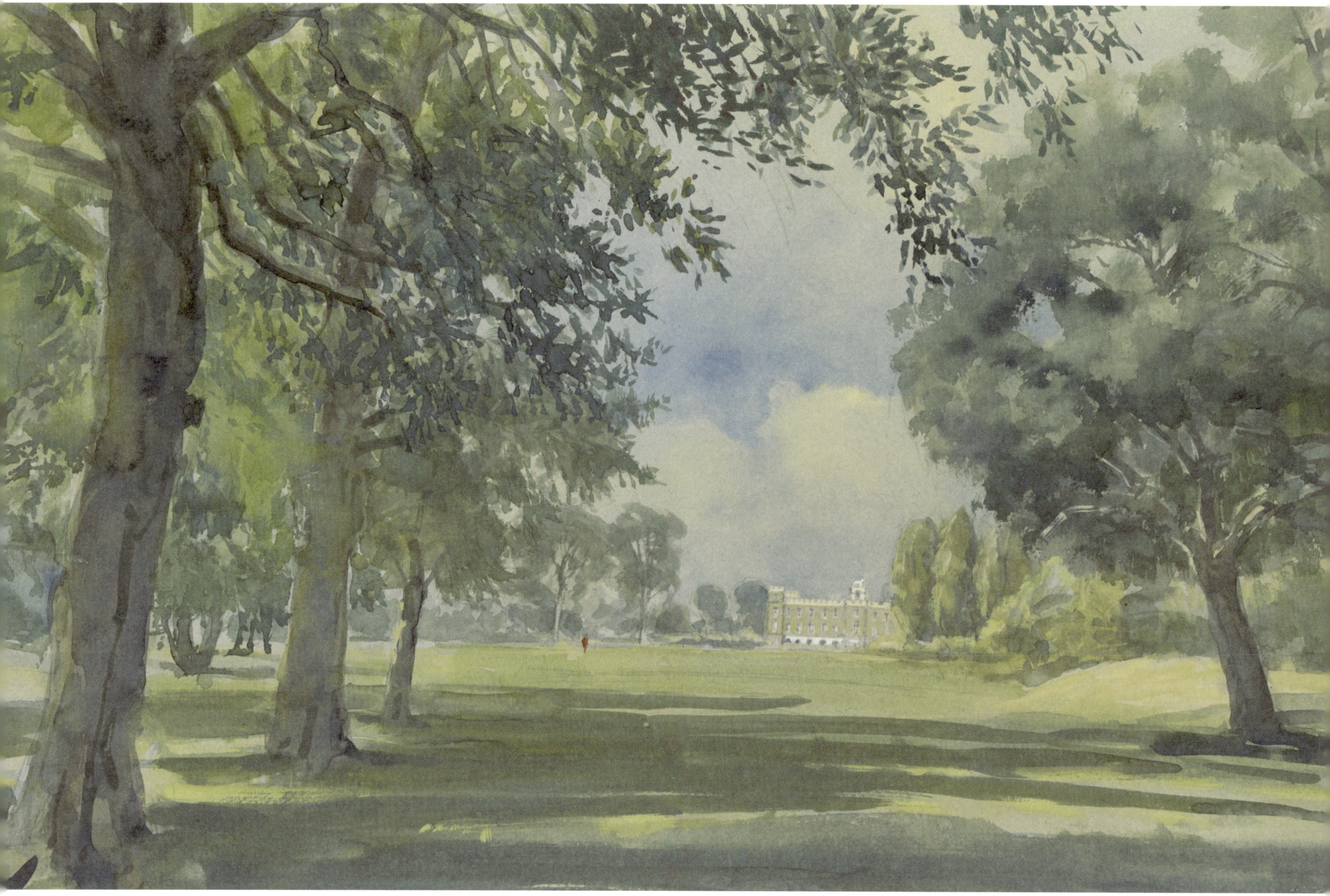

*Syon House from Kew Gardens (gouache/watercolour).*

# SYON HOUSE

## Greater London 1754

BROWN's professional life was one of continual journeying to distant estates, so work nearer to Hammersmith and home must have been welcome to both him and his long-suffering wife. Their marriage, as far as we know, was solid and conventionally Christian and they must have savoured those quiet family times.

In 1754 Brown was commissioned to undertake work at Syon House, an hour's ride away on the north bank of the Thames. The house belonged to the 1st Duke of Northumberland, whose wife Elizabeth was the daughter of the Duke of Somerset, for whom Brown had worked at Petworth. These complex tribal alliances, built round marriage and land, oiled the wheels of the eighteenth century aristocracy and helped put a signature to many of the commissions on which Brown was to work.

At Syon, Brown set to with gusto. The views towards the river were opened out and the River Brent diverted to create a series of linear lakes. A new lakeside walk meandered through shrubberies. An arboretum was planted with rare and exotic trees. In the park most ancient trees were retained but sometimes clumped up with new planting. The Syon Reach is the only unbanked stretch of the Thames in Greater London. Because of its continual grazing and conservation without 'improvement' over the centuries, Syon Park has become a recognised conservation area for both fauna and flora. For example, more than 150 different species of fungi have been recorded in its 140 acres and it harbours a diversity of insects, birds and bats.

My visit to Syon started on a wet August day, making painting impossible. As compensation I was treated to a private tour of the house, whose main state rooms, including the magnificent Long Gallery and the Great Hall, remain as Robert Adam designed them. Once the rain stopped, I went into the park, attracted by a view with the cattle. Unfortunately I also attracted them and had to beat a hasty retreat over a rather aggressive barbed wire fence, retrieving my painting equipment later: it is amazing how the old limbs can be activated when necessary.

It was not until after 1764 that Brown, following his appointment as the royal Master Gardener, became involved with the adjoining Kew Gardens, then a Royal Park.

There is a fine view from Kew to Syon across the Thames, which I painted from the comfort of a perfectly placed garden bench. After some thought I decided on gouache, using a grey paper as a mid-tone ground so that the light areas can be superimposed rather than leaving them out, as happens in pure watercolour. The picture is given an overall unity by the consistent colour of the paper and a pleasing effect is more easily obtained.

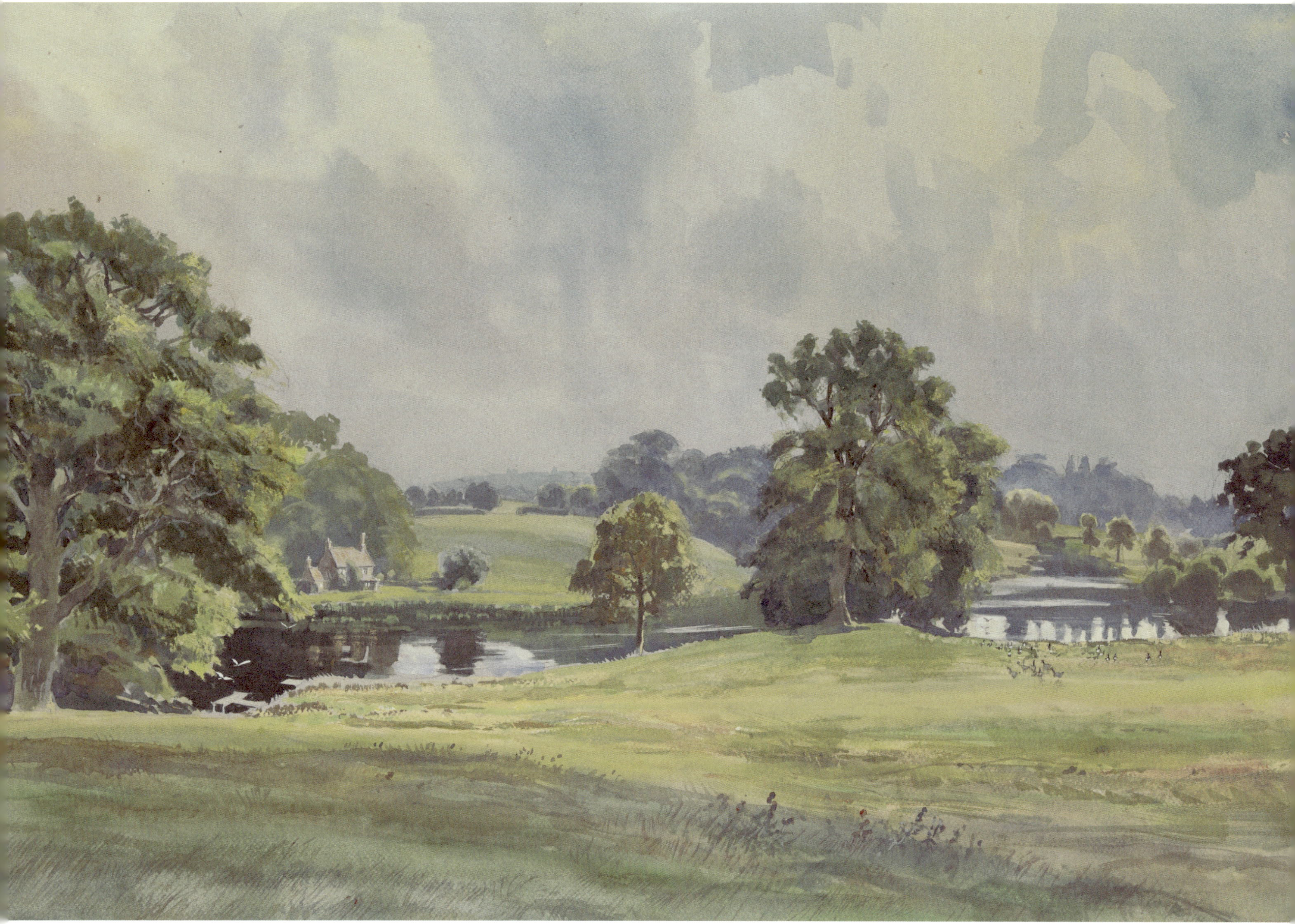

# BOWOOD HOUSE

## Wiltshire 1757

THE 1ST EARL of Shelburne initially asked Brown to draw up plans for Bowood in 1754, the year he bought the estate, but it was not until after his death seven years later that the work started. His son William, the 2nd Earl, and briefly prime minister in the 1780s, soon commissioned Brown to make a start on the inevitable lake, which in Bowood's case was almost half-a-mile long.

Bowood was one of Brown's most extensive projects. The park was of over 2,000 acres, with lawns sloping gently down from the house to the lake, and drifts of mature trees. An arboretum of rare trees was planted in the pleasure grounds behind the walled garden. A small village was moved (traces can still be found at the bottom of the lake), leaving a solitary picturesque cottage to be viewed from the house.

The Earl's wife Sophie was an enthusiastic gardener, regularly noting in her diaries the progress of the work. The original large scale plan drawn up by Brown is framed at Bowood, whilst his boundary plantings of beech are now one of the great features of the park.

In the 1770s the two parts of Bowood, the 'Big' house and the 'Little' house were joined by an enormous drawing room. It was in the 'Big' house that Joseph Priestley had a laboratory and where he 'discovered' the existence of oxygen in August 1774. During the Second World War the 'Big' house was requisitioned by the RAF, later becoming dilapidated before finally being demolished in 1955. Today, the elegant orangery and 'Little' house are the main residence. The Adam dining room was dismantled and now occupies the eleventh floor of the Lloyd's of London headquarters, the modernist Richard Roger's building. I wonder if that is a happy marriage?

The picture collection at Bowood was especially interesting to me because of the many watercolours of supreme quality, which include works by John Varley, William Callow, J. M. W. Turner and Richard Parkes Bonington. I was inevitably drawn to those by Edward Lear and David Roberts because of my life-long passion for travel and painting in the East, especially India. The 5th Marquess of Lansdowne (as the family title became) was Viceroy of India in the late nineteenth century, and it was he who accumulated the large collection of pictures of the subcontinent.

From the Victorian terrace where I painted, an Arcadian view leads the eye through a landscape that might have come from a canvas by Claude Lorrain, with every feature seemingly random, but in fact carefully placed. Groups of ancient trees in the foreground break up views of the lake beyond. A cottage, rusticated, nestles by the water. Trees, clumped or in bigger blocks, regress into the distance. Bowood's park has altered little since Brown's designs were completed, and to this day it remains one of the great examples of his genius.

OPPOSITE *Bowood House. The park from the terrace (watercolour).*

# CHARLECOTE PARK

## Warwickshire 1757

CHARLECOTE PARK is near Stratford-on-Avon, and was one of the houses Lancelot visited in 1750 when touting for business after first leaving Stowe. He would have found an ancient deer park, within a paling fence, which had once been part of the Forest of Arden, famously where Shakespeare was reputed to have been apprehended poaching. The old Warwick Road then ran past the fine Elizabethan gatehouse and beyond lay the sprawling house built by Thomas Lucy in the 1550s, and where at great expense he entertained Elizabeth I.

The estate had been owned by the Lucys since at least the thirteenth century. The then present incumbent, George Lucy, was only two years older than Brown, and the two men became good friends. In her book about the house, a recent chatelaine, Alice Fairfax-Lucy, described George as a man who 'feared boredom, loved his dogs and pretty women, and abhorred marriage but constantly talks of it.'

As his mentor and friend the Dowager Countess of Coventry observed, he had no need to 'take so irrevocable a step as marriage to solve his servant problems.' His domestic life was run by a widow, Philippa Hayes, to his total satisfaction.

George Lucy also 'bumped all over Europe', which meant that Brown did not return to Charlecote until 1757. By then the old Warwick Road had been moved to its present position on the other side of the deer park and a new bridge built over the River Dene. Initially 'Capability' did some work on the flow of the river where it joined the Avon. Three years later a formal contract was agreed:

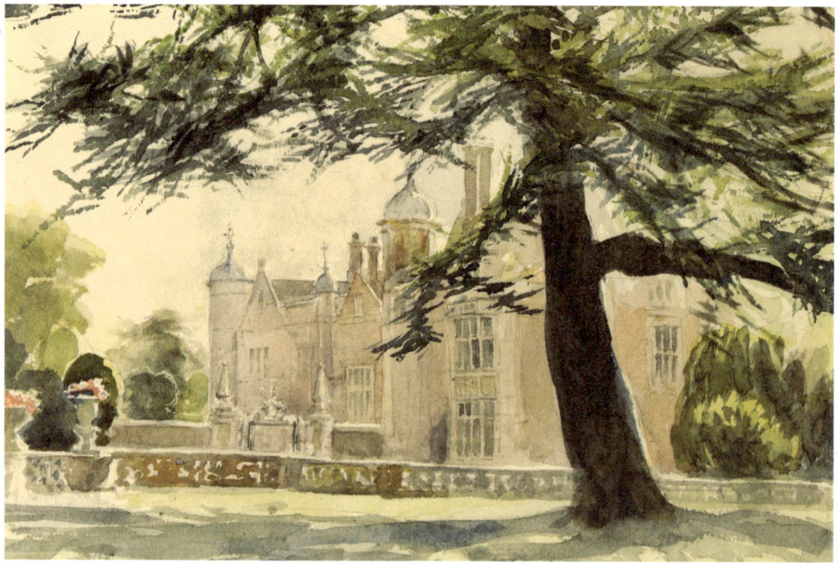

*Charlecote Park from the Orangery, now the National Trust restaurant (watercolour).*

> Article 1. To widen the River Avon and lay its banks properly . . . giving them an natural and easy level.
> Article 2. To sink the fosse [ha-ha] quite round the Meadow . . . to make sufficient fence against the deer.
> Article 3. To fill up all ponds on the north front of the house, to alter all slopes and give the whole of natural easy, and corresponding level with the house on every side.

A final article concerned the replacement of dead trees and sowing 'the altered ground with clean hayseed and Dutch clover'.

By and large this is how it is today. The house itself was consider-

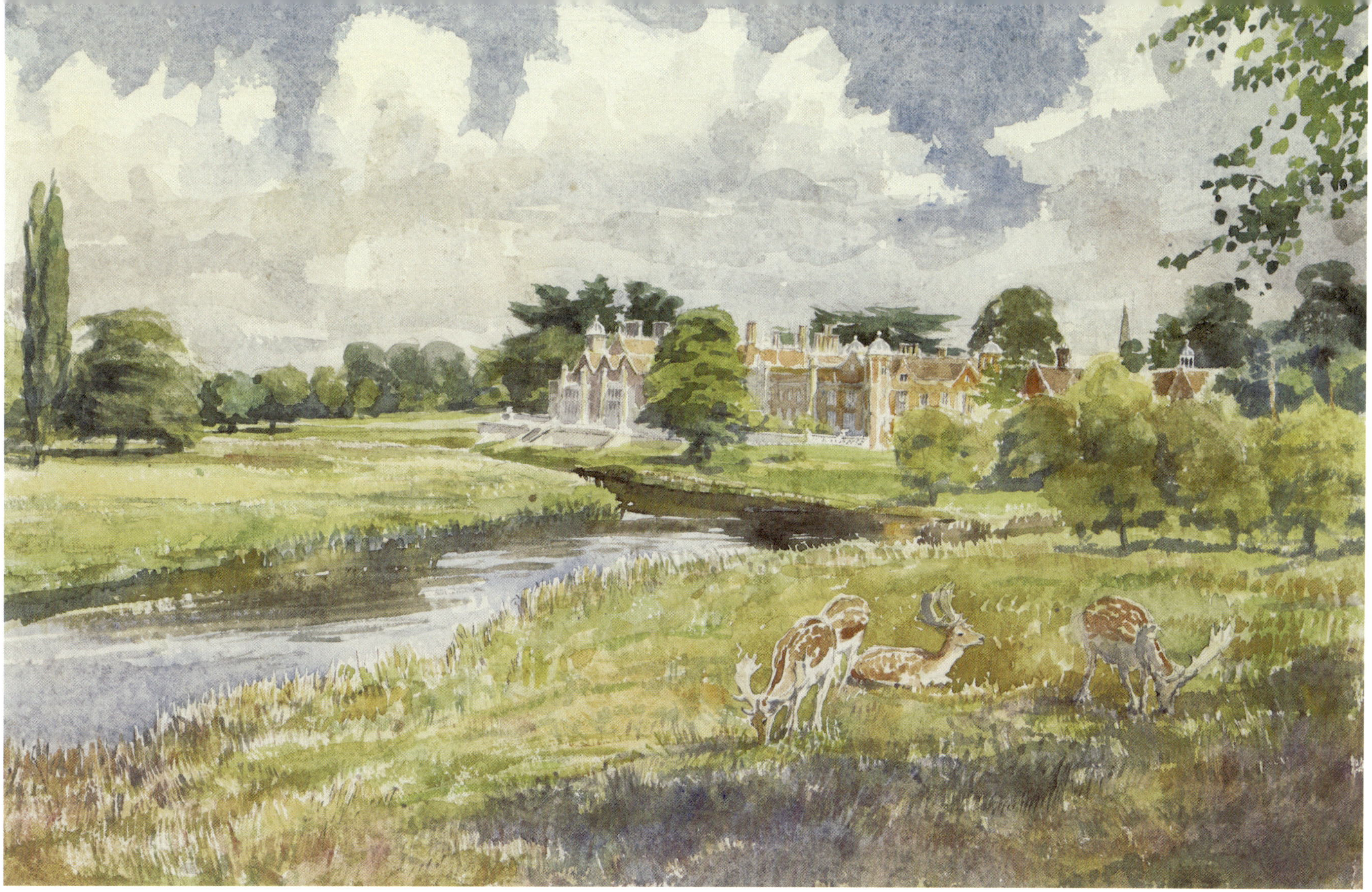

*Charlecote Park from the River Avon (watercolour).*

ably restored and altered in the early nineteenth century by George Hammond Lucy, but the overall view is still of a rose pink Elizabethan mansion set in an ancient park. Although the National Trust took over the house in 1994, the family still live there. Alice Fairfax-Lucy's son, Sir Edmund Fairfax-Lucy, the present incumbent, is a fine painter who trained at the Royal Academy schools under Peter Greenham, who tutored many good artists.

The day I visited Charlecote I walked through the ancient park to the lodge. Fearless fallow deer grazed as I passed, laden with a rucksack bulging with painting gear. Finally I found a fine viewpoint by the Avon and did my preparatory drawing. This took several hours. I had to sort out the composition and draw to scale Charlecote's many towers, chimneys and windows (all of which had to be measured). I had just finished when I was politely told I had strayed beyond a notice forbidding entry and was bade move some 30 yards; another prospect, another drawing. A bad setback, but artists have to soldier on, and so I resettled in the safe lands beyond the notice: a pity though about the pictures that might have been.

# LONGLEAT

## Wiltshire 1757

In 1558 Sir John Thynne laid the foundation stone to what was to become one of the great Renaissance houses of England. He was already 53, and had spent much of his resources renovating and extending the old priory buildings at Longleat, but in 1557 all this was destroyed in a disastrous fire. Despite his mean and grasping disposition, Sir John's energy must be admired. He was determined to start anew.

In this he was helped by Robert Smythson, later the predominant architect of the Elizabethan building Renaissance, but who arrived at Longleat as a young master mason. Quite how much of the plan and complex building operations were Smythson's and how much Sir John's is not known, but surely there was a certain synergy between the two in the creation of this great Wiltshire masterpiece? Smythson's 18 years working at Longleat had a profound influence on his future career. His crowning achievement was Hardwick Hall, more glass than wall, built at the end of Elizabeth's reign.

Longleat's site is low-lying, but the house dominates a great bowl of land between two ridges of hills. An engraving of about 1704 by Leonard Knyff shows extensive formal gardens and parterres – even a rectangular deer park and radiating avenues of trees. Canal-like waters connected squared fishponds, and the whole sits stiffly in the surrounding rolling countryside.

In 1754 Thomas Thynne, the twenty-one year old 3rd Lord Weymouth, re-inhabited Longleat after the house had been abandoned for 15 years. The once spectacular formal gardens were overgrown, the house was dilapidated and the whole estate was run down and in debt. One of his first acts was to appoint 'Capability' Brown to redesign the landscape, and the ink was barely dry on the contract before work began. The parterres, formal gardens and overgrown fish ponds were swept away, to be replaced by lawns and a series of lakes.

Sadly, since then much of the woodland has suffered. A great elm avenue stretching from the house to the Horningsham Lodge fell victim to Dutch elm disease in the 1970s. The storm of 1987 felled many of the mature chestnut and beech trees planted by Brown on a promontory overlooking the house, known now as Heaven's Gate. I remember painting there some years ago, and the watercolour on the opposite page records beech trees that are no more. However do not grieve, the loss of a great old tree allows new saplings to flourish – and so the circle of life continues.

The result of Brown's work, which cost £8000, was noted by one of the periods great gossips, and a compulsive letter writer, Mary Delany. She was astonished to find no evidence of the £30,000 spent by the 1st Viscount on his gardens and 'water works'. 'They are succeeded by a fine lawn, a serpentine river, wooded hills, gravel paths meandering round a shrubbery, all modernised by the much sought after Mr Brown.'

It is easy to concentrate on the park, lakes, statues, follies and great houses that Brown created, ignoring his contribution to the evolution of the kitchen garden. In such places as Longleat fruit and vegetables were originally grown within the formal pleasure gardens immediately around the house. Fruit trees would be in espaliered rows along

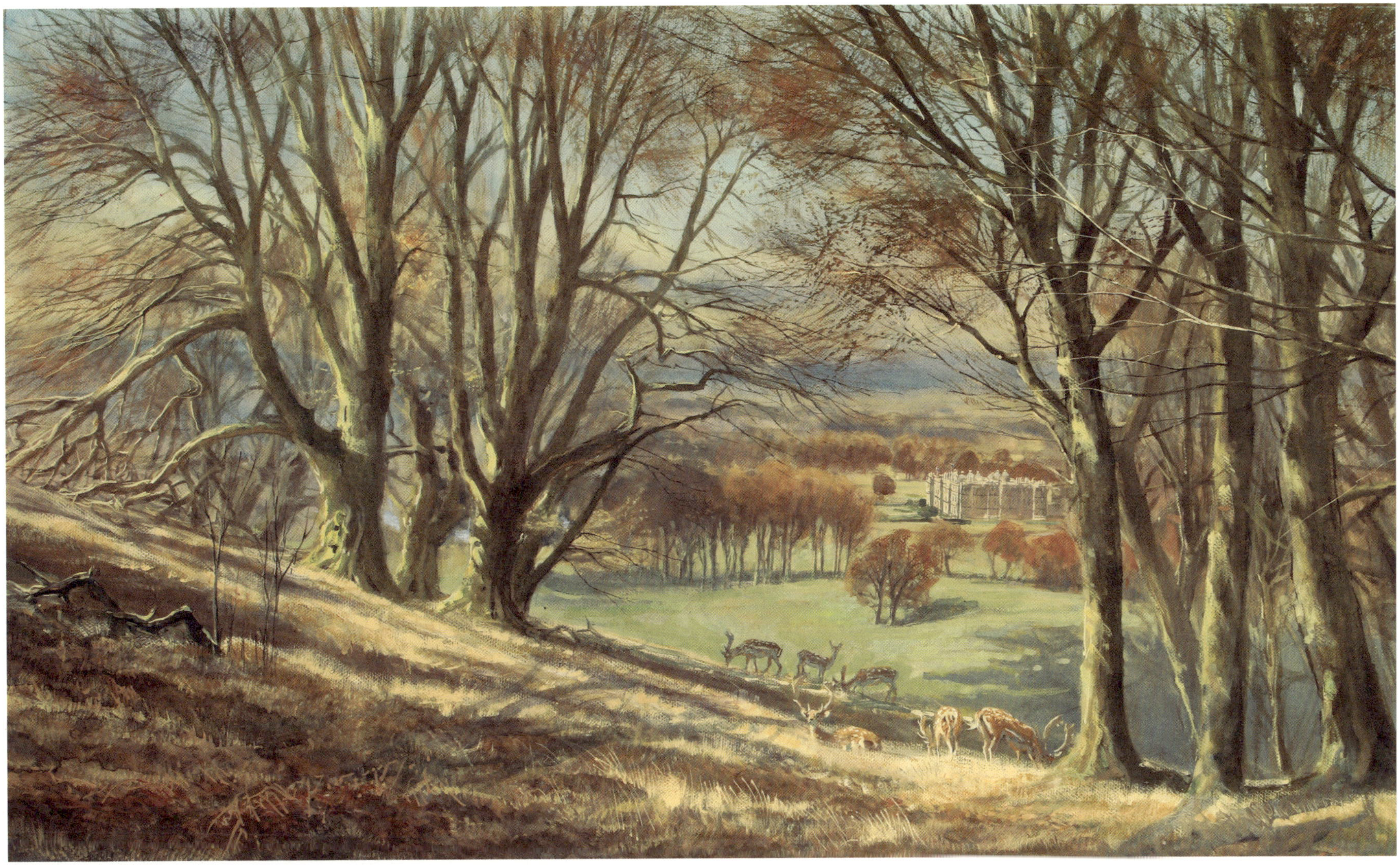

*Longleat. The park and house from Heaven's Gate painted in 1982. Most of the trees in the view were blown down in the great gales of 1987 (watercolour).*

the paths, whilst vegetables grew in geometric beds conforming to an overall pattern. Perhaps these beds might have been contained within tightly-cut box hedging. Roses and other flowers might be interspersed and the character and colour of the vegetables themselves gave form to the garden. A fine example can still be seen in France in the great formal gardens of Villandry in the Loire valley.

The eighteenth century marked the start of a revolution in domestic food production. It was realised that a microclimate could be created by surrounding a garden with a high wall, whilst developments in glass production and ironwork meant that tender plants and shrubs could be nursed through an English winter. Immense glasshouses became scented with new and exotic fruits – pineapples, pomegranates, peaches, vines, oranges and lemons.

However, the geometric walls and the subsidiary buildings required for almost industrial fruit and vegetable production were not a happy companion to the landscapes being created by Brown and the other disciples of the natural garden. How out of place a walled garden would have looked in a Claude Lorrain painting. The now unfashionable kitchen garden was tucked away somewhere unseen, often a long way from the main house.

At Longleat these gardens are about half-a-mile away, hidden by heavy planting. They are about 4 acres and are surrounded by high walls with a dividing wall in the middle. They include a number of buildings, many of a later date, whilst others built as lean-tos line the northern exterior wall. A delightful company called Simpsons Seeds now manage the gardens with an artistic mixture of good order and overgrown chaos. They grow everything organically, resulting in a continual battle with nature, but the garden is buzzing with bees. 250 years ago it would have been a very different place. All would have been meticulously tended by a dozen or so gardeners, priding themselves in growing the exotic at a time when a pineapple on your table was the ultimate status symbol.

In present times art and love have flourished at Longleat. Alexander Thynn, the present marquis, has devoted his energy to both. On a visit some years ago he showed me with pride his portraits of his multitude of 'wifelets' and his other murals, some depicting the Karma Sutra. The subject matter displayed a rude medieval vigour and the overall effect of the thickly applied paint was of Elizabethan stump work. The scale was magnificent and unfashionably I am not a voice to deride his achievement. My paintings by comparison seem very small as I try to convey 'Capability' Brown's much bigger canvas.

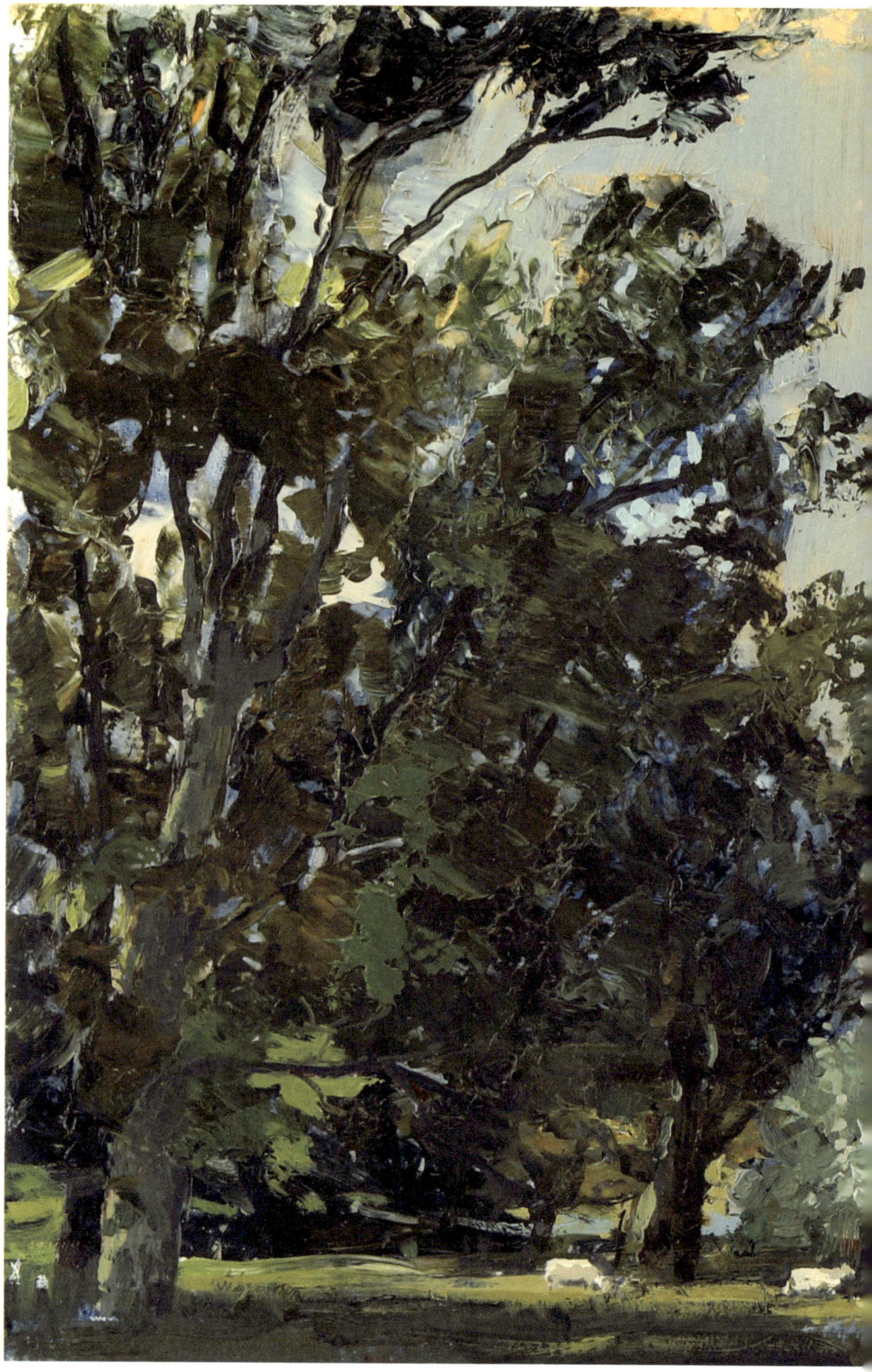

*Longleat (oil).*

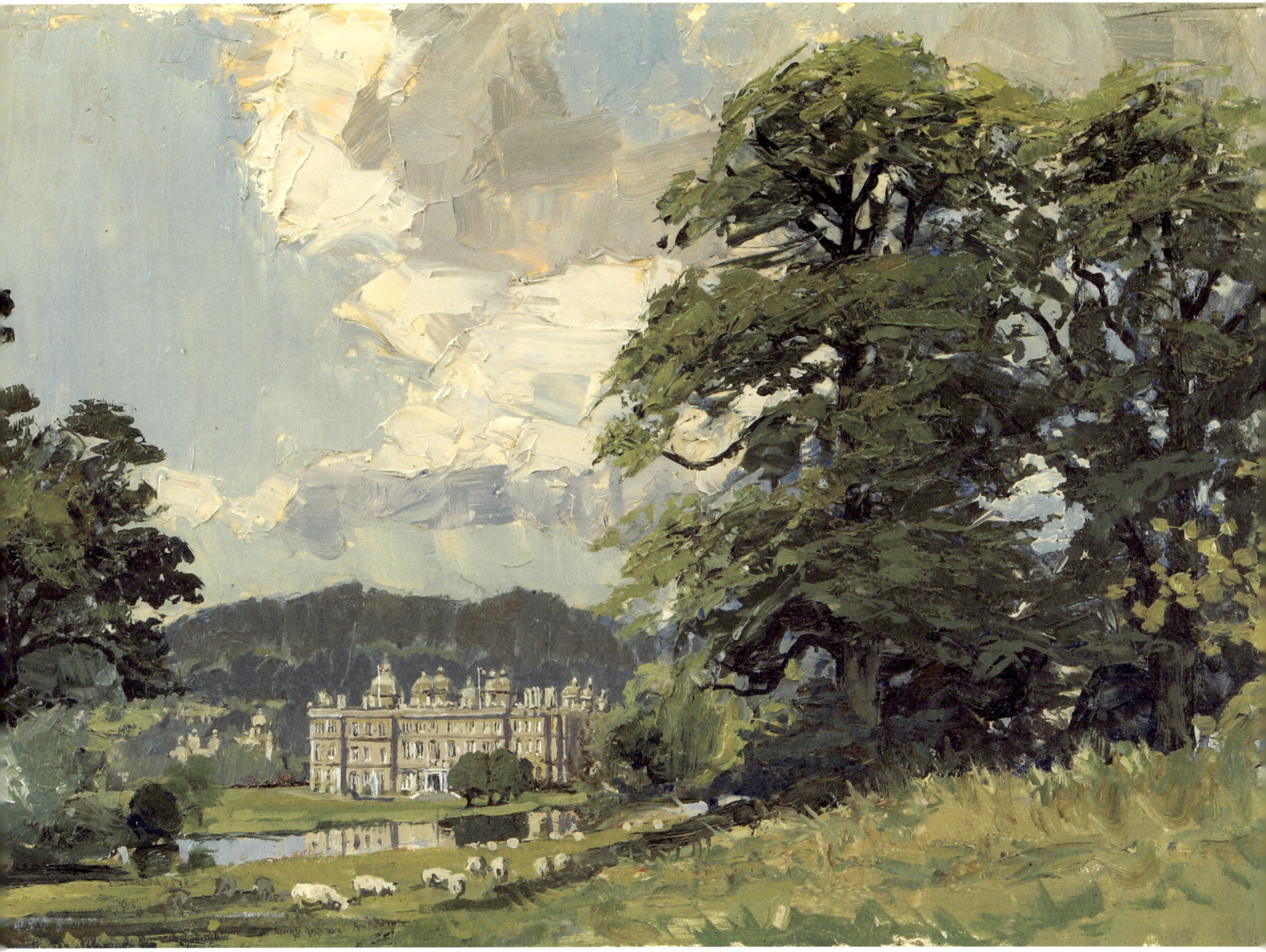

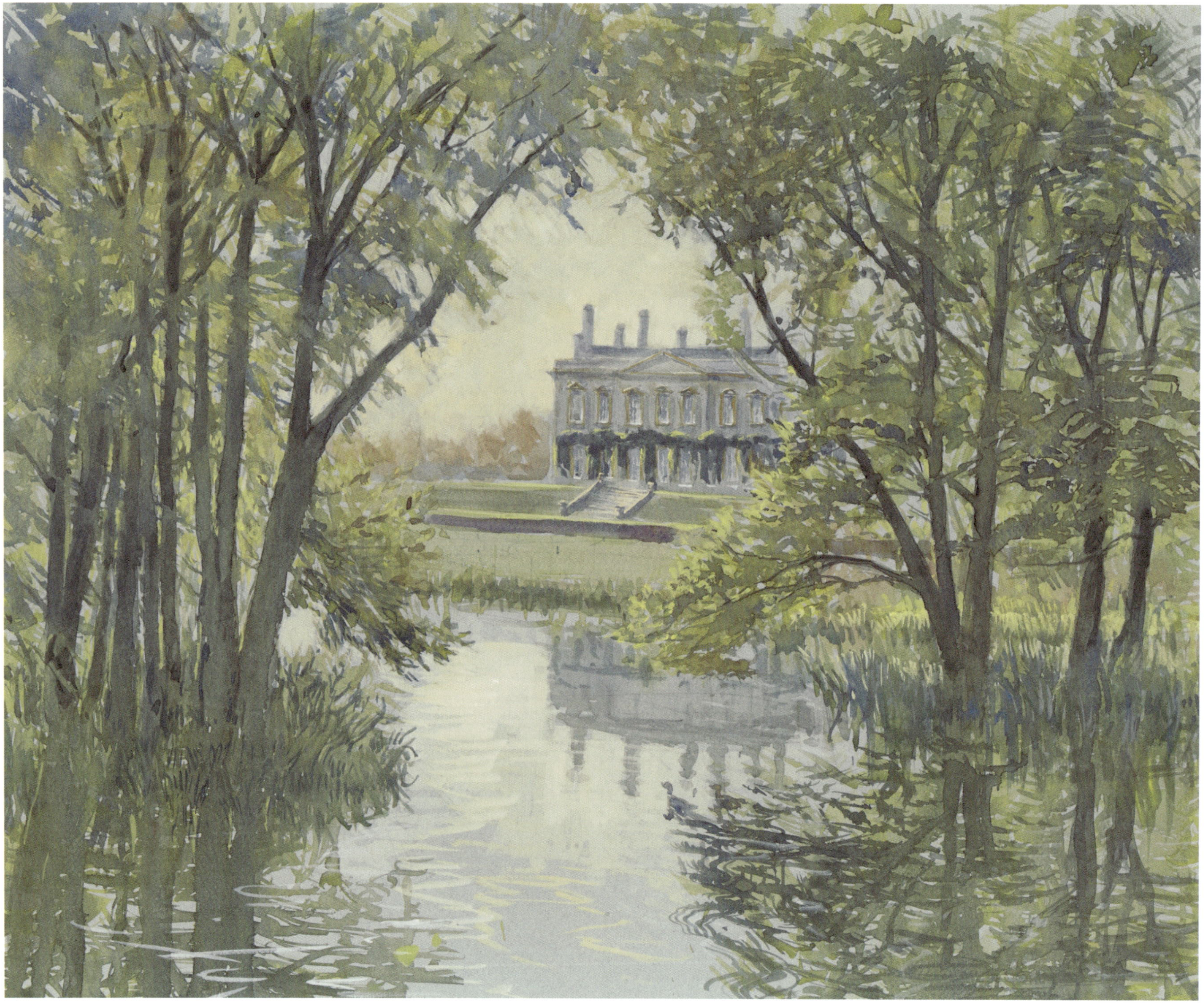

# ASTROP PARK

## Northamptonshire 1758

THIS MANUSCRIPT poem was found at Corsham Court in the Methuen Collection and referred to Astrop thus:

*At Astrop Brown his skill display'd*
*In Woods and Lawns and clear Cascades,*
*The first from fetter'd Rules set free,*
*And made the Lawns with these agree. . . .*

This classical house, built by the Smiths of Warwick in the 1730s, lies in the Cherwell Valley. It was here that Brown designed a long lake and shelter belt for the lawyer and MP, Sir John Willes, the elderly Chief Justice of the Court of Common Pleas.

Near the house is a spring surrounded by a small spinney. In the eighteenth century this was known as St Rumbold's Well and a celebrated place to take the waters. Thomas Short, writing in 1740, found it a 'certain cure in all female Obstructions, and singularly good in the first, and beginning of the second stage of consumptions; seldom fail in the Jaundice, or begining Dropsies, effectually restores a Constitution Shattered by hard Drinking, they are Sovereign in Rheumatic pains Stone and Gravel; and have restored several who have been melancholly or maniac.' One distinguished visitor was William Pitt the Elder, who wallowed in the ironstone mud.

The late owner of Astrop, John Ewart, hunted into his eighties. His wife, Susie, was a professional photographer and good painter. Tragically, she broke her back in a riding accident. She could move her arms but not her hands, but through sheer determination she retaught herself how to paint. While helping her in this, I gave the matter a lot of thought. Beyond my admiration for her spirit in overcoming her physical limitations, I realised that in painting by far the most important aspect is the vision. The dexterity and finesse in the execution of a picture are worth nothing if you cannot analyse honestly what you see and find a way of interpreting it to convey some truth about the subject matter – whether it be a landscape, a nude, a still life or an abstract. In some ways her pictures gained a strength and clearer vision when the distractions of detail were less easily achieved.

The opposite can apply; how often has the student who could draw brilliantly ceased to observe because his or her virtuoso skill obstructed observation? Skill, and the 'knowledge' of how to paint, should be a servant and not master in your act of creation. To put it more simply, be suspicious of anyone who says 'this is how to paint a tree'.

*Astrop Park. The walk around the lake gives Brownian glimpses of the house and park (watercolour).*

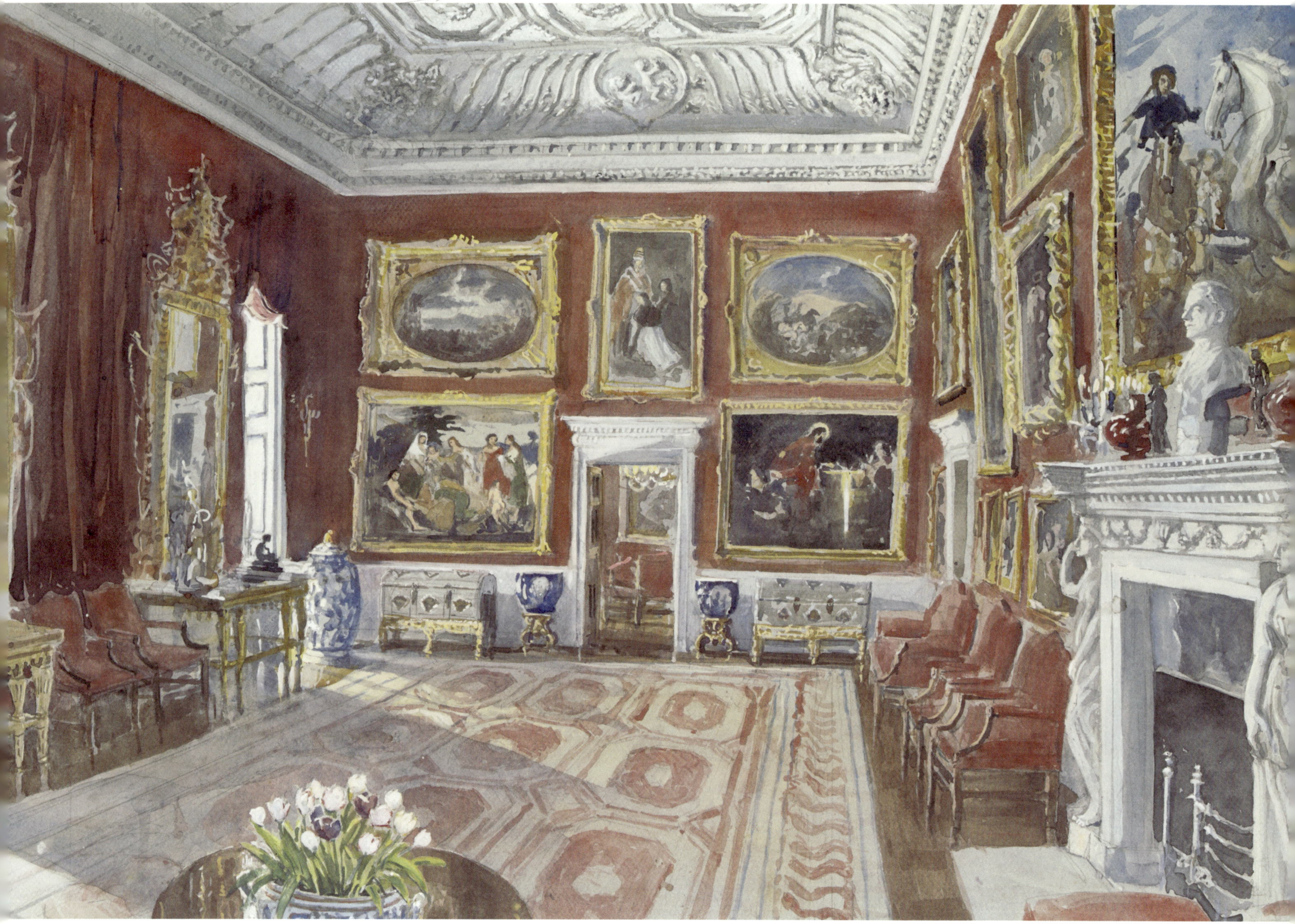

# CORSHAM COURT

## Wiltshire 1760

ALTHOUGH 'Capability' Brown visited and submitted a plan for Corsham Court in 1760 no work started until a year later, due to his ill health. He apologised to the owner, Paul Methuen, for 'My health which has been extremely bad is now on the mend and I hope to be quite stout'.

Once recovered, Brown embarked on what was to become one of his most successful undertakings, involving both enlarging the house and landscaping the park. His schedule of work still survives:

> Making the great Walks and sunke Fence between the House and the Chippenham Road.
> The draining the ground between the Sunke Fence and the line of the garden.
> To making the Water in the Parks, as also the levelling round it.
> The levelling round the House, as also on Front the New Building.
> The Sunke Fence on the Front of the Church-yard. All the planting included, Mr Methuen to find trees . . . the Above Articles comes to one Thousand and twenty Pounds.

Only part of this work was completed in Brown's lifetime. For instance, the lake was undertaken by Repton to Brown's plan some years later.

This was soon followed by a second contract to substantially alter the Elizabethan house and build a gallery, needed to accommodate the promised inheritance of important Renaissance pictures from Methuen's cousin and godfather, the well-travelled diplomat Sir Paul Methuen.

Much of the park and building work have been substantially altered since Brown's time – among others by Nash and Repton – but the gallery remains unchanged; many of the paintings hang where they were originally placed over 250 years ago. It is a fine room, measuring 72 x 25 x 20 feet, with four large windows and walls hung with crimson silk damask (700 yards at 13s 6d per yard). The care Brown took over the ceiling can only be appreciated by studying the detail, for each swag of fruit and flowers has its own unique form. The design was originally intended for Burton Constable in Yorkshire but was not used.

In 1959 the 4th Lord Methuen commissioned from the royal tapestry and carpet factory in Madrid a carpet which mirrors the ceiling's design. Pictures by van Dyck, Rubens and Guido Reni are closely hung, but it is work by lesser-known artists that caught my eye. The small head of a cavalier by William Dobson, and the two sisters and brother of the artist by Sofonisba Anguissola, particularly attracted me.

The Christian name Paul recurs generation after generation in the Methuen family, but their characters were very different. The 3rd Lord Methuen was a Field Marshal, whilst his son, who dissuaded his father from selling the picture collection, became an eminent artist and was elected a full RA in 1959. The formative influence on his style was Sickert, and although not a member of the

OPPOSITE *Corsham Court. The picture gallery is one of Brown's most distinguished interiors and many of the paintings are still in the place where they were originally hung (watercolour).*

Camden Town group his paintings are imbued with their quality.

I was particularly interested to see the modern collection, which the present owner, James Methuen-Campbell, went to much trouble to show me. Pictures had been removed to various storage rooms from their previous hanging place and it was like exploring an Aladdin's cave with a new delight at every turn. The many Paul Methuens were spiced by Sickert, Augustus John and William Nicholson and augmented more recently by James's acquisitions, which include works by Thomas Hennell (a writer and illustrator killed at the end of the Second World War) and S. R. Badmin, who did intricate and delightful pictures for the Shell posters.

Painting an interior presents particular challenges, especially when there are so many pictures, chairs, tables (designed by Adam), marble busts, elaborate candelabra, ginger jars and a highly patterned carpet. Other complications were the architectural details of the room with its ornate ceiling, marble chimneypiece with intricate carving, the pedimented doorframes, the crimson of the wall and furniture and the way the light cascades through the two windows that remain open (two have been curtained off).

In the drawing I had to initially forget all this detail and concentrate on the proportion of the room. I personally like to make a little sketch to decide on the parameters of the picture. In this case I wanted a broad perspective of the room with the chimneypiece and light coming through at least one window. Having done this I can fairly accurately draw where the horizon is on my paper. Everything in the room is either above or below your eye level or horizon. It is a hypothetical line in that it does not actually exist (unless you can actually see something like the sea where it meets the sky) but in the drawing it is the only line from which you can measure and fix all the features in the room. This of course assumes you keep your head in a fixed position because as soon as you move the whole perspective changes. It helps if you can directly measure (sight size method) where various points are in relation to the horizon and draw to scale. The other important point is to establish the central vanishing point in the room, which will determine the angle of every parallel line coming towards you. This is easy because it is the point on the horizon immediately opposite you on the far wall. Having established the outline drawing it is then much easier to fix the position of all the ornaments, furniture, pictures and other details, which immediately attract the eye and which one instinctively wishes to depict first.

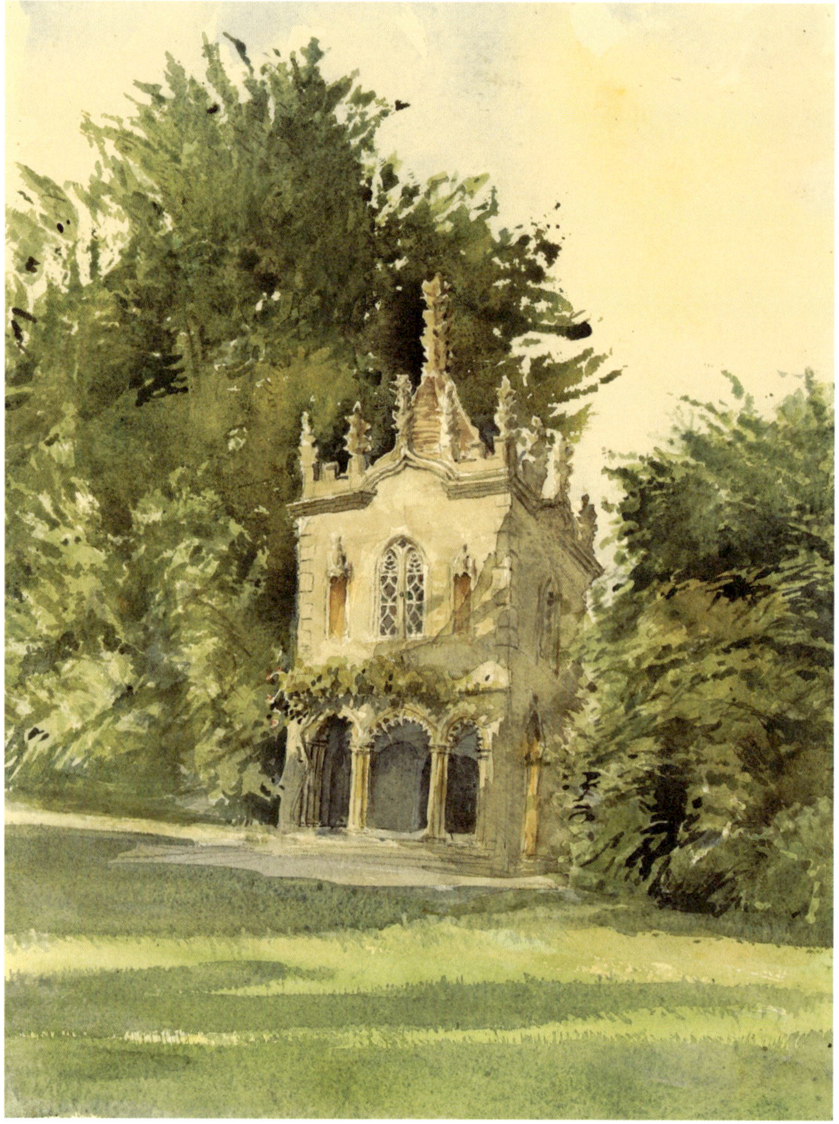

*Corsham Court. The Bath House built by Brown but Gothicised by Nash (watercolour).*

# PRIOR PARK

## Somerset 1760

There is only circumstantial evidence that Brown was involved in the landscaping of Prior Park, in that in 1760 £100 was paid into his Drummonds bank account by its builder, Ralph Allen. It could be considered an indulgence to include it as a Brown landscape, but William Pitt was a close friend of Allen and might well have promoted Lancelot's interests. Also, he had done much work locally, at Corsham and Longleat, and the hanging woodland on either side of the valley at Prior Park has the characteristic stamp of his work.

Prior Park is interesting, not only for its breathtaking natural situation above Bath, with fine views over the city and a deep valley below, but also because of the rags-to-riches story of Ralph Allen, its creator. Allen was a Cornish postmaster's son, who aged 19 joined the postal service at Bath, rising to become deputy postmaster. He is credited with eventually reforming the entire postal system, shrewdly realising that by creating a network of postal routes that avoided London he could cut back on fraud and inefficiency, thereby making himself a fortune on the way.

He then used part of his wealth to buy stone quarries round Bath, persuading his quarrymen to cut the honey-coloured Bath Stone in regular squared-off blocks, which he then marketed by constructing a small ornate building in the centre of the city. With the proliferation of building in Georgian Bath he made a second fortune. With this he bought the Prior Park estate and built a substantial Palladian mansion at the top of a valley 'to see all Bath and for all Bath to see.'

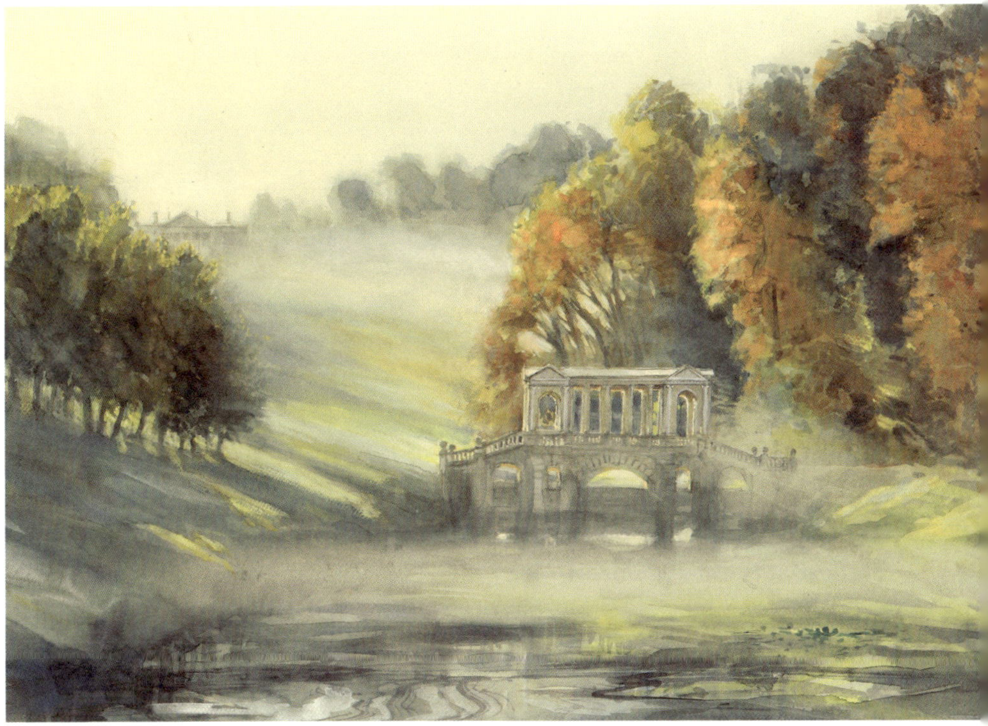

*Prior Park with the Palladian Bridge (watercolour).*

The Palladian bridge of 1755, one of only four in existence (the others are at Stowe, Wilton, and St Petersburg), acts as a dam between the upper two lakes and is a spectacular viewpoint from the terrace of the mansion above.

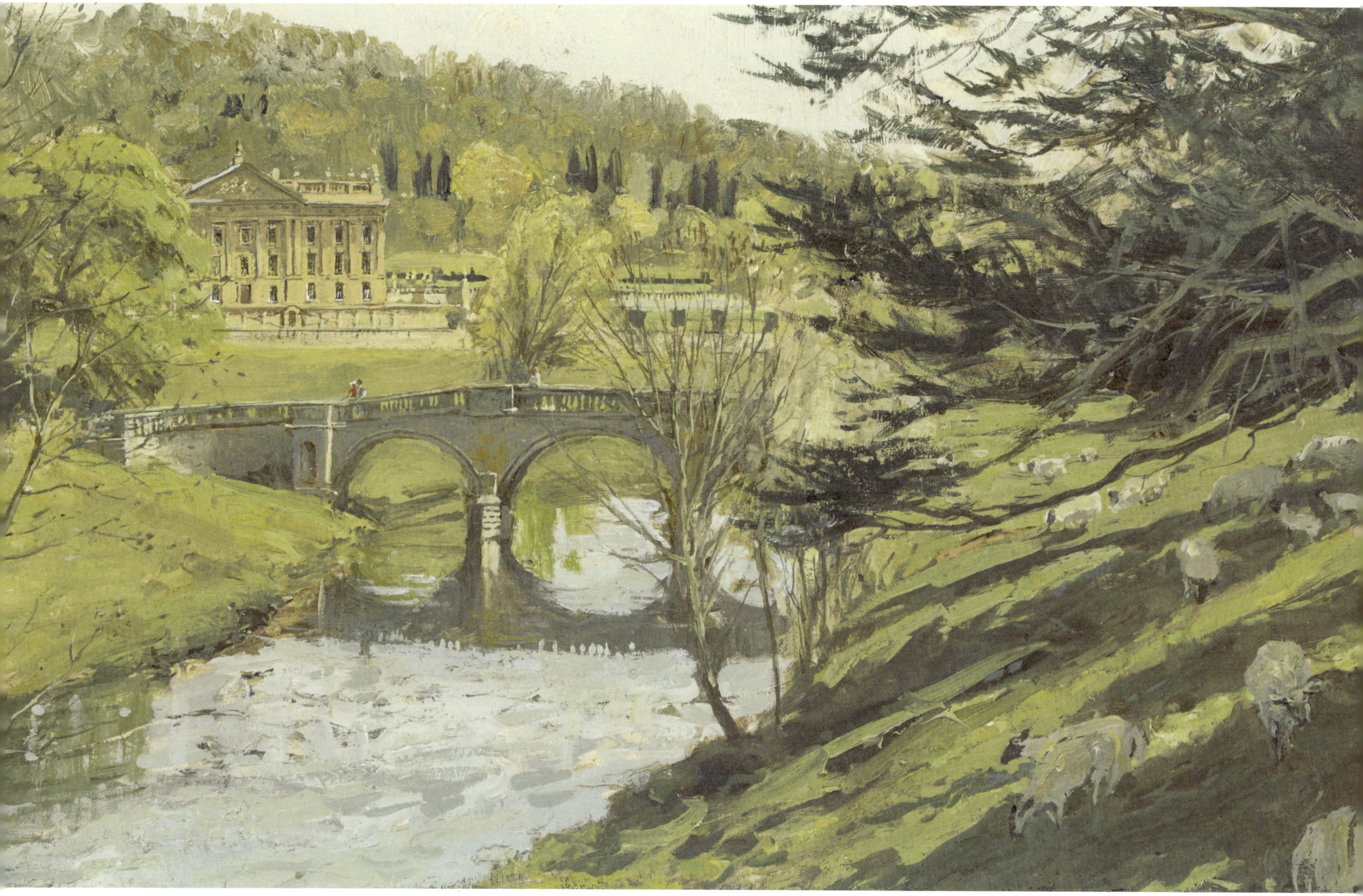

*Chatsworth House with James Paine's bridge (oil).*

# CHATSWORTH HOUSE

## Derbyshire 1760

Daniel Defoe described visiting Chatsworth in the 1730s as riding over 'a vast extended moor or waste, which for 15 or 16 miles together presents with neither hedge, house or tree, but a waste and howling wilderness.' 'What could be more wondrous,' he went on, when from that 'comfortless barren the traveller looks down into the most pleasant garden and the most beautiful palace in the world.' With the motor car one has a slightly different impression, but even now it is hard not to feel a real sense of surprise when one first glimpses this great house, which sits so well in its rolling park.

The original Elizabethan house was transformed by the 1st Duke of Devonshire at the beginning of the eighteenth century, and the formal gardens were set out by London and Wise. Jan Siberechts's painting of 1707 shows them as lush and green, but beyond the encircling wall a rough, bare bank dropped steeply down, hiding the River Derwent from the house.

In the mid 1750s the 4th Duke engaged William Kent, who began the naturalization of the gardens by sweeping away much of the formal elements. James Paine undertook work on the house and, after altering the route of the drive and surrounding approach roads, built two new bridges – one whose three arches span the Derwent and is adorned with sculpture. Brown followed in Paine's wake, principally to landscape the park and reduce the likelihood of flooding. It was not the first time the two men had worked together, but there is no clue as to their relationship.

'Capability' Brown retained the terraced gardens to the north and west of the house, but radically shaped the contours of the land to the south and east, so that the Derwent could be seen from the house. Brown's mastery of water was once again employed to full effect. After levelling out the steep bank by the river, he raised the water level with a weir, which still exists downstream by the classical mill – now a romantic ruin. A once rapid torrent subject to flooding became a tranquil sheet of water reflecting the sky, house and James Paine's fine bridge.

Next Brown turned his attention to the planting of trees. Wedge-shaped clumps were strategically placed in the park. The great ridge behind the house was heavily planted to define the soft green nest in which Chatsworth sits (the accounts for 1760/61 include 71,500 thorns, 15,000 rowans and 10,000 oaks).

Even Paine was impressed by 'Capability's' handiwork at Chatsworth. 'In justice to Mr Lancelot Brown,' he wrote, 'it would be an omission not to say that he has executed his part in a masterly manner and has, by his skill, contributed to making it one of the noblest palaces in Europe.'

Houses seem to take on the persona of those who live there. Despite its grandeur, Chatsworth is one of the 'warmest' houses imaginable. The 11th Duke of Devonshire inherited unexpectedly. With the house came an enormous burden of death duties, which could easily have broken up the whole establishment. With shrewd guidance and great energy and determination the estate enjoyed an unlikely renaissance. The public were embraced almost as guests and 'Debbo', as the world knew the Duchess, wrote books, opened shops and became a great publicist for the brand. The tradition of

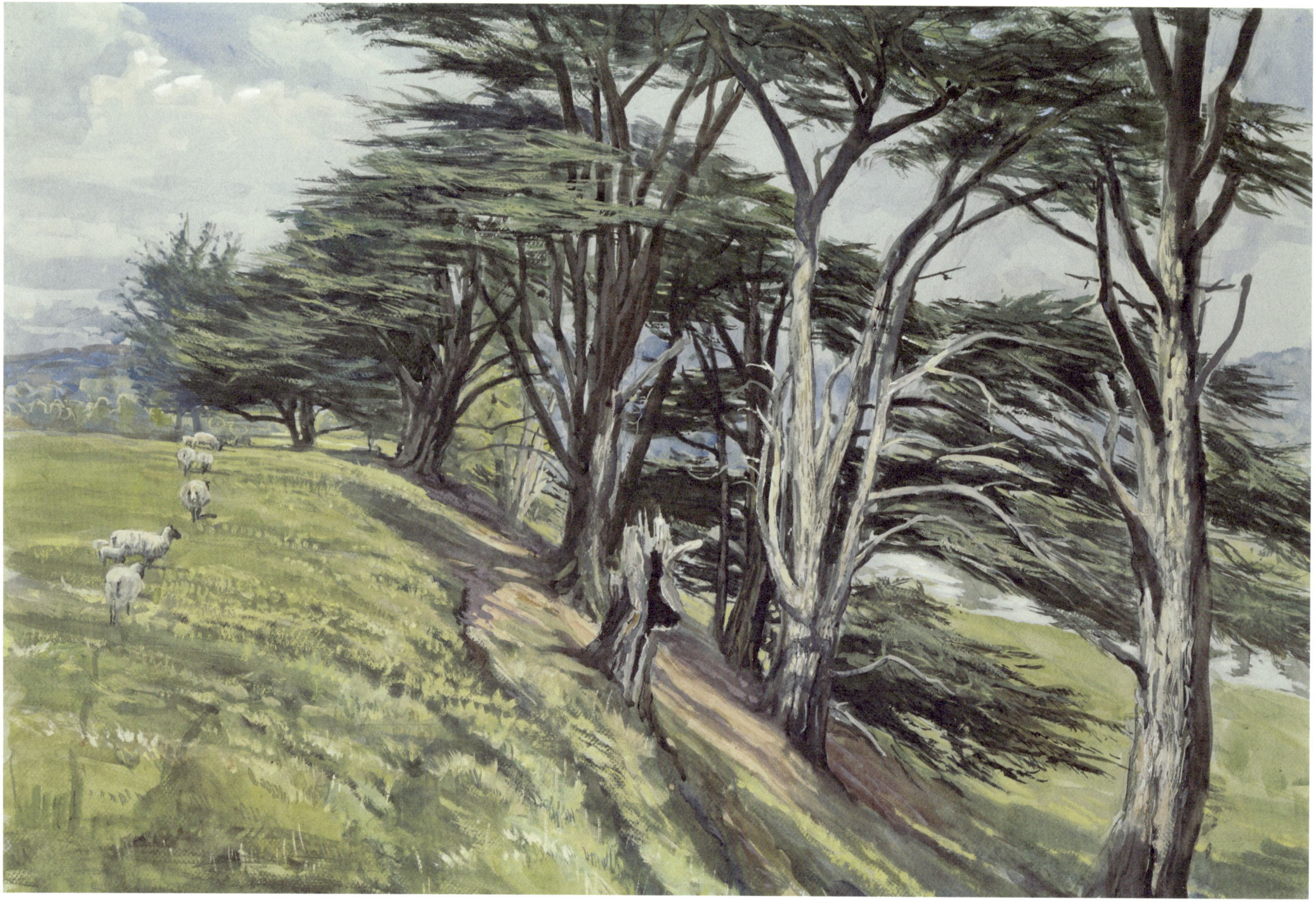

*Chatsworth House. Great cedars of Lebanon probably planted by Brown on the banks of the River Derwent (watercolour).*

collecting art was revived. Lucien Freud was a friend and did a number of paintings of the late Duke and Duchess, which are in their collection. The tradition continues, for the 12th Duke is a keen collector of the avant-garde, thus enlivening the eclectic treasures of the historic permanent collection.

In 1988, I received an anonymous commission to paint the funeral of David Cecil, the historian, who had died in 1986. No sensible artist would have taken this on but I looked at my leaking roof and launched into the task. On completion, still without knowing who had commissioned the picture, a letter came from Andrew Devonshire asking me to record various scenes on his properties, which included not only Chatsworth but Bolton Abbey and Lismore Castle in Ireland. So coming back to paint was like revisiting an old friend.

Since my last visit, generations of industrial grime have been removed from the house (over the moors are Chesterfield and the South Yorkshire coalfields). The windows have been gilded to emulate one of the great palaces in St Petersburg: with their gold leaf beside the rich cream stone of the walls it now glows in the evening sun. I felt an oil painting tingling in my fingers and imagined mixing yellows, reds and a touch of umber with pure cadmium yellow for the gold leaf. The woods beyond were coming into leaf, forming a more subdued but similar palette to the house. Suddenly the sun lit Chatsworth's western face, picking out the columns and lower window ledges. Afterwards I discovered that the great cedars Brown planted by the Derwent were probably to be felled. As a requiem, using gouache and watercolour, I painted their tortuous forms dramatically clinging to the steep riverbank.

# CASTLE ASHBY

## Northamptonshire 1761

Castle Ashby was developed as a major house by Henry Compton in 1574 out of a crenellated medieval manor belonging to the Bishop of Coventry. Compton's son, created Earl of Northampton, continued the project. Queen Elizabeth came here in 1600, and on James I's visit a few years later the castle was described as 'Lord Compton's princely mansion'.

Monarchs have left their mark. The house was originally built as an 'E' shape building to celebrate the coronation of Elizabeth. William III (William of Orange) persuaded the then earl to adopt the Dutch customs of planting avenues, one opposite each face of the house. Only two remain today (one of them 3½ miles long), the others falling victim to the more naturalistic fashion which Brown introduced in his landscaping. Today, surrounded by its 10,000 acre estate, it remains one of the most magnificent and beautifully maintained of all English country houses.

'Capability' Brown's first contract in 1761 was with Charles, 7th Earl of Northampton, and work was begun immediately. Following the young Earl's death in Naples two years later, whilst on the Grand Tour, Castle Ashby passed to his younger brother, Spencer. The 8th Earl honoured his predecessor's determination to modernise the old-fashioned gardens. Their old boundary wall was replaced by a ha-ha. Two lakes were created from a series of ponds, round which Brown laid out extensive plantations, retaining as many of the old trees as possible. He built an ice house, a menagerie, and a bridge at the north end of one of the lakes, whilst Robert Adam designed a domed temple to present a classical facade to the water.

Brown's work at Castle Ashby led to a crucial change in his circumstances. Involvement in local politics and the substantial expenditure on Castle Ashby left the Earl short of money. The rumour of the possible sale of an estate he owned at Fenstanton to Mr Drummond (of the bank) came to Brown's attention. He immediately wrote and said that he would be interested to purchase the property if the sale to Drummond fell through – which it did. With the result that Lancelot Brown, a Northumberland farmer's son, paid £13,000 to become Lord of the Manor of Fenstanton and join the ranks of the landed gentry. There is an irony about all this, as Dorothy Stroud has pointed out: 'the foremost exponent of landscape, the devout disciple of Palladio, thus came to reside in a small, old-fashioned gabled manor house, standing virtually on the edge of the road, with a pair of clipped yew trees growing either side of a modest front door.'

Castle Ashby is only the second home of the Marquess of Northampton, the other being Compton Wynyate, probably one of the most romantic houses in Britain. But the present heir, Earl Compton, lives at Castle Ashby and was immensely kind in patiently showing me the many attractive aspects that might be painted. The view I chose was just in front of a shrubbery which, unknown to me at the time, concealed a romantic folly built there for the fine prospect. I longed to wield the billhook to restore this vantage point.

I had the usual quandary whether to paint oil or watercolour. Bright sunshine and vibrant autumn colouring decided me, and my oils were squeezed out onto the palette. James McNeill Whistler

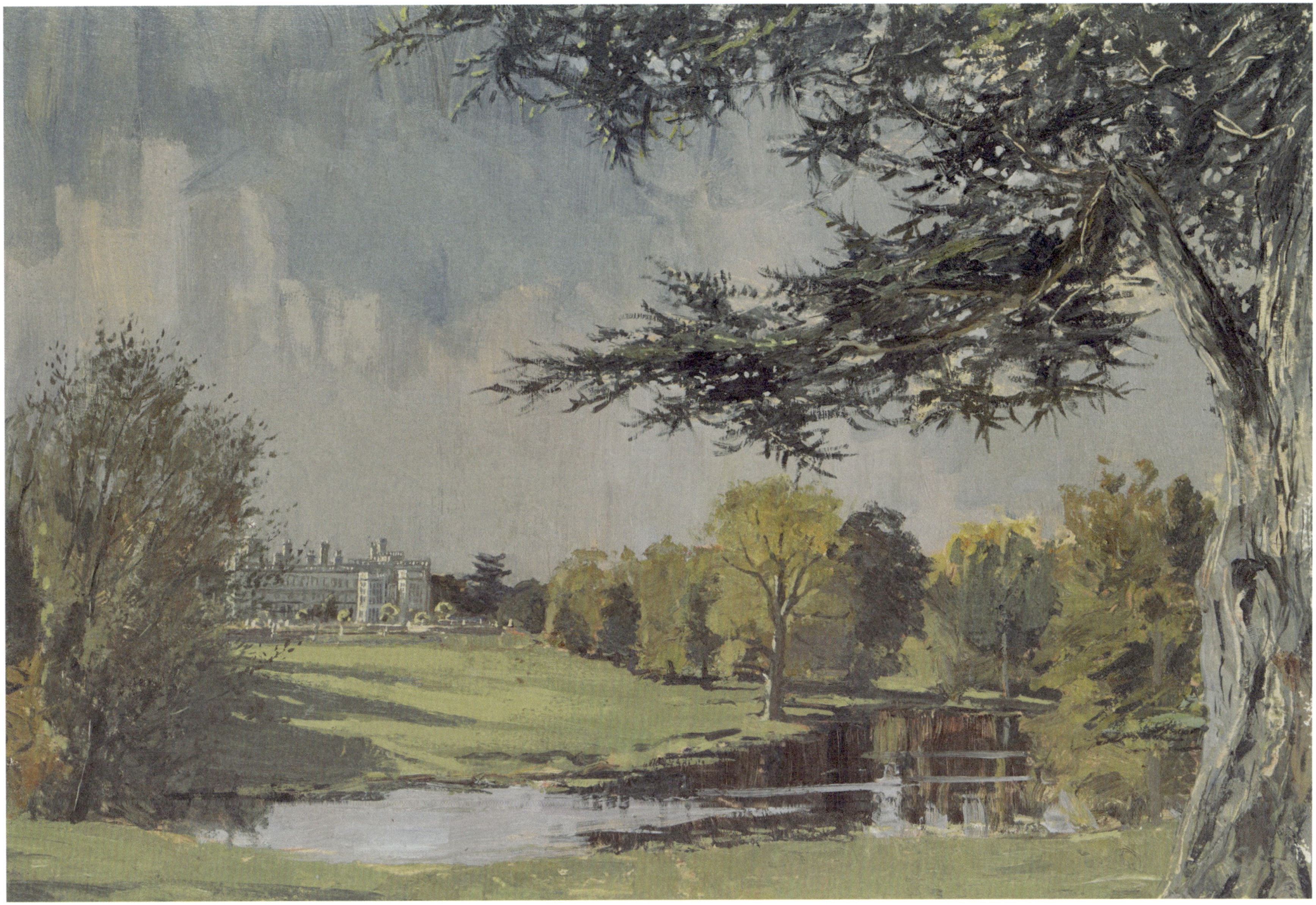

*Castle Ashby from one of the viewpoints perhaps created by Brown (oil).*

spent as much time mixing his colours on his palette with a knife as painting the picture. This might seem tedious in the short term, but saves much time and energy in the long. Moreover, you think about your colours dispassionately and compare hue and tone critically as piles of paint. The mixed pigment is then transferred from palette to painting surface, again with a knife blocking in the main colour areas. I push around this paint with brushes, fingers, or if necessary an old twig, and finish the painting with finer brushes as necessary.

# AUDLEY END HOUSE

## Essex 1763

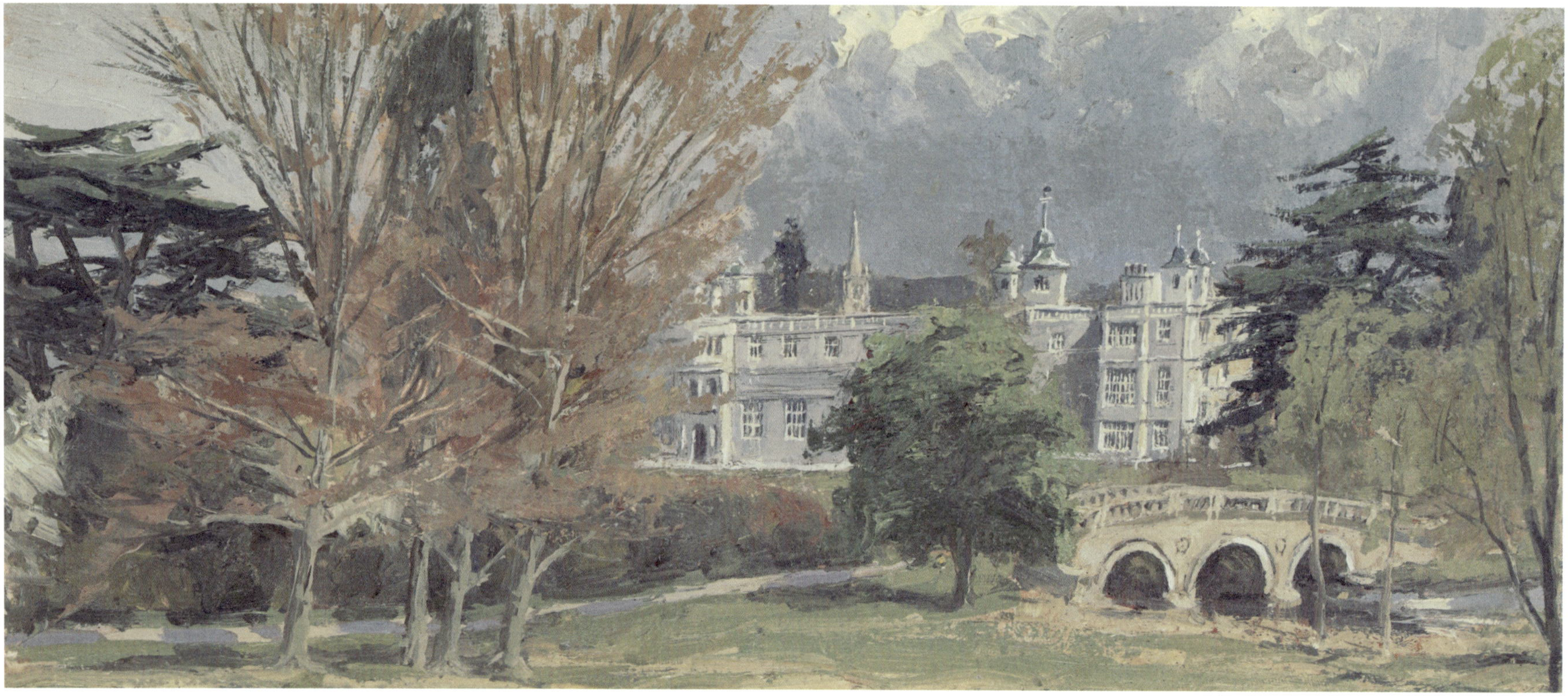

*Audley End with the Adam road bridge (oil).*

Following the Dissolution of the Monasteries Henry VIII granted Walden Abbey to his loyal Speaker of the House of Commons, Sir Thomas Audley. The abbey sits in the low-lying valley of the River Cam in Essex, and Sir Thomas converted it into a courtyard house around the original cloisters. As Lord Chancellor and a peer, Audley confirmed Henry's divorce from Catherine of Aragon, passed the death sentence on Sir Thomas More and presided over the trial of Anne Boleyn, whose execution he witnessed.

In 1603 his grandson, Thomas Howard, 1st Earl of Suffolk, demolished the abbey and started to build what became one of the most magnificent Jacobean mansions in Britain. The cost of the house was prodigous, reputedly £200,000 – money Suffolk lacked. Both the Earl and his countess were imprisoned in the Tower for embezzlement until released by paying a fine, and the 1st Earl died in disgrace at the house which had all but bankrupted him.

After the Restoration Charles II bought Audley End for a princely £5, principally as a base for parties when attending Newmarket races. William III had less inclination for the turf and returned Audley End to the Earls of Suffolk, the last of whom died in 1745 without a direct heir. By then much of the house had been demolished.

Thanks to a redoubtable aunt, Elizabeth, Countess of Portsmouth, who used the money from two marriages to buy the house and estate at a bargain price, Audley End passed to Sir John Griffin. Her nephew was then a colonel in the 33rd Regiment of Foot, based in Hanover, where the regiment saw service during the War of the Austrian Succession. The countess's only condition was that Griffin add a second Griffin to his name, which he duly did.

Once back in Essex, Sir John Griffin Griffin threw himself into the task of improving the house and estate, spending about £100,000 between 1762 and 1792, and personally involving himself tirelessly in the work. In 1763 'Capability' Brown was summoned to create a landscape worthy of the house.

It was a difficult time for Brown, who was badly overstretched. He was already working on Luton Hoo in Bedfordshire and a number of other schemes. He hastily drew up an ill thought out contract with Sir John, whose clauses included widening the River Cam, making new drives, tree planting, building a ha-ha, and laying out and seeding various lawns. Brown agreed to complete the work in thirteen months, which allowing for the vagaries of the weather was completely unrealistic. Sir John was an exacting client. The outcome was one of 'Capability's' rare disputes over fees, which culminated in a famously damning letter from Lancelot which ended, 'Mr Brown will never labour more to convince Sir John as he knows that there is none so blind as him that will not see.'

None of this turmoil is reflected in the calm beauty of the landscape we see today. The great house itself sits on a flat lawn running to the river, where the limpid water reflects fine clumps of trees and the rambling red brick wisteria-clad Elizabethan stables that lie on the other bank. Robert Adam designed the elegant road bridge, and beyond to the west on Ring Hill is the Temple of Victory.

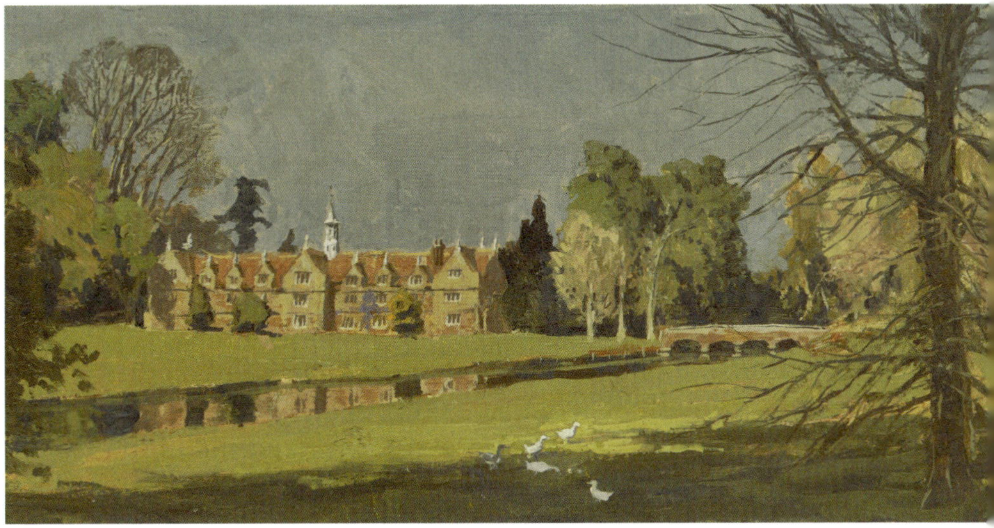

*Audley End, the Elizabethan stables (oil).*

English Heritage now owns Audley End and the immediate grounds. The once derelict walled gardens have been admirably restored by Garden Organic and perhaps look now as they did in the eighteenth century. Teams of volunteers attend to the peaches, pears and apples cordoned and espaliered on the high mellow brick walls, and the glasshouses burgeon with fruit and flowers.

The view of the house I chose is obscure, perhaps because I was feeling lazy about painting all those windows! I am however often more attracted by something only partly seen, because the mind then conjures something even more magnificent than that which exists. The fleeting glimpse might haunt and evoke the desire to see more. I feel this is in the spirit of Brown and the landscape movement, where views were interrupted by judicious planting of clumps of trees so that only part can be seen at any one time. We live in an age of immediate gratification and full revelation, deadening the imagination.

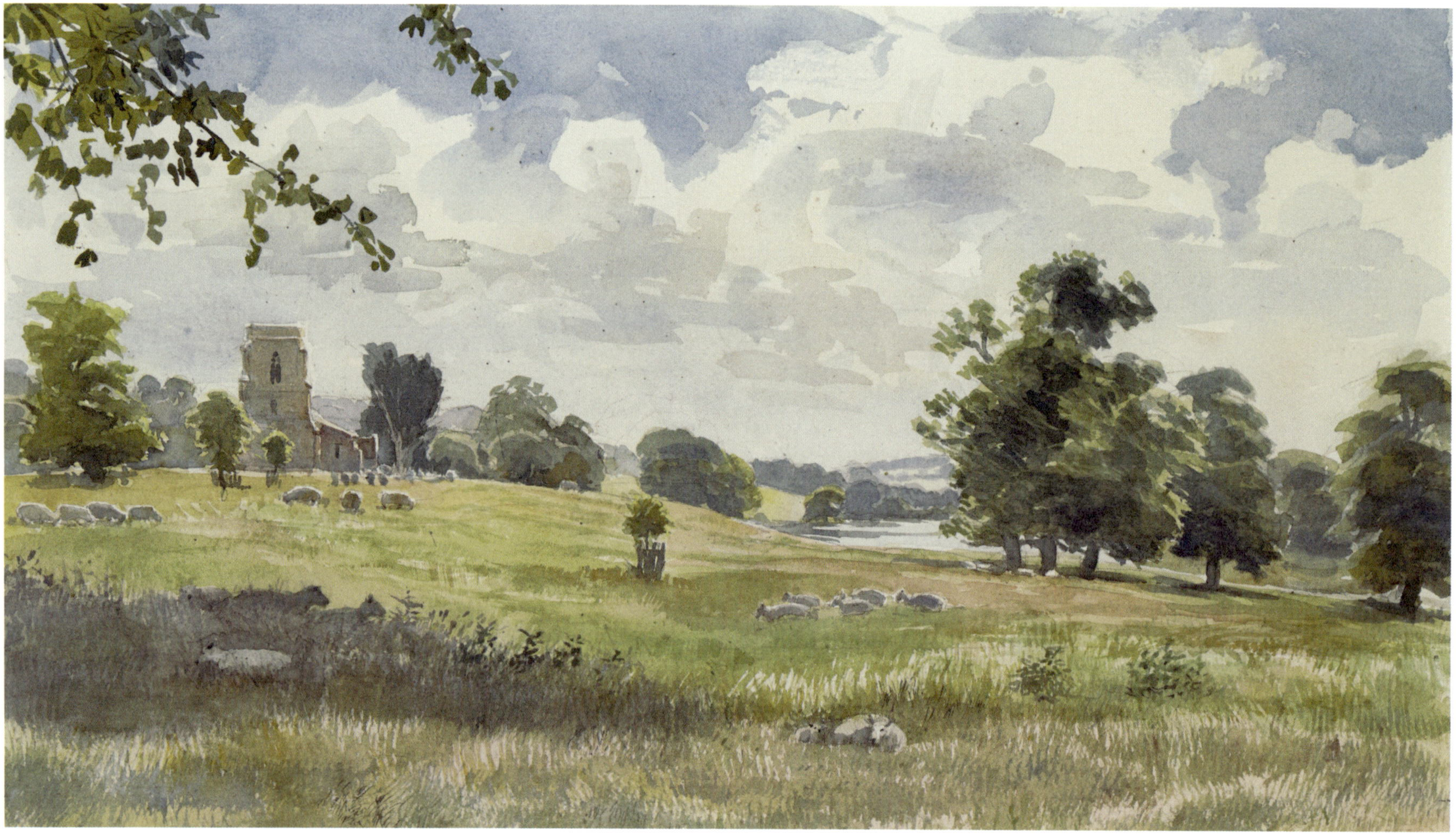

*Fawsley Hall, the view from the terrace (watercolour).*

# FAWSLEY HALL

## Northamptonshire 1763

The Knightley family acquired land west of Northampton at Fawsley in 1416. Over 300 years later, the then owner of the estate, Lucy Knightley, commissioned Brown to draw up plans for its improvement: the unusual male Christian name, which Knightley loathed, was due to a connection with the Lucy family of Charlecote.

Brown's original contract dates to the early 1760s. Horace Walpole wrote in 1763 that 'the ground Brown is laying out, and making a large piece of water . . .' The lake still survives in a well-watered valley below the hall and church. The extensive undulating landscape is dotted with attractively situated clumps of trees on every prominence, and generally its characteristics have Brown's signature. Only his plan has been lost, for it was last seen in 1943.

Lancelot often stayed at Fawsley when heading north or working in the Midlands. After spending the night there in 1775 he wrote to his wife Bridget, 'I came to Mr Knightley's, where I stay'd one night and met a cheerful domestic wife that never wishes to stir from home – she looks after her birds and makes her husband's pleasures her own – she had all the wifely virtues etc'. Tell that to 'Woman's Hour'!

I arrived at Fawsley in the evening at the end of a long journey from Yorkshire. There was enough light to embark on a preliminary reconnaissance, thus avoiding wasting time trying to find the right spot the next day. The site is amazingly picturesque and almost too many options presented themselves. The hall is a handsome building, the oldest part dating from Henry VII's reign and the latest Pugin Victorian Gothic, with a large chunk of Elizabethan and a smattering of Georgian in-between – a real archaeological jigsaw of a house.

The medieval church sat alone on a knoll a little distance away, surrounded by a fine park and ha-ha with a little bridge leading to the porch. Inside a feast of Knightley tombs and memorials gave a haunting feeling of the family's presence – they at least still inhabit this small corner of what had once been theirs, for the house is now an exclusive hotel run by 'Hand Picked Hotels'. The last Knightley died in 1913 and the estate, excluding the hall, is owned by the Gage family of Firle in Sussex through inheritance.

The view I eventually chose was from the lawns in front of the hall, looking across the park's ancient oaks towards the church. The church is a lonely beacon and the sole evidence of a now lost village, which was swept away for sheep grazing some 200 years before Brown came here. Below, the long waters of 'Capability's' lake disappear into the distance.

The painting I did of this scene is in pure watercolour on 'Arches Not paper' – a confusing term best explained by a description of watercolour paper and their surfaces. 'Smooth or Hot Press (HP)' is obviously a smooth even surface, ideal for detailed work such as botanical painting, but does not suit my more spontaneous style. 'Not' is an intermediate textured surface which will effectively take generous washes of watercolour and is good for most purposes, including rendering of distant landscape. 'Rough' is a much more characterful surface with greater texture, allowing a more expressive approach to watercolour painting, sometimes on a large scale.

# MILTON ABBEY

## Dorset 1763

The monastic lands at Milton Abbey were bought by the Tregonwell family on the Dissolution of the Monasteries, who in due course built a new mansion incorporating a proportion of the original Benedictine monastery. Prior to that, a small town complete with market square, inns, almshouses and a celebrated school had grown up to the south of the abbey along the course of a small river. The Tregonwell family eventually sold the estate in 1752 to Joseph Damer, later to become Lord Milton. Walpole described the abbey's new owner as 'moderately sensible, immoderately proud'. Quarrelsome and high-handed, he was soon at loggerheads with the local community.

On Brown's first visit in 1763 the monastic house still stood. He was engaged to lay out a park, landscape the grounds around and to the south of the abbey, create a lake, and plant woods on the tops of the two valleys that look down on the abbey – which lies in a bowl. There was then a lull while Lord Milton decided the fate of both the old house and the adjoining town. It soon became apparent that his intentions were to raze the entire town and build a completely new village in a secluded valley not visible from the house. As he bought up individual properties, or as his tenants' leases expired, their houses were demolished. Brown levelled and landscaped their sites, and their residents were moved to the new cottages as they became available.

Lord Milton also decided to demolish his house, except for a portion of the abbey, which has been retained as a church to this day. William Chambers was appointed to design a new mansion. The two men soon fell out. The house was only partly built when Chambers refused to do any more, describing it 'as a Cursed Gothick house for this unmannerly Imperious Lord, who has treated me, as he does everybody, ill.' The more amenable James Wyatt was brought in to complete it.

Contention continues as to whether both Brown and Chambers were involved in designing the new village of Milton Abbas. Forty double houses were built between 1773 and 1779, each with a garden. Jane Brown has persuasively argued that no one blessed with Lancelot's practical commonsense would have placed a village in a deep east-west valley, so that every house was in the shade for at least half the day. Whoever the designer, Milton Abbas today is much visited as a 'chocolate boxy' classic English estate village.

Two further obstacles remained to Lord Milton. The first was the school, which after much rangling and argument was finally moved to Blandford. The second was a lawyer called William Harrison, who owned two houses in the old town, knew his rights and refused to be budged. Lord Milton responded by opening the sluices in the stream and deliberately flooding his house. Harrison then took Lord Milton to court, and won. Only after Harrison's death were the park and lake completed. Despite the expense, the lake has never fulfilled its desired effect and although there is still water in the valley it seems a separate entity to the house. An active fishing club is now the beneficiary.

I was lucky enough to paint at Milton Abbey on a bright late autumn day. The picture turned out to be chromatically relatively

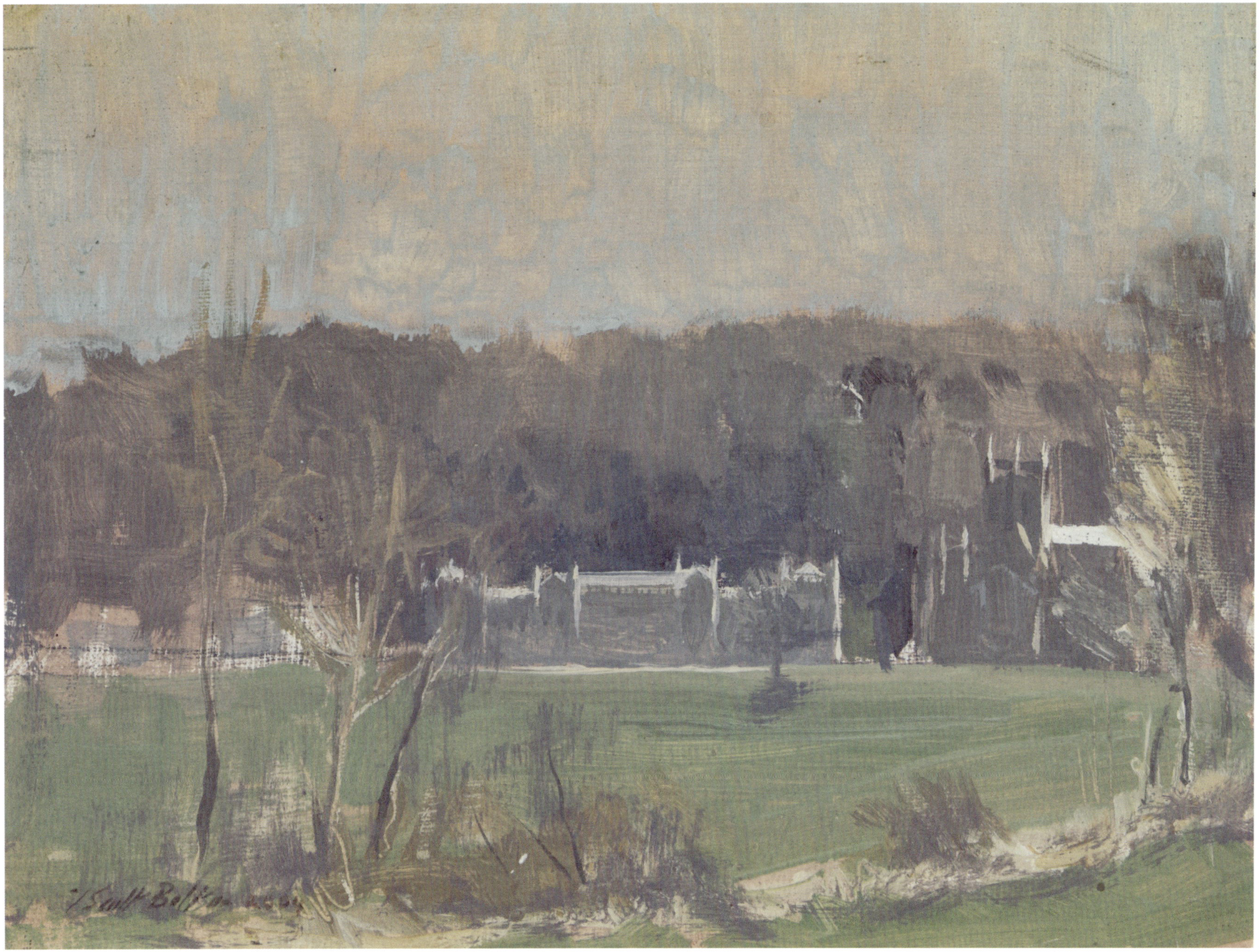

*Milton Abbey evening sketch (oil).*

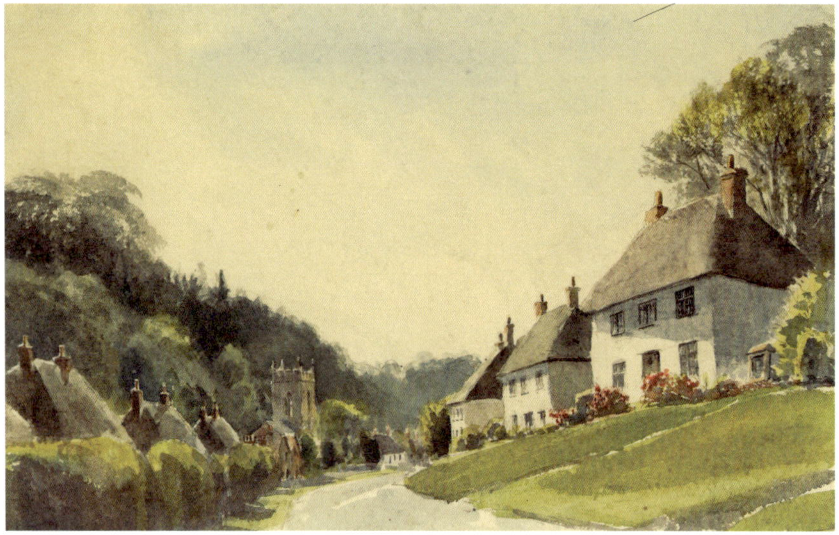

*Milton Abbas (watercolour).*

high for me, with a blue sky and splashes of red which were complementary to the green foreground. Of course, unless painting in the style of the Fauvists, the artist often uses muted colours in landscape painting. An exception are flowers, which give areas of pure colour so radiant they are difficult to reproduce. Constable was noted for adding a splash of red to enliven an otherwise dull green area. In nature the green lawn is never as green as emerald green out of a tube, and a so-called red tree likewise would look subdued when compared to cadmium red.

The background of my picture was framed by the great woods that Brown planned and were planted on the ridges. These merged in the distance to grey blues and mauves. The pale yellow Portland stone of the abbey seemed very pure. Its creamy colour shone in sunlight, contrasting with the bluey purple of the same stone in the shade.

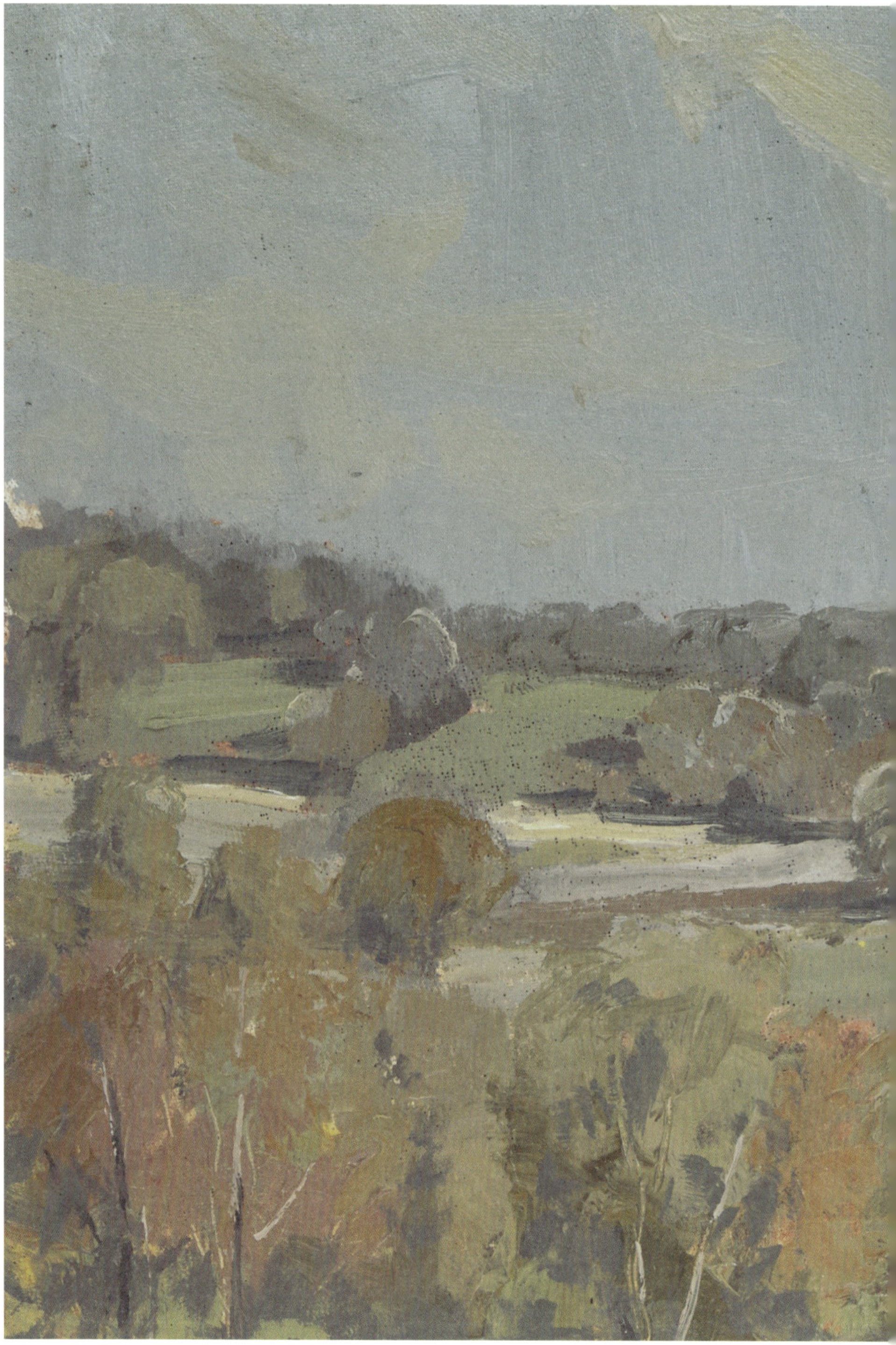

*Milton Abbey (oil).*

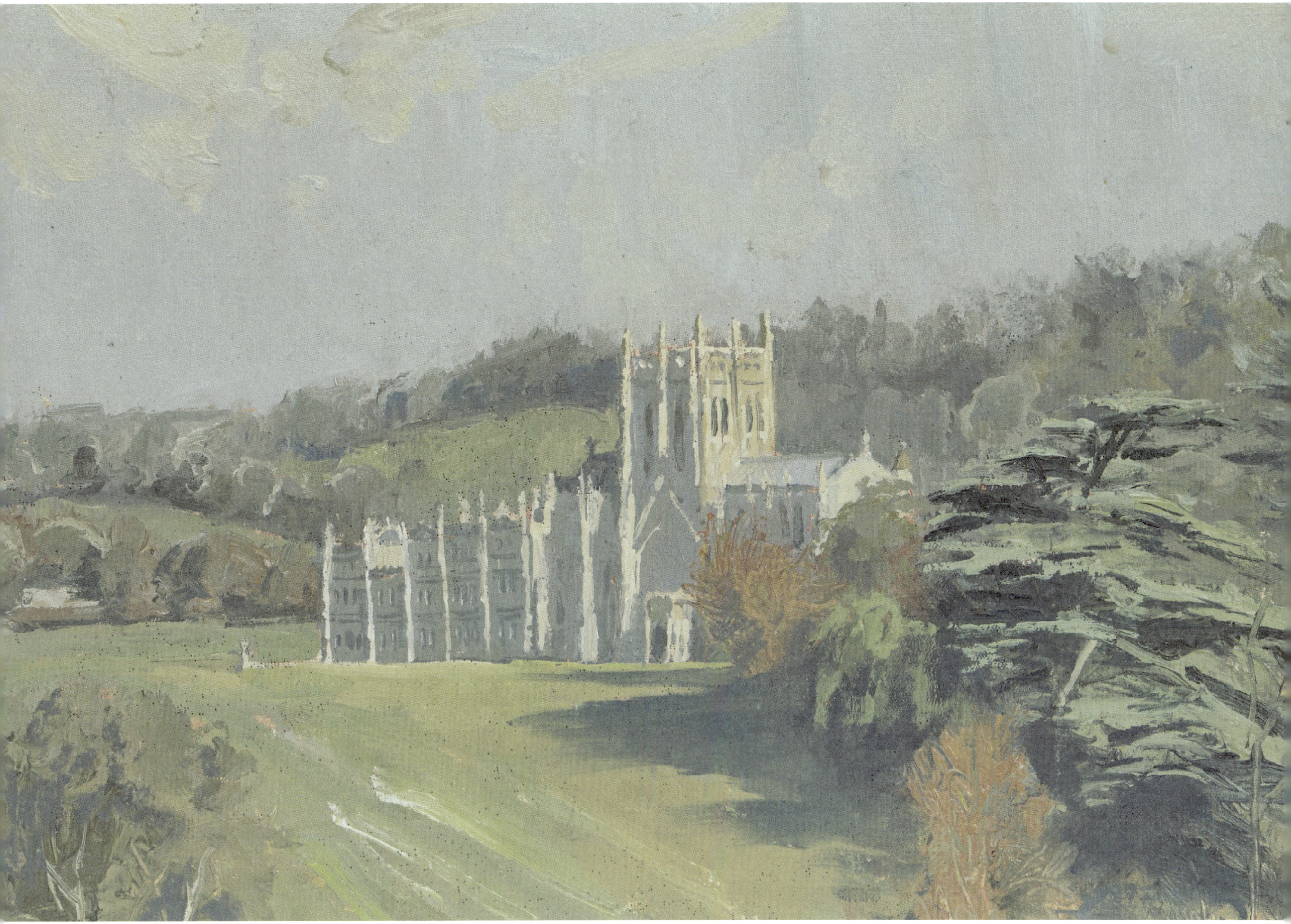

# LUTON HOO

## Bedfordshire 1764

John Stuart, 3rd Earl of Bute, was a renaissance man; a patron of the arts, a horticulturist trained at the University of Leiden in botany (he was largely responsible for the foundation of the Royal Botanic Gardens at Kew), as well as a courtier and 'special' friend of the widowed Augusta, Princess of Wales. In 1762 he briefly became prime minister, before resigning the following year and devoting his energies to botany and building, principally at Luton Hoo.

The Earl acquired the Bedfordshire estate in 1764, engaging Robert Adam to remodel the house and 'Capability' Brown the landscape. The house sits proud on a crest above the River Lea. Brown's first task was to open out an expanse of grassland to give a wide prospect of the string of lakes he formed by damming the river.

Arthur Young described a new wooden bridge over the Lea in *A Six Months Tour through the North of England* in 1769, continuing, 'A little further is the cascade, which is yet but a capability . . . .' It has been suggested that this is the first use of the word 'capability' in connection with Brown, hence his nickname.

Brown planted trees on the hill on the opposite side of the lake, beyond which, peeping over the brow, can be seen the buildings of Luton airport. The planes fly like clockwork across the valley in a similar fashion to the former flushes of pheasants of its Edwardian heyday, when the estate was owned by the fabulously rich South African diamond magnate Sir Julius Wernher.

Bute's proclivity for plant collecting was reflected in his development of the gardens at Luton Hoo. The five acre octagonal walled garden, built by Brown, was as much a place for his collection as for

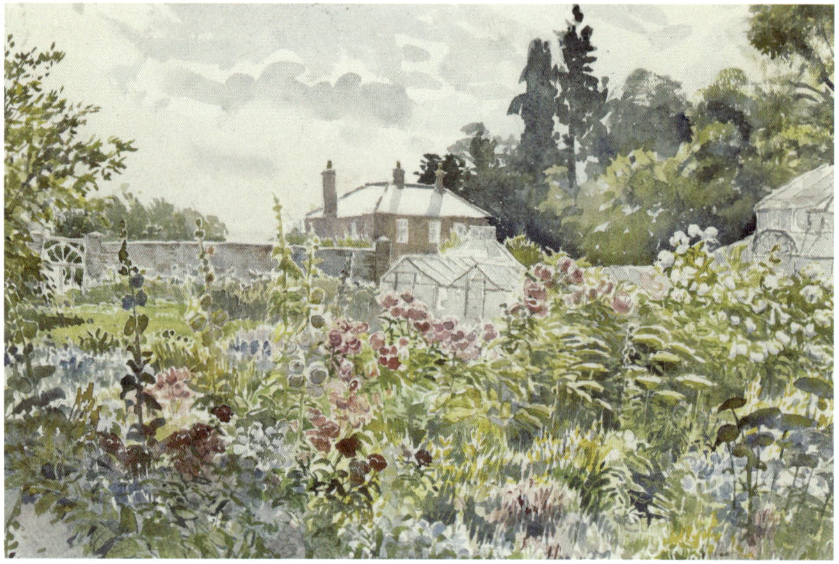

*Luton Hoo walled garden which accommodated Lord Bute's famous plant collection (watercolour).*

the growing of fruit and vegetables. Many rare plants were obtained from Augusta, Princess of Wales, including sophora, gingko, zelkova and oriental plane. He meticulously kept a list of plants as they flowered, and this numbered over 1000.

In recent years great efforts have been made to restore the gardens, which up to a few years ago lay totally derelict. The great Wernher glasshouses, a ghost of their magnificent Edwardian apogee, are now covered with sheets of plastic, but heroic strides have been made in reintroducing plants appropriate to its historic

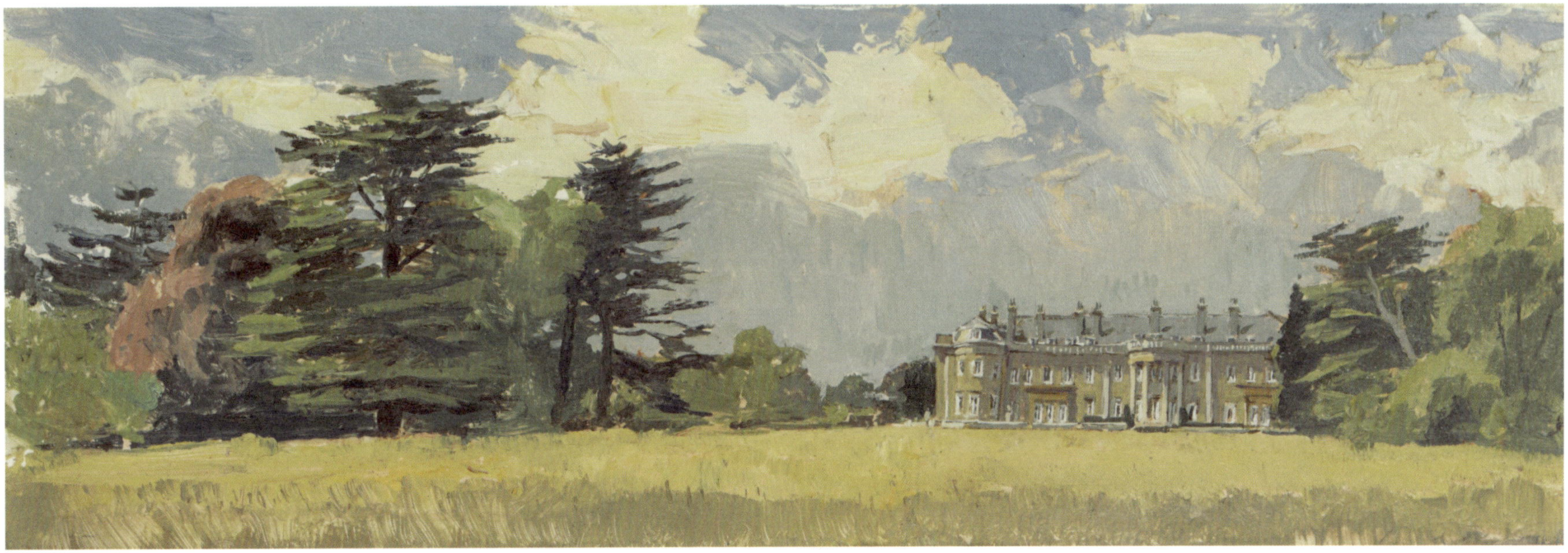

*Luton Hoo (oil).*

associations. One section particularly attracted me. An area was planted up with eighteenth century varieties listed by the Earl in 1777: amongst the roses were *Rosa Gallica Officinalis* (the apothecary's rose), *Rosa de Meaux* (used to make rose oil), *Rosa Kazanlik* (used to make fragrance) and *Rosa Alba* (the White Rose of Lancaster), and all had a herbal or symbolic significance. Many other plants as well as being decorative were of medical use. This area is still owned by the Phillips family, who inherited from the Wernhers. The gardens have a wonderful feel. Much of the restoration is being done by a team of volunteers willing to share their knowledge and enthusiasm for the gardens.

I have never pretended to be a botanical painter, but do enjoy painting flowers as part of a landscape. Claude Lorrain gave his landscapes a sense of perspective and distance by both colour (blues tend to dominate the distance) and by creating a series of dark and light areas through the picture. I treat more intimate pictures like the flowerbed on the opposite page in the same way, but on a more constricted scale. The area of shadow where the hollyhocks and roses dominate the foreground has been made up so that the middle ground will have its own identity, shining brightly in the sunshine. This gives the picture a better structure and a sense of space.

The main house and about 1,000 acres of parkland and lakes containing the principal works done by Brown now belong to a privately owned hotel group, Elite Hotels, and they in their turn could not have been more helpful in giving me access to paint. The manager, Charles Long, took me on an adventurous off-road motorised ramble in search of a good view. At lunchtime, a liberal hamper of food was brought to me by the charming head gardener, who had been originally employed by the Phillips family. From my viewpoint I looked two ways and decided to do a pair of paintings, one of the palatial house framed with prominent clumps of trees, including Brown's trademark cedar of Lebanon. Turning round, the second painting was a pure 'Capability' landscape of undulating open fields with clumped trees in the foreground, the long lakes snaking along the course of the river and beyond layers of field and woodland to the skyline. The magician's touch made the view perfect in a subtle way, an essay of understatement with no pompous or dramatic affectations of grandeur.

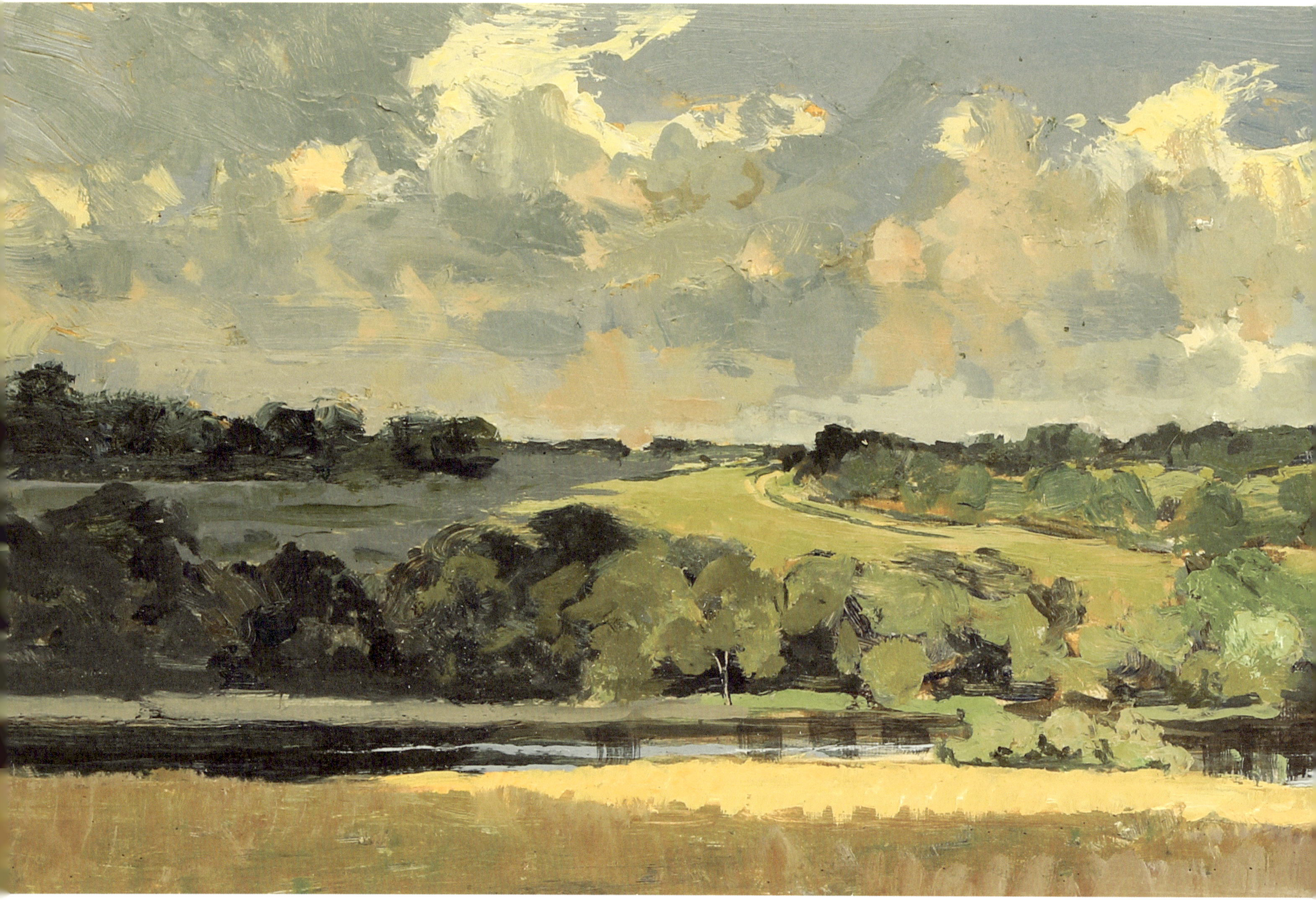

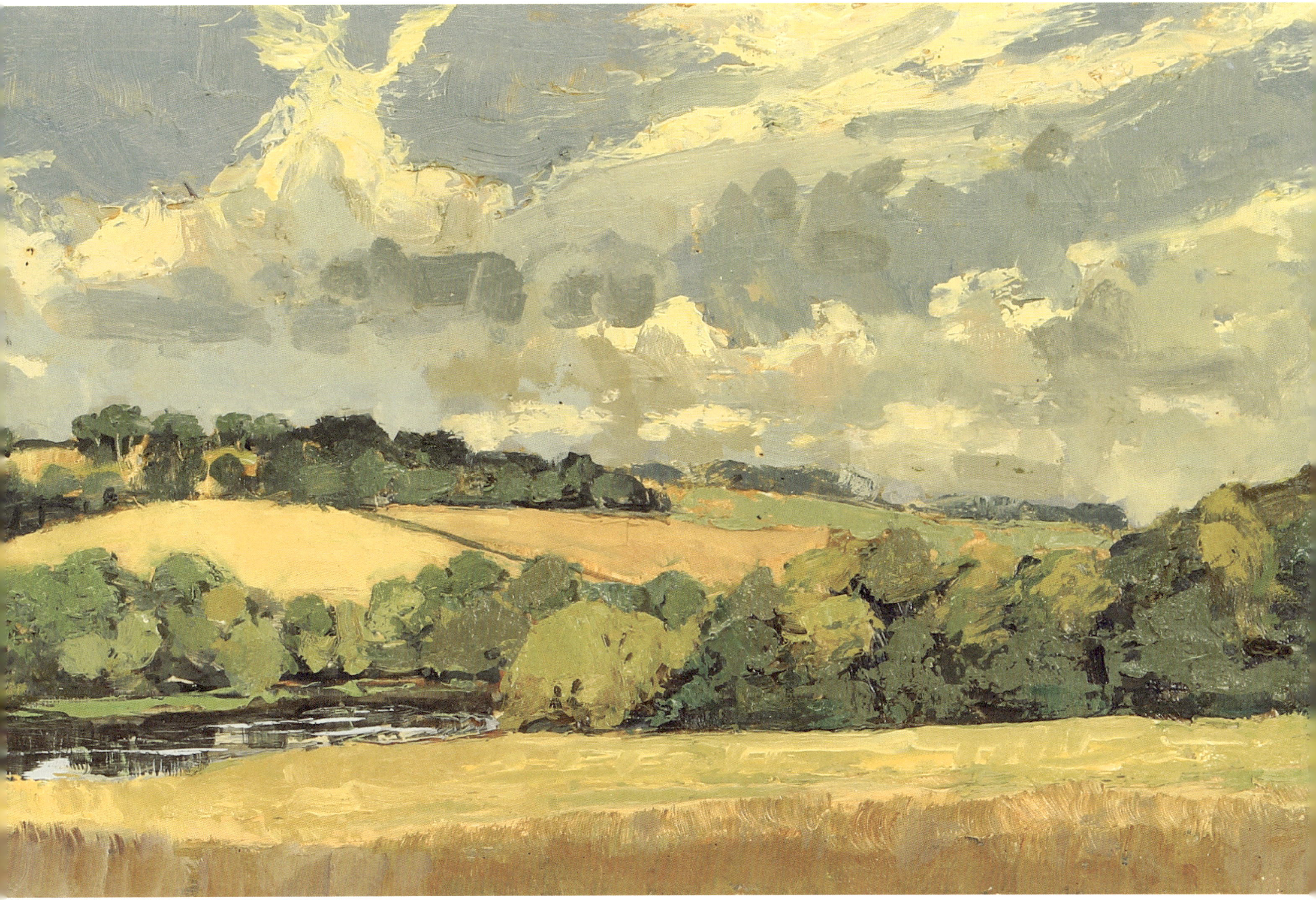

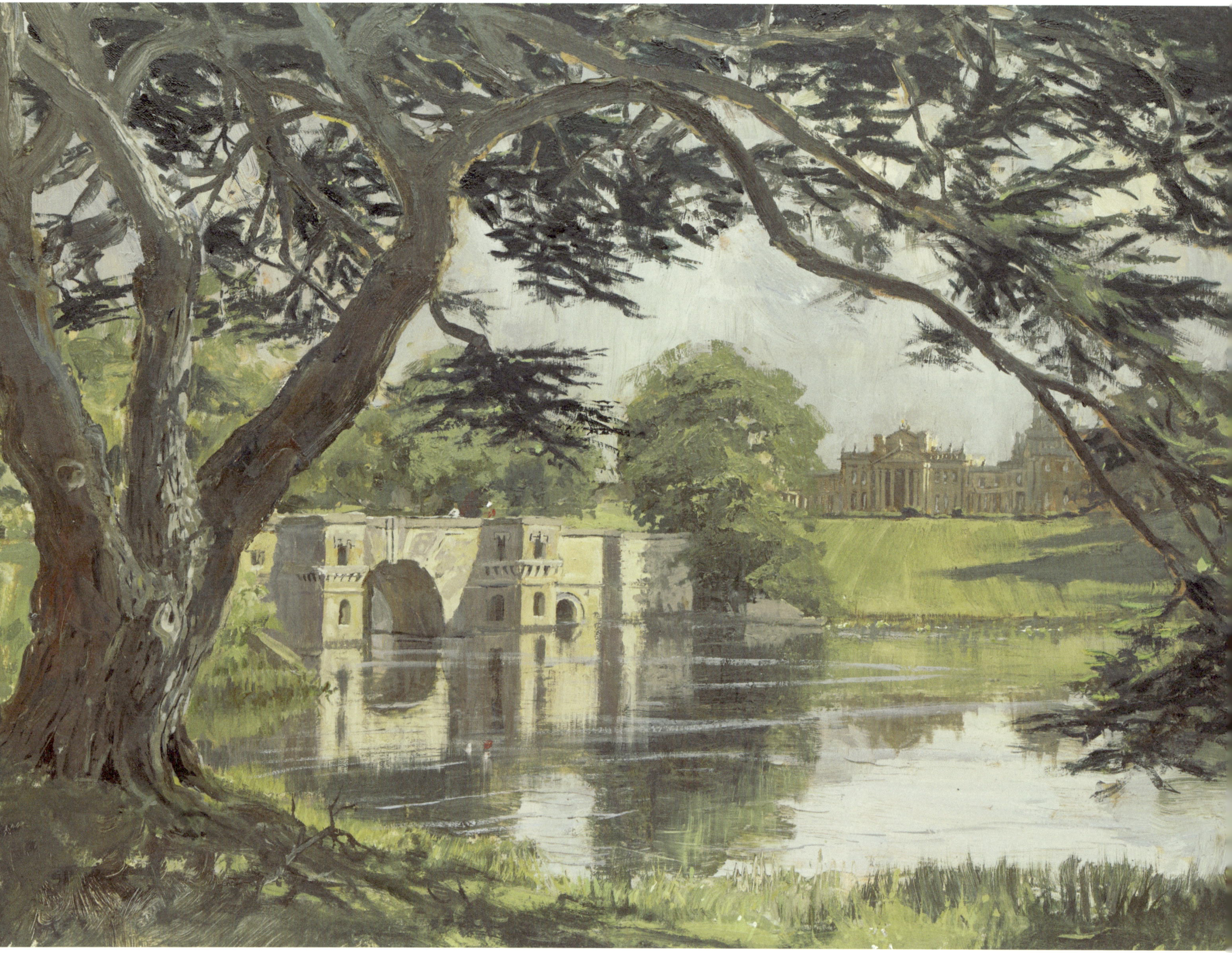

# BLENHEIM PALACE

## Oxfordshire 1764

1764 WAS a year of triumph for 'Capability' Brown: not only was he appointed Master Gardener at Hampton Court but he also purchased the Manor of Fenstanton – thus underlining both his pre-eminence as a garden designer and his new status as a member of the rural gentry. As so often happens, other things fell into place. For 1764 was the year he started work at Blenheim, widely considered his greatest landscape, at the behest of George, 4th Duke of Marlborough, who as well as being Lord Privy Seal was a keen astronomer, building his own observatory at Blenheim and conversing widely with other European scientists. In a letter written to Brown the previous year, the Duke ended, 'I have a notion I shall begin here immediately, so that the sooner you come the better.'

Happily, Brown's ten years of working at Blenheim were more harmonious than those between it's original architect, Sir John Vanbrugh, and the flamboyantly combative 1st Duchess, Sarah. The two soon fell out, principally because the Duchess thought Vanbrugh's plans unnecessarily extravagant. Another point of dispute was Vanbrugh's wish to retain old Woodstock Manor as a picturesque feature in the landscape. Sarah disagreed. The manor house was demolished, Vanbrugh was banished from the site and was never to see his most ambitious work, which was finally completed by Sir Nicholas Hawksmoor.

The genius of the place and Blenheim's grandeur inspired Brown to produce one of his most successful plans. His masterpiece was the lake, which, such was his flair for managing water, he managed to conjure from the meagre waters of the River Glyme. On his first visit he saw a marshy stream, of which one visitor condescendingly wrote, 'you might, without straining yourself, jump over'. Brown knew what he was doing, for it was upstream on this same river that he had created a lake at Kiddington 24 years earlier – his first commission. The course of the Glyme could be a reflection of his own progress from obscurity to greatness. By the time Brown finished at Blenheim he had reshaped the contours of the valley and created a massive and picturesque lake divided into two by Vanbrugh's Great Bridge.

The Great Bridge was one of Blenheim's principal monuments. Although incomplete, and regarded by the 1st Duchess as an extravagant folly, it spanned the valley of the Glyme with towering arches, whose buttresses contained more than two dozen rooms in three stories, some with plasterwork and fireplaces. Brown raised the water level by 15 feet to where the arches sprung from the top of the tall columns, thereby flooding the ground floor rooms. As I painted the bridge, I imagined the reflections I saw in the water to be part of the now submerged structure, the realm of pike, carp and tench. The necessary dam gave Brown the opportunity to create another feature, the Cascade, which still gives air and life to this tributary of the Thames.

If the lake was 'Capability' Brown's main achievement at Blenheim, he also swept away much of Henry Wise's formal parterres,

OPPOSITE *Blenheim Palace. Sir John Vanbrugh's bridge was never completed and is now partly submerged by Brown's great lake (oil).*

designing a more spacious landscape to replace the formal avenues, lakes and ponds laid out when the palace was built. He did little building work except for adorning existing structures with Gothic ornament.

The vastness of the place easily absorbs the teeming crowds. The dread I felt as I unpacked my painting gear in the unending car park evaporated when I strode into the magnificent landscape. I found a quiet place to paint, by yet another noble cedar tree, which might well have dated from Brown, and which a passer-by was convinced could be seen in a Harry Potter film.

It was the perfect place to sit and paint. The tree's arching branches almost touched the water, framing the scene. The light played across the broken facade of the bridge with its inhabitable buttresses. To my right, the great palace showed only its shaded face, but sudden chinks of sunlight caught any stonework protrusions on its succession of columns and parapets.

*Burton Pynsent (see overleaf). The great Burton Pynsent column erected by William Pitt in memory of Sir William Pynsent dominates the Somerset Levels (watercolour).*

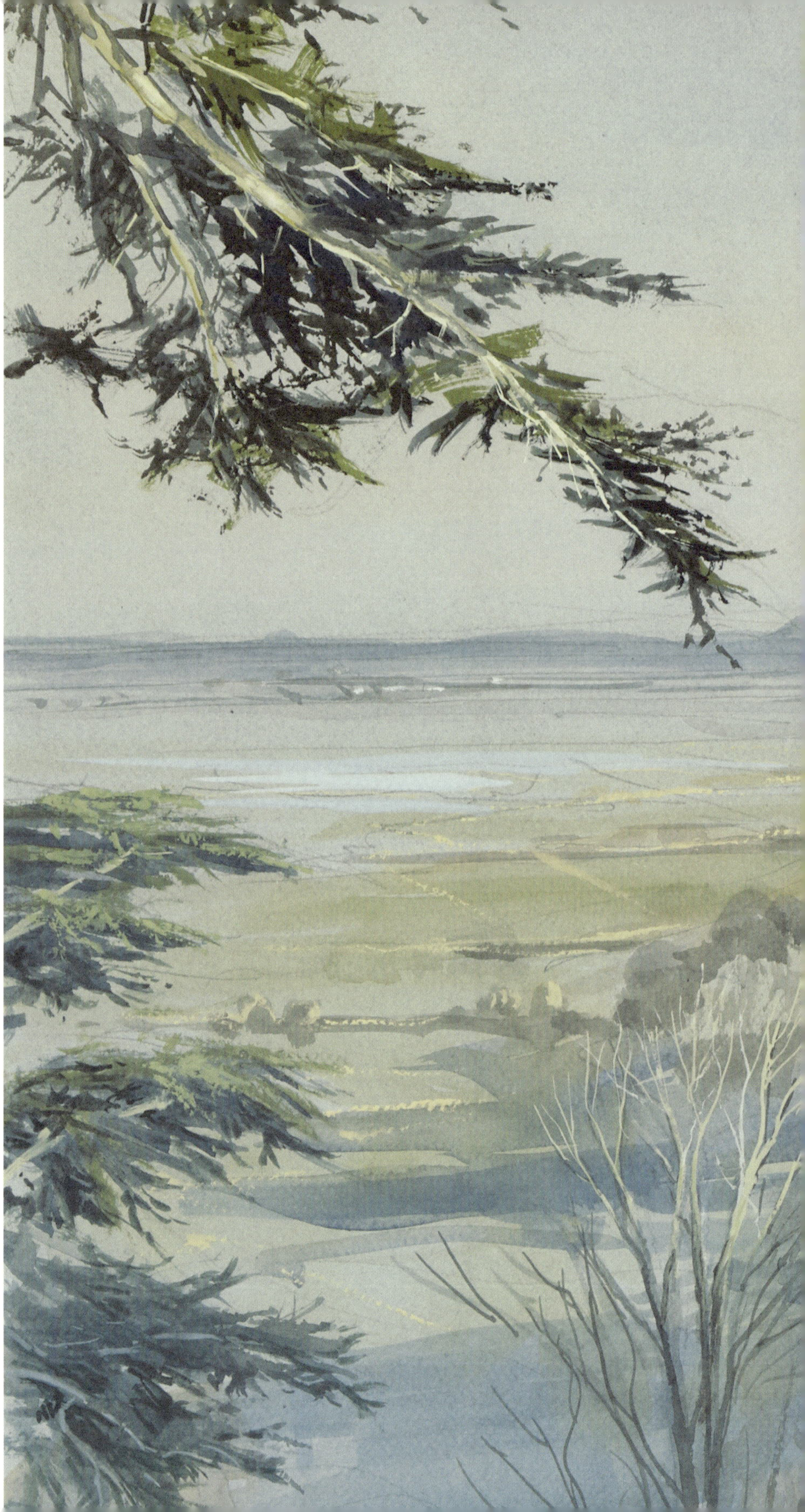

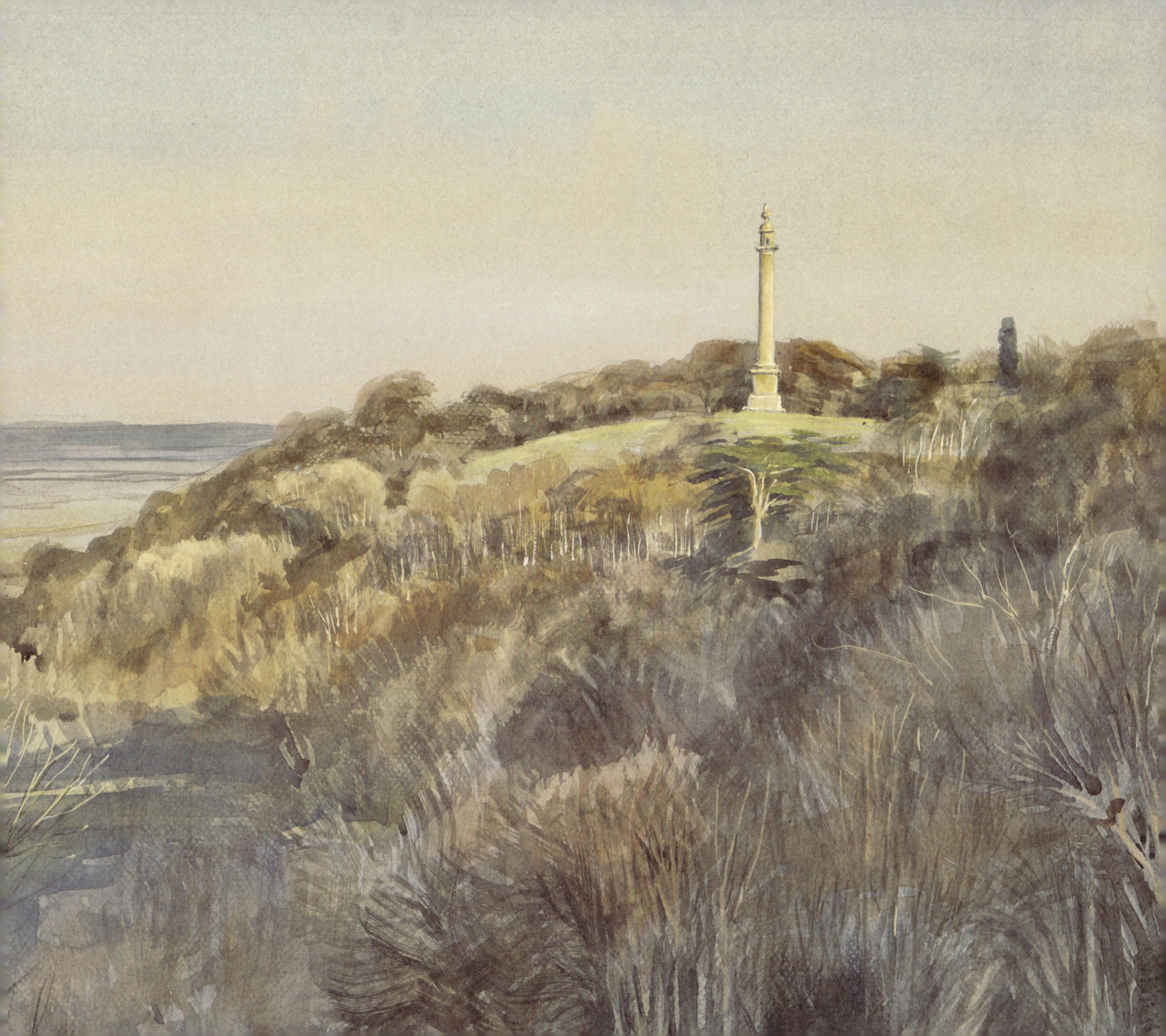

# BURTON PYNSENT

## Somerset 1765

Even the aloof William Pitt, 1st Earl of Chatham, must have shown some surprise when Sir William Pynsent, a wealthy unknown admirer, left him his Somerset estate of Burton Pynsent because of a political disagreement with his heiress over the taxation on Somerset cider! In recognition of this benefaction, Pitt asked Brown to design a column in memory of Sir William and undertake other landscape improvements, including the planting of a number of his favourite cedar of Lebanon.

A country house landscape is in a constant state of change, thanks in part to the desire by successive owners to implement what is new and fashionable – and it was this which gave Brown the freedom to create so many landscapes in the style of the naturalistic movement.

Most properties have seen radical changes since Brown's time. Modern farming has meant larger rectangular fields to accommodate large modern machinery. At Burton Pynsent, the Victorians planted linear flowerbeds and manicured hedges as a separate entity to the landscape beyond. This looked back to the seventeenth century for inspiration and was later taken to a further stage by the influential garden designer, Gertrude Jekyll, who regarded the immediate garden as an extension of the house, with 'rooms' created by hedges.

In 1909 another garden designer, Harold Peto, laid out a terrace and formal gardens around the eighteenth century house, which by this time had been reduced to about a third of its former size. It is from this terrace that the Pynsent Column can be best observed, and the present owner, the eminent silver expert, Tim Schroder was kind enough to let me paint from this viewpoint. What a view! The column shone in the warm light of a clear winter's day on a bluff of land above the flat and partly flooded West Sedge Moor, with the Quantock Hills a blue smudge in the distance. As a contrast, frost iced the shaded foreground, while the sunlit woods were a patchwork of yellows, reds and greys with two cedars, perhaps planted by Brown, giving structure, the stiff lateral branches leading the eye back into my picture.

I find when composing a picture that strong foreground shapes can give tremendous depth of field when painting distance. The nearer the object is to the viewer, the greater is the contrast in tonal values, and colours tend to be stronger (i.e. less grey) and warmer. By contrast, distant objects have less tonal disparity and become cooler. If you observe distant mountains they merge into a blueish mono-tonal layer. However a tree in the foreground will have much deeper shadows, and the areas where the sun is shining on a branch might be lighter than anything in the distance. Also any colours here will be chromatically stronger. By consciously being aware of this in painting a sense of space and distance can be achieved. The main thing is to observe closely what is there before you.

# WESTON PARK

## Shropshire 1764

CONTRACTS between Brown and Sir Henry Bridgeman (later Earl of Bradford) dated 1765 and 1766 are still preserved. They cover creating ha-has to keep out deer, preparing a pleasure ground for planting 'trees and shrubs for ornament or use', levelling an area of park and 'lowering the hill in the manner agreed by Sir Henry'. Some work was also done on the alignment of the drive, which in a Brownian way gave glimpses of landscapes and buildings – including the house and an eighteenth century granary. At a similar time, James Paine was commissioned to build the Temple of Diana and the Roman Bridge.

Since then much has changed at Weston. The main drive has been realigned to arrive to the east of the house rather than to the south. Brown's extensive lawns were transformed into large and intricate formal gardens during the Victorian period. Unlike Croome Court, the old parish church lying to the east of the house was retained, but the uncomfortable manner by which it was connected to the house by the addition of a late Victorian orangery is not architecturally satisfactory – specially in the context of the earlier buildings. One benefit, typical of an age obsessed with status, was that it allowed the Bridgeman family access to their private pew without entering via the church porch.

The park extends to nearly 1,000 acres and there are clumps of oak attractively dotted around. A particularly fine stand of great chestnuts frame the Temple of Diana as one approaches along the sinuous path from the house.

A twentieth century intrusion is a quaint narrow gauge railway line that snakes through the woods, but no train was running on the January day when I was painting. Happily, fallow deer still roam the park, where both black, Jacob and commercial sheep are kept in their separate flocks by temporary fencing.

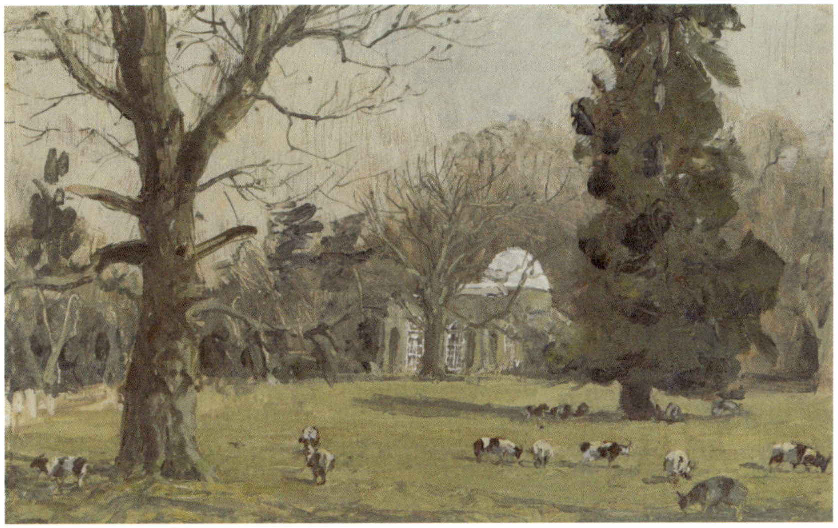

*Weston Park. The Temple of Diana (oil).*

The granary, which until a few years ago was a farm building with two square towers gracing it's entrance front, has now been turned into an excellent shop, restaurant and art gallery, which holds a new exhibition each month.

Painting at Weston was in many ways difficult. So many have had a hand in its creation that it was impossible to paint anything that was predominately Brown. His contracts were mainly concerned

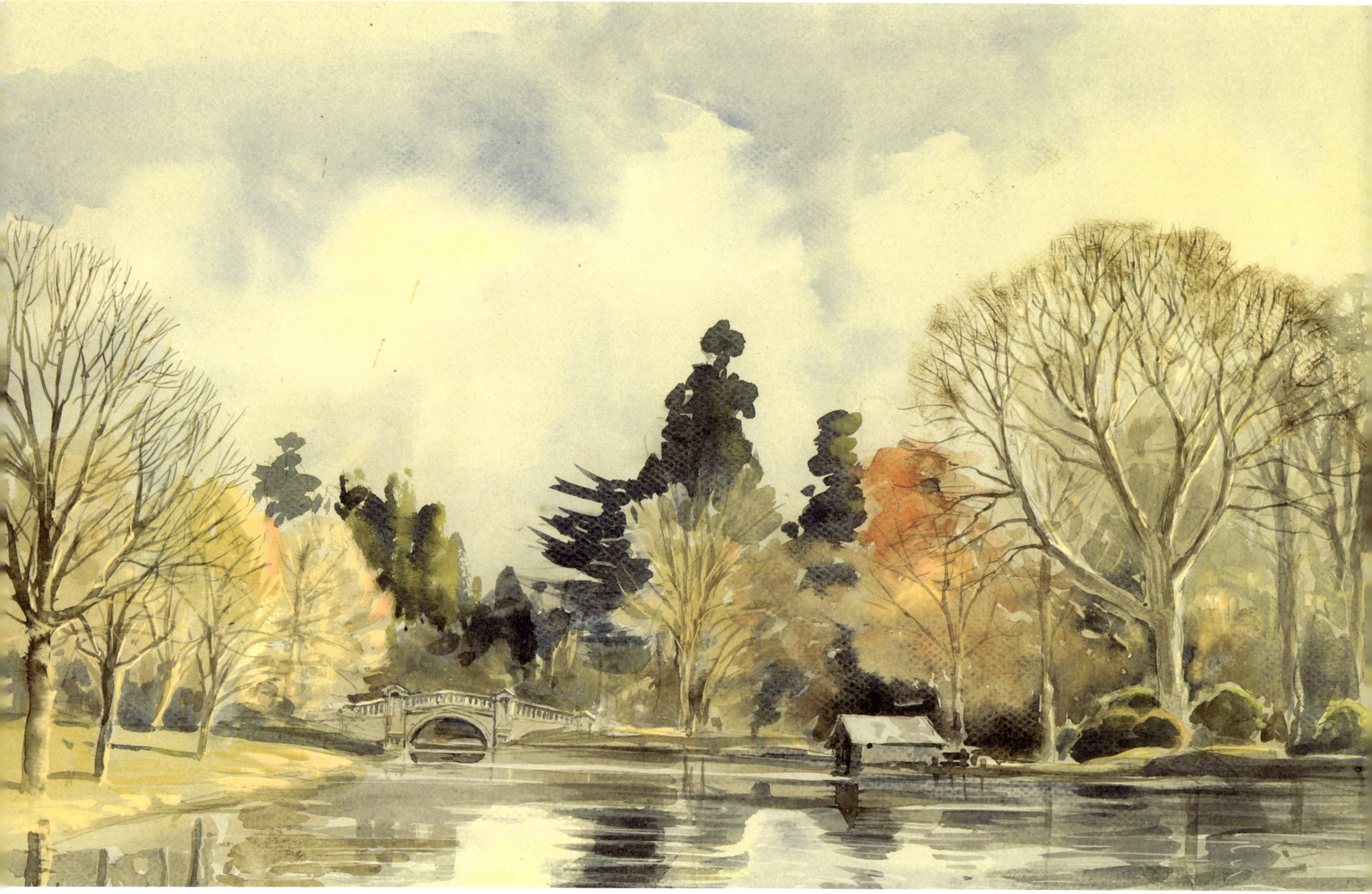

*Weston Park, the lake and bridge (watercolour).*

with the structural alteration of the landscape and others designed the lake, temples and bridges. The oils I painted were done with a very limited palette: raw umber, light red, French ultramarine, cadmium yellow and Titanium white. It is often easier to achieve a satisfactory result with these limited resources – the eighteenth century artist, when pigment had to be ground, satisfied himself with few colours.

Brown also worked at Tong Castle, which sits just over the Shropshire border with Staffordshire, but no evidence of his landscaping survives. The twelfth century castle was replaced in the 1760s by an extraordinary Gothic fantasy for George Durant, an army paymaster who made his money in Havana, Cuba. Sadly, the castle was gutted by fire shortly before the First World War and finally demolished in the 1950s. The M54 now runs over its site.

But the village of Tong is worth a detour, if only for its remarkable church. St Bartholomew's is a fine example of perpendicular fifteenth century Gothic architecture. The real surprise lies within. Described as a 'treasure house of tombs and effigies, products of the Nottingham shops of alabaster workers,' it houses one of the finest collections of medieval tombs in the country. All the male figures wear armour and their wives look calm and beautiful, serenely lying there through the centuries. They range from the earliest, the tomb of Sir Fulke de Pembrugge, through various Vernons, to finally a sophisticated Elizabethan two storey edifice commemorating Sir Thomas Stanley, his son Edward, and their respective wives, with an epitaph written supposedly to them by Shakespeare. I was truly moved by finding this unexpected wonder, seen in the mysterious gloom of a winter's evening.

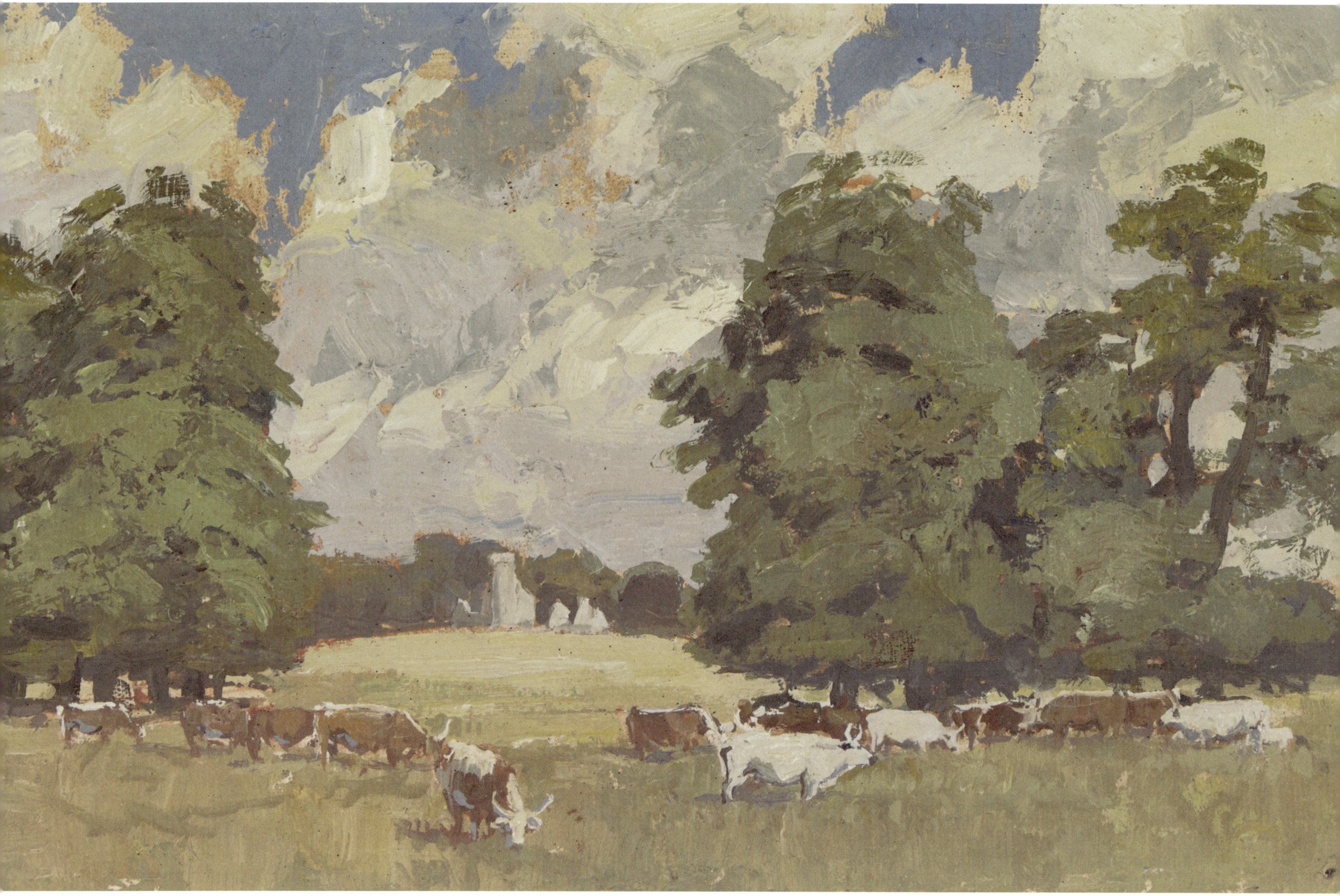

ABOVE *Wimpole Hall. The view from the house with old English cattle (oil).*
OPPOSITE *Wimpole Hall. The Sham Castle designed by Sanderson Miller (watercolour).*

# WIMPOLE HALL

## Cambridgeshire 1767

THE WIMPOLE ESTATE was acquired in 1428 by Henry Chichele, Archbishop of Canterbury and founder of All Souls College, Oxford, remaining with the family for the next 250 years. The core of the present Wimpole Hall was built in 1632 for Thomas Chiceley, only to be considerably altered and extended nearly a century later by James Gibbs for Edward Harley, 2nd Earl of Oxford and Mortimer.

At the same time, Charles Bridgeman was commissioned to redesign the gardens and more distant landscape. One of Bridgeman's lasting legacies is the great avenue stretching for some two miles on the southern axis of the house. Even now it gives an awesome feeling of space as it cuts its swathe into the far distance. It was originally a double bank of great elms, but sadly these are no more, having succumbed to Dutch elm disease, and limes have been planted in their place. A contemporary engraving by Jan Kip shows avenues radiating out as far as the eye can see, with parterres and geometric planting on all sides of the house. The earl's glittering life of artistic patronage ended badly in financial chaos, drink and death.

Philip Yorke, 1st Earl of Hardwicke, purchased Wimpole in 1742 and immediately set to work on yet more improvements with the Palladian architect Henry Flintcroft, who like Brown had risen from humble stock, redesigning and unifying the exterior of the hall.

There is evidence that a gentleman gardener called William Shenstone, a close associate of Sanderson Miller, advised the 1st Earl on creating the beginnings of an 'improved' naturalistic landscape. His son and heir married Jemima, Marchioness Grey, who had formerly lived at Wrest Park, where 'Capability' Brown had been working, and on the death of the 1st Earl Brown was immediately brought in to complete the park.

The Marchioness soon fell under Lancelot's spell, writing to her daughter, 'Break off, Break off, we tread Enchanted Ground, Mr Brown has been leading me such a Fairy Circle and his Magic Wand has raised such landscapes to the Eye – not visionary, for they were all there, but his Touch has brought them out with the same Effect as a Painter's Pencil upon Canvass.'

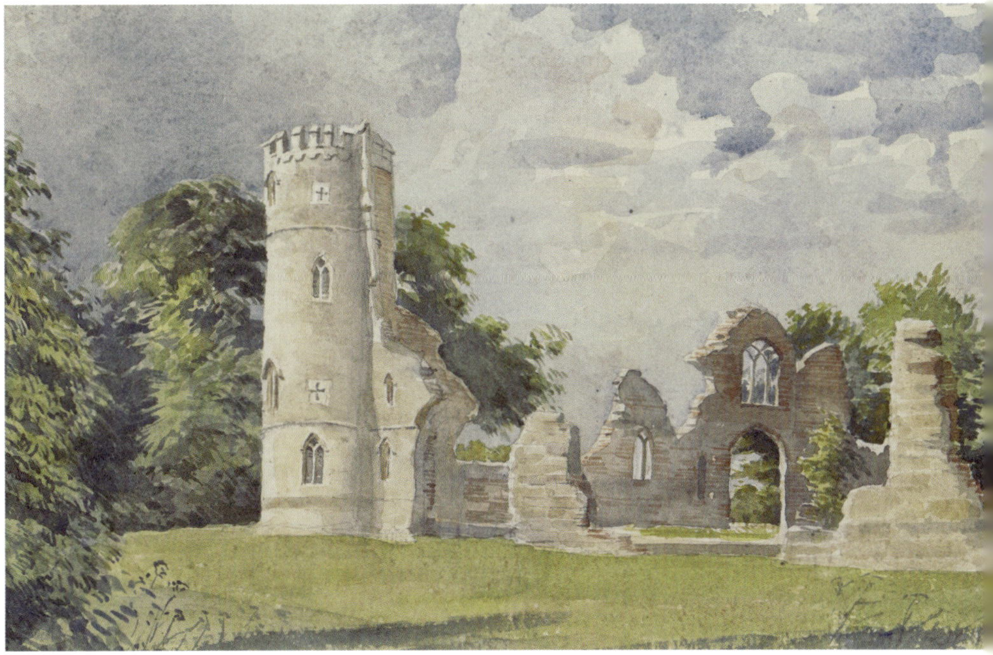

Brown's principal contribution was a wider extension of the park, further clumping of the old formal avenues and a new lake in the valley to the north of the house. He also built the Gothic sham castle, originally designed for the 1st Earl by Sanderson Miller a generation earlier. This has recently been restored by the National Trust, who now own the house and park, and I couldn't resist painting a watercolour of what is still an impressive jumble of mock ruins, with its comical castellated tower.

The natural landscape created by Brown is often today inhabited by the beasts of the the chase or field depicted in the ideal classical scene. With a sunken ditch or ha-ha invisibly dividing the park from the immediate policies of the house, the cattle, sheep or deer grazing among ancient oaks, are important aspects of the landscape garden. Here at Wimpole the home farm has become a designated centre for rare breeds, thus helping preserve varieties of cattle, pigs, sheep, goats and poultry which might otherwise become extinct. As I painted, Longhorn and Park White cattle grazed with their impressive bulls, who mingled freely, reminding me of the famous wild herd at Chillingham that I painted many years ago.

*Alnwick Castle (see overleaf) with the River Aln (watercolour).*

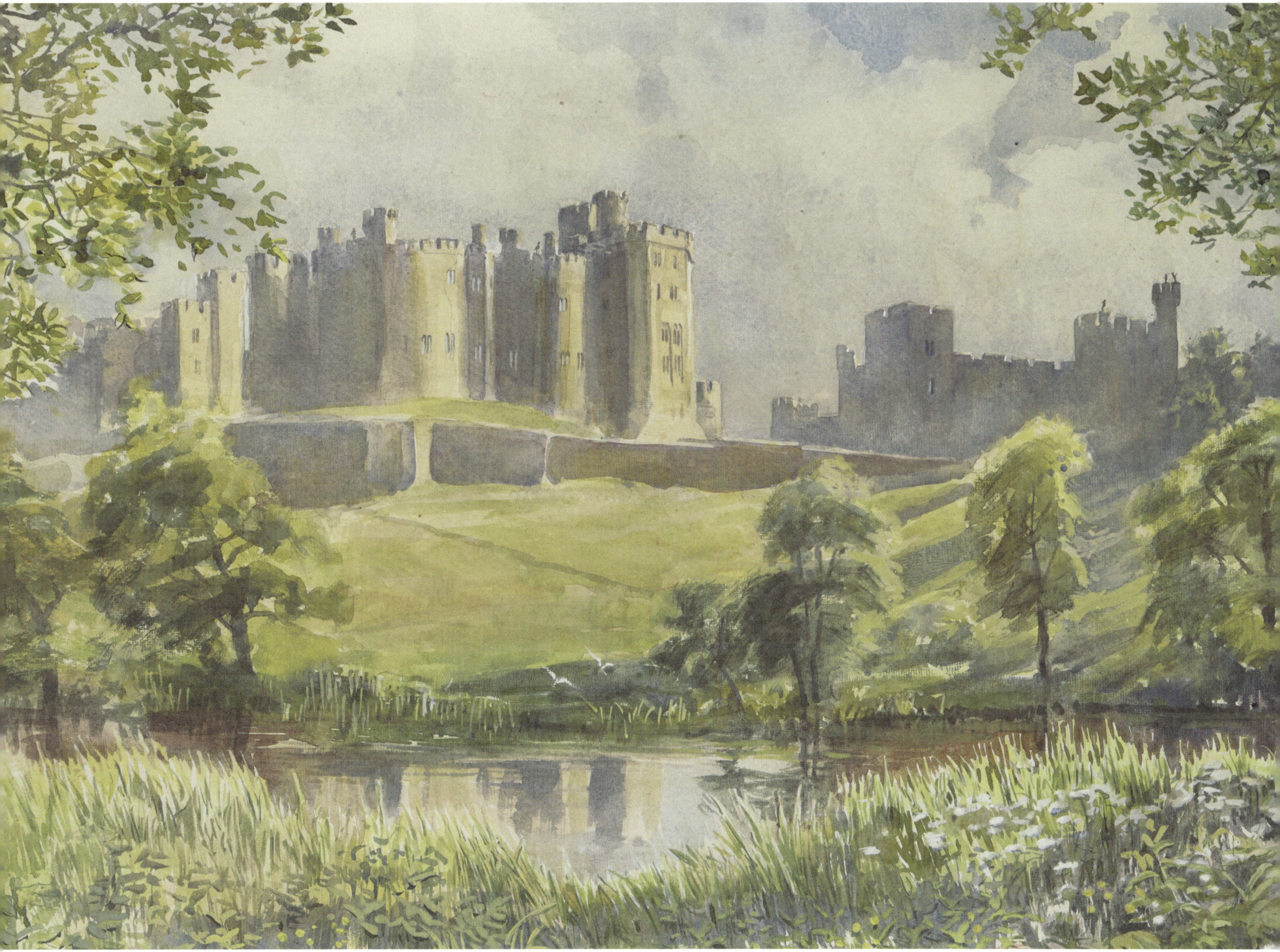

# ALNWICK CASTLE

## Northumberland 1769

THE GREAT Northumbrian castle on the Scottish border was built shortly after the Norman Conquest, and has been owned by the Percy family since the late thirteenth century. It marks the most northern of all 'Capability' Brown's landscapes, though the exact date when he first visited the castle is uncertain. Horace Walpole provides a hint, for in 1752 he observed that the Duke and Duchess of Northumberland were 'building at Northumberland House, at Sion, at Stansted, at Alnwick and Wentworth Castles. They live by the etiquette of the old peerage, have Swiss porters, the Countess has her pipers – in short they will soon have no estate'. It transpired that the Duke's fortune exceeded Walpole's expectation.

Canaletto painted the castle in 1752 and showed it to be on a boulder-strewn hillside. When Brown embarked on the main body of his work at Alnwick, in July 1769, he cleared and turfed the hillside, filling and levelling part of it to form a terrace walk below the castle walls, where formerly the little Bow Burn cut its way through. Most of the planting was concentrated on the further slopes of the River Aln, which meanders down the valley below. A Yorkshire landowner, visiting a decade or so later, wrote enthusiastically of Brown's improvements: 'I never saw plantations so large, better disposed, or that flourished more . . . .'

The landscape created by Brown reminds one of the more prosperous south and its gentle parks rather than the barren wilderness of Northumberland. But his changes reflected the period. Peace with the unification of Scotland and England, a growing prosperity and the ideas of the Age of Enlightenment, together with their own more cosmopolitan outlook, allowed the Duke and his Duchess to soften the castle's original purpose as a fortress and make it a family home. James Paine made various internal alterations. Robert Adam decorated the state rooms. Brown's only regret was the lake, which although intended, was of necessity abandoned when the great flood of 1771 swept through the valley.

As I was painting by the river I was amused to see a row of fellow artists setting up. In the centre ground below the castle a medieval style tent was erected. I wandered over but everyone was very cagey and I was dismissed by the producer of an arty T.V. programme saying 'these are serious artists.' So I wandered back to my amateurish daubs!

HULNE PARK and its ruins of a Carmelite priory retains a more rugged aspect than the castle. Again situated on a bluff above the River Aln, it has been made into a pleasure pavilion and the destinaton for a ride or walk. Brown might have been responsible for its conversion into a romantic banqueting hall, but there is no evidence for this. One can easily imagine the duchess and her friends whiling away a summer afternoon in this Arcadia.

I painted three pictures, all in different mediums. I chose the first, a large watercolour on white paper of the castle, because, despite the low evening sun, the view seemed full of light. I painted *contre-jour*, or against the light, and somehow the dark brooding castle beyond exacerbated the brightness of the sun – catching the trees, reeds and

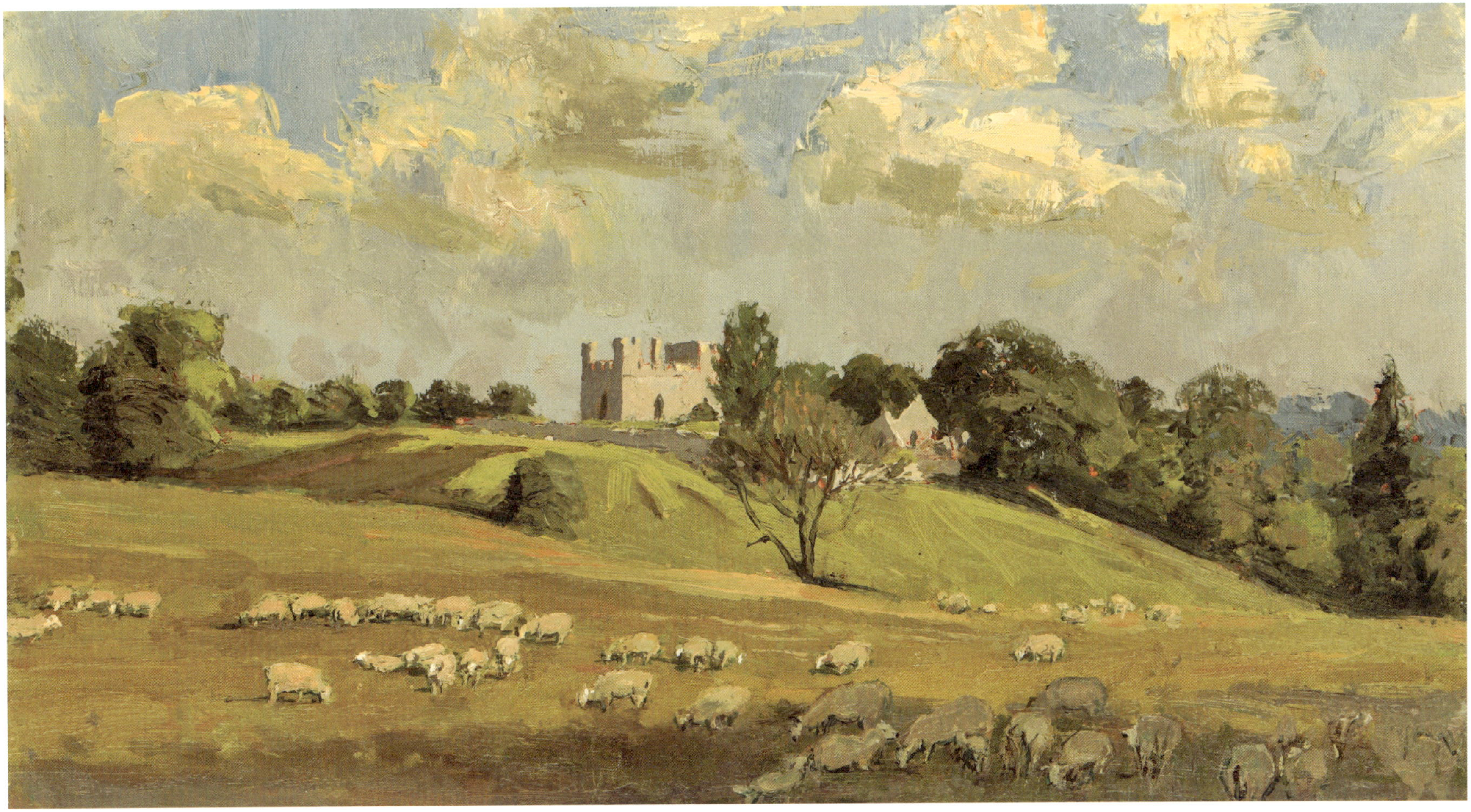

*Hulne Priory (oil).*

grass in the foreground. In painting, the darker the shadows, the brighter the light areas appear.

The second was a gouache of Hulne Priory in a big landscape, chosen because I also wanted to paint a second softer picture (*see page 12*). A group of fallow deer lay inconspicuously in the dappled shade as I painted looking down over the river to the priory, with the blue landscape rolling off into the distance. The grey paper gave an overall unity and I could gently work either side of this mid-tone ground. With this type of painting it is difficult to emulate the brightness of a pure watercolour because even white paint never quite has the resonance of white paper.

The third picture (*see above*) is a study of the priory, which I painted in oil on a smaller scale. Using the paint thickly (impasto) it enabled me to almost use sculptural qualities to give the picture strength and vivacity.

# CLAREMONT

## Surrey 1769

In 1708, the playwright and architect Sir John Vanbrugh bought land near Esher in Surrey, then known as Chargate Farm, 'the situation being singularly romantik', and developed a small 'box' for his own use. The site's potential was not lost on Thomas Pelham-Holles, the Duke of Newcastle, who, at the age of 21, taking advantage of Vanbrugh's impecuniosity, purchased the property for himself. Vanbrugh substantially enlarged the house for the Duke and built the sham castle, which still exists as a belvedere today.

The grounds were first developed by Charles Bridgeman in a formal way, with avenues and a round pool. The National Trust now manage the gardens, and have restored Bridgeman's amphitheatre into a turfed grassy bank. As at Stowe, William Kent adjusted Bridgeman's formal layout and created clumps of trees out of the avenues. He also made a larger informal lake from the circular pool, complete with an island, pavilion and grotto. None of this could be seen from the house, but were pleasure grounds beyond the mount (hence the original name, Claremount).

In 1768 Robert Clive, 'Clive of India', bought the estate from the Duke of Newcastle's widow. The hero of Plassey, who had established the power of the East India Company in Bengal, had returned to England with a fortune worth £300,000 (perhaps £120 million today). Despite his wealth, his health was not good. He thought Vanbrugh's house too damp and low-lying, so decided to pull it down and build a new classical mansion on higher ground.

Sir William Chambers, who was also working for Clive at Styche Hall in Shropshire, was asked to draw up plans. But so was 'Capability' Brown, and much to Chambers anger it was Brown who was given the contract. It was a real feather in Brown's cap. The site was within easy reach of London, and Brown could combine his genius for landscape with a talent for architecture for a client who was one of the richest men in the country.

Once again Brown turned to his son-in-law, Henry Holland, to oversee the building and detailed internal design. The house is built of pale yellow bricks, with Portland stone for the cornice surrounding the windows and the rooftop balustrade. The park provided the clay to make about 1.5 million bricks.

The house cost £30,000, then a king's ransom, but small change to Nabob Clive. Riches do not always bring happiness. The circumstances of his death in 1774 remain shrouded, but recent biographers have suggested that he probably had a heart attack whilst on opium. He was only forty-nine, and had little time to enjoy his creation. A local legend tells of a rare night spent there during a storm, which so rattled the casements Clive jammed them with golden guineas, which were then squirreled away by the chambermaids.

On my visit I first walked around the lake and up to the belvedere before realising that it was hidden from the house, which lay beyond a heavily wooded ridge and is now the Claremont Fan Court School. In due course I presented myself at the school and asked the deputy headmaster for permission to paint it. Such requests fall on deaf ears these days. Painting was out of the question without a month's notice and consulting the sex offender's register; even taking photographs on school premises was frowned on. He did point out a

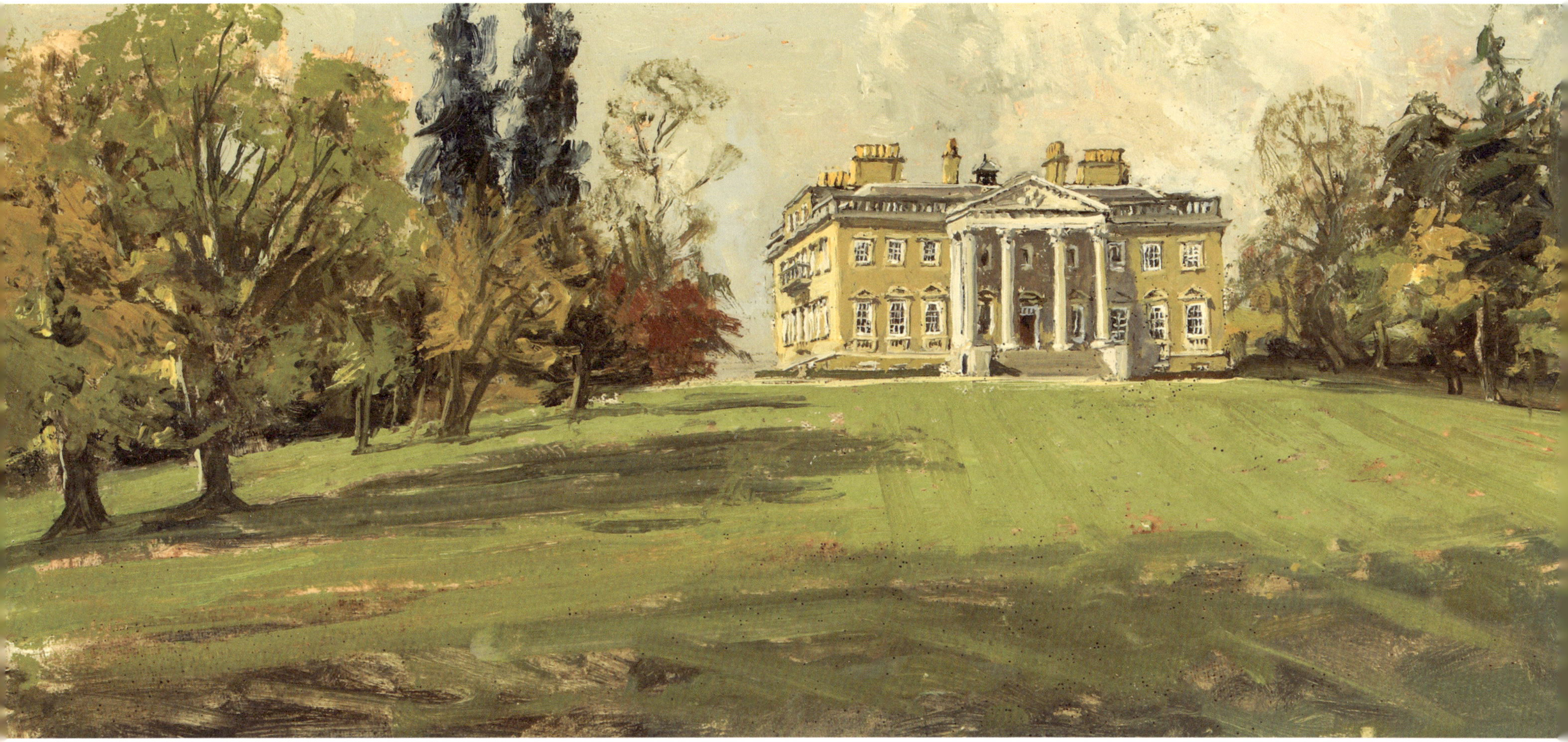

*Claremont House, designed by Brown and built by Henry Holland (oil).*

distant view beyond the school grounds, which I set off in search of amidst a desolation of stockbroker belt gated communities, with cameras eyeing me suspiciously from every post. In the end I gave up, but managed to paint surreptitiously from the front of my car in a school car park.

Great houses when institutionalised are like some grand old dowager fallen on hard times, who still displays a gracious face to the world but lives in cramped and reduced circumstance. The one room I saw at Claremont was the oval entrance hall, a beautiful space with black pillars and ornate plaster medallions celebrating Robert Clive's achievements with an inlaid marble floor inspired by that at Syon. Utilitarian desks and chairs now grace the space.

Ideally I paint standing at an easel, but where space is cramped or where the artist wishes to be invisible a pochade box is an excellent alternative. Working off your knees sitting down, the box lid contains the canvas or board, the palette fits below this and acts as a lid to the paints and brushes below. Everything you need is in this one container and it is ideal for doing quick small sketches, such as the situation I found myself in at Claremont.

# COMPTON VERNEY HOUSE

## Warwickshire 1769

In 1769 Brown redesigned the 120 acre park at Compton Verney for John Verney, 19th Lord Willoughby de Broke. It was classic 'Capability' Brown, involving his ability to manipulate water, and his skills both as a landscape designer and architect. The old ponds were transformed into an L-shaped lake. A new drive approached the house over a new classical bridge (whose bronze sphinxes are similar in design to those at Croome Court). The inevitable cedars of Lebanon were planted and the old chapel, which stood a stone's throw from the house and blocked the best views, was demolished and replaced by a classical chapel, designed by Brown and built on the other side of the house.

Compton Verney was originally built by the Smiths of Warwick in about 1714. It was requisitioned during the Second World War and thereafter remained empty and dilapidated. In 1993 it was bought by the Littlewoods football pools millionaire Sir Peter Moores, who subsequently transformed the house and grounds into one of the leading centres of art in the Midlands. It is now a charity, run by the Compton Verney House Trust.

On my visit, sculptures by Henry Moore and Rodin glistened wet with rain in the sunshine, complementing each other in their monumentality and casting long shadows across the manicured lawns. The smaller Moores and Rodins were shown in the contemporary gallery designed by Stanton Williams, which – surprisingly – is a happy bedfellow to the classical Robert Adam interiors in the main mansion.

My painting time was punctuated by heavy thundery showers and periods of sunshine when the cumulonimbus clouds rose high in the sky. Fortunately I had my fishing umbrella, under which I crouched with my easel as I quickly brushed on thick oil paint to catch a moment of light on a changeable day. Changing light conditions offer opportunities as well as a challenge. A pattern of light and shade, if well conceived, will give the picture a structure. Timing is all. The precise moment when all seems right has to be retained in the mind and painted. Once I've decided the light and shadow that best suits the composition, I try to avoid being continually diverted by the ever-changing scene.

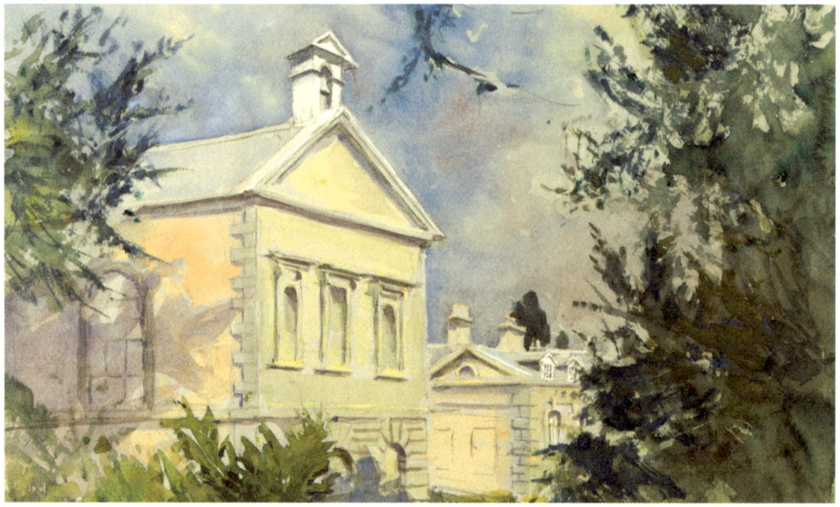

*Compton Verney. The chapel built by Brown to replace a medieval church (watercolour).*

OPPOSITE *Compton Verney with the Sphinx Bridge and fine cedar (oil).*

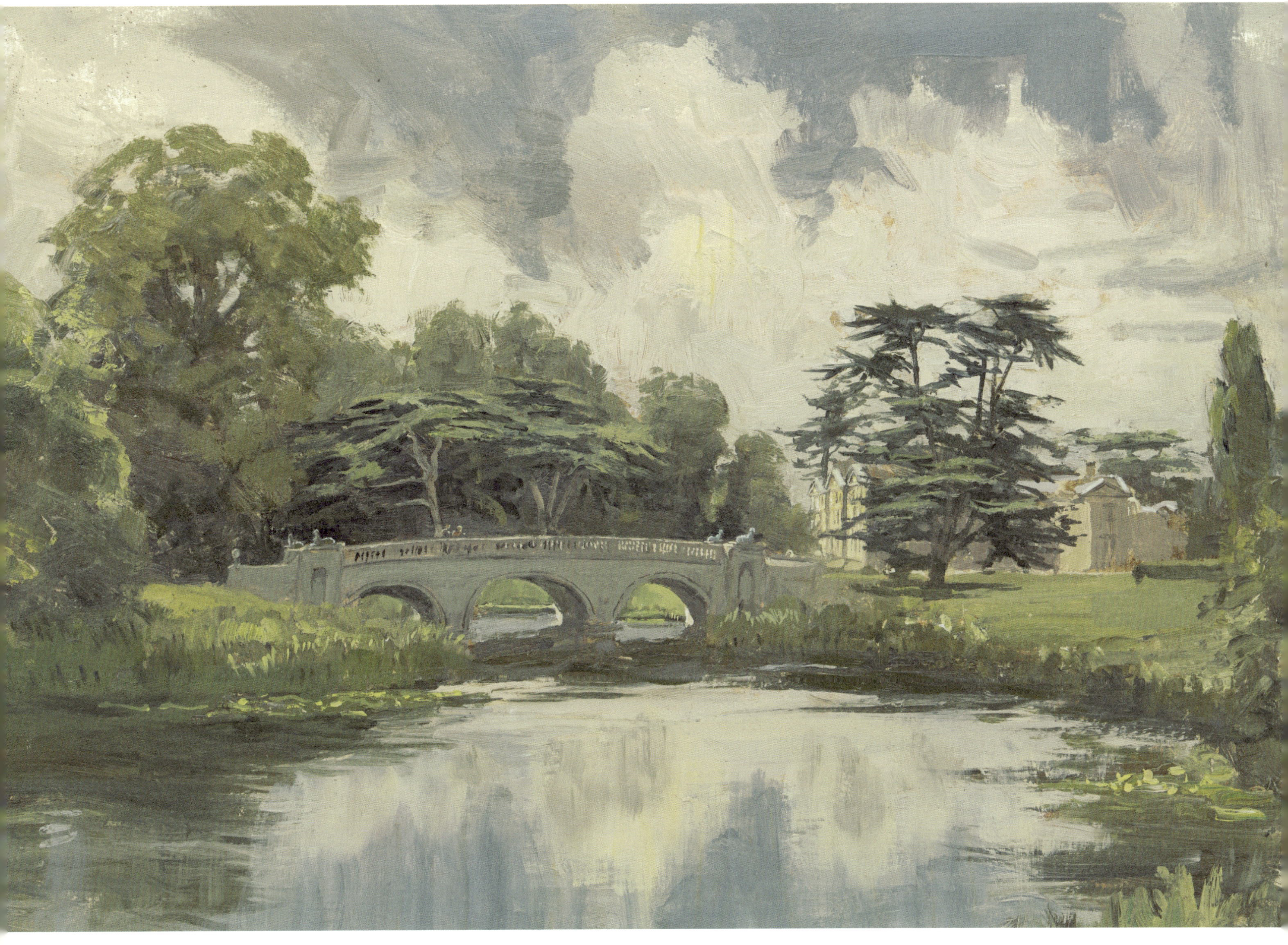

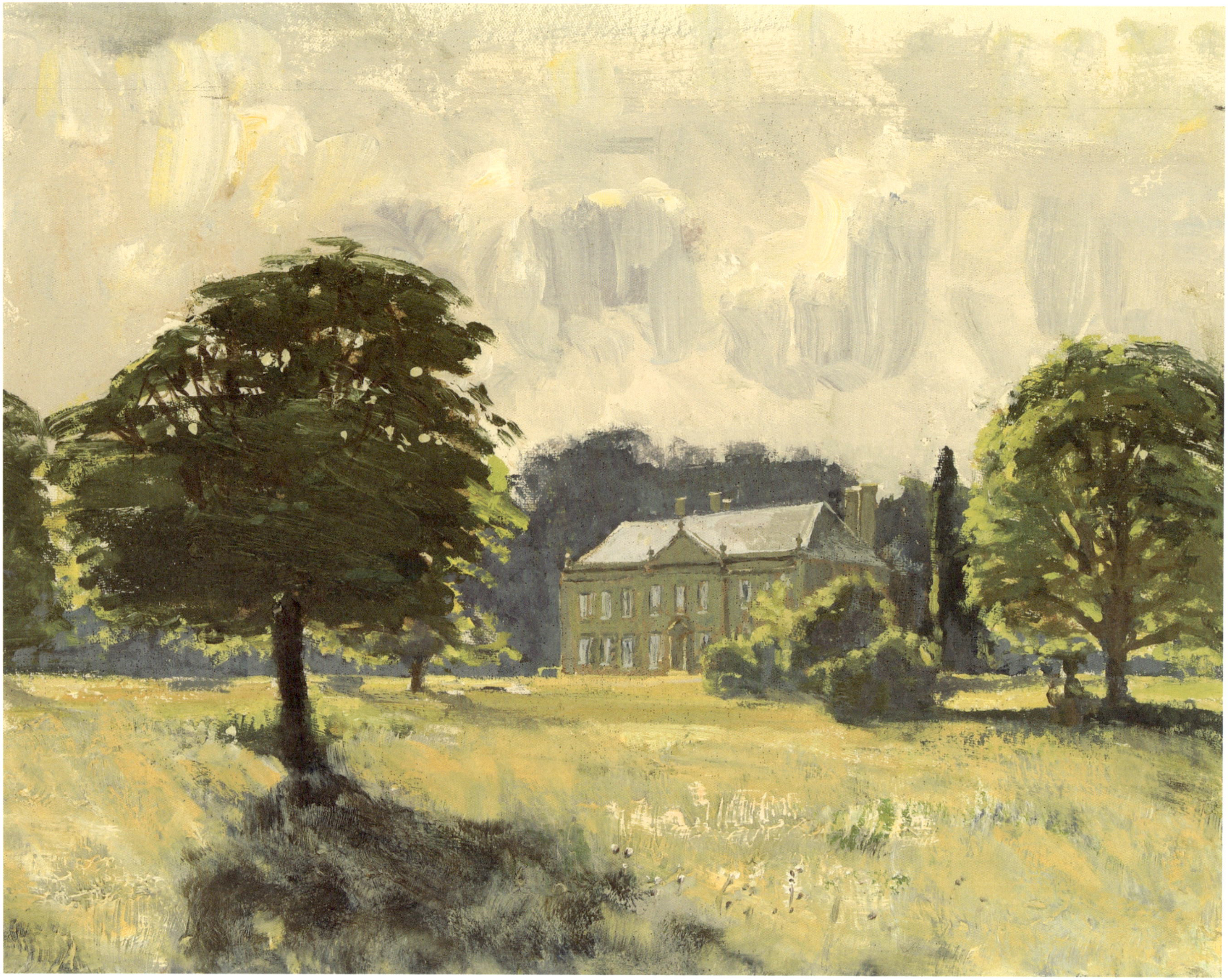

*Wallington Hall (oil).*

# WALLINGTON HALL & ROTHLEY PARK

## Northumberland 1770

It was a glorious May evening. After the heat of the day painting little St Wilfrid's Church at Kirkharle (*see page 8*), I drove the few miles to Wallington, where the delicate classical house was mysterious in the evening light and trees in the park shed long shadows. I painted from the top of the ha-ha, which has all the hallmarks of a Brown creation.

The Blacketts of Wallington prospered because of considerable mining and other interests in Newcastle, spending liberally on improving their house and park. It was probably here in 1737, when he was still only twenty-one, that Brown met William Joyce, a freelance layer-out of gardens and skilled in the use of a theodolite – then a rare and valued instrument that substantially reduced the time spent surveying and measuring. It was Joyce who could have sown the seed in the young gardener's mind that it might be possible to make a living doing something similar. Now, in 1770, Brown, aged fifty-four, returned to the countryside of his childhood as the most famous landscape gardener in Britain. Both Sir Walter Blackett and Lady Loraine requested Brown's services, and he drew up plans which still exist for both of them.

A few miles from Wallington is Rothley Park, which also fell within Brown's brief for improvement. There was a lower lake which existed when Lancelot came and is now heavily wooded. Besides this is a pretty Regency house called Lake House in a most spectacular position, which is run as a bed-and-breakfast. I parked my car here and headed for the upper lake, which is immediately above the road and which Lancelot designed. By contrast here there is grass running down to the water's edge. Clumps of trees punctuate the landscape, whose reflections gives a shimmering mirror image. Above, on an outcrop of rock called Codger Crag, a miniature fort, designed by Thomas Wright, had been constructed and is still there today.

If landscape gardeners were saints Lancelot Brown would be the patron saint of fishing. It is hard to gauge how much pleasure and peaceful moments he has given to so many in piscatorial pursuit. Here at Rothley, several fishermen pottered about trying to catch the wily trout.

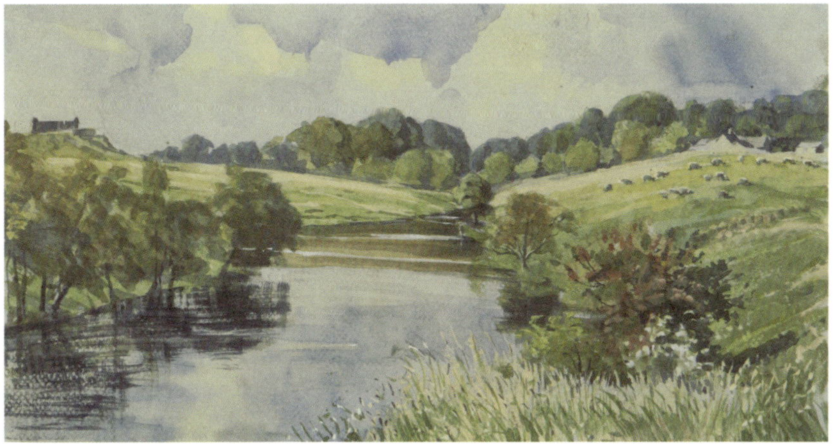

*Rothley Park. The lower lake with the dam hidden by the road bridge (watercolour).*

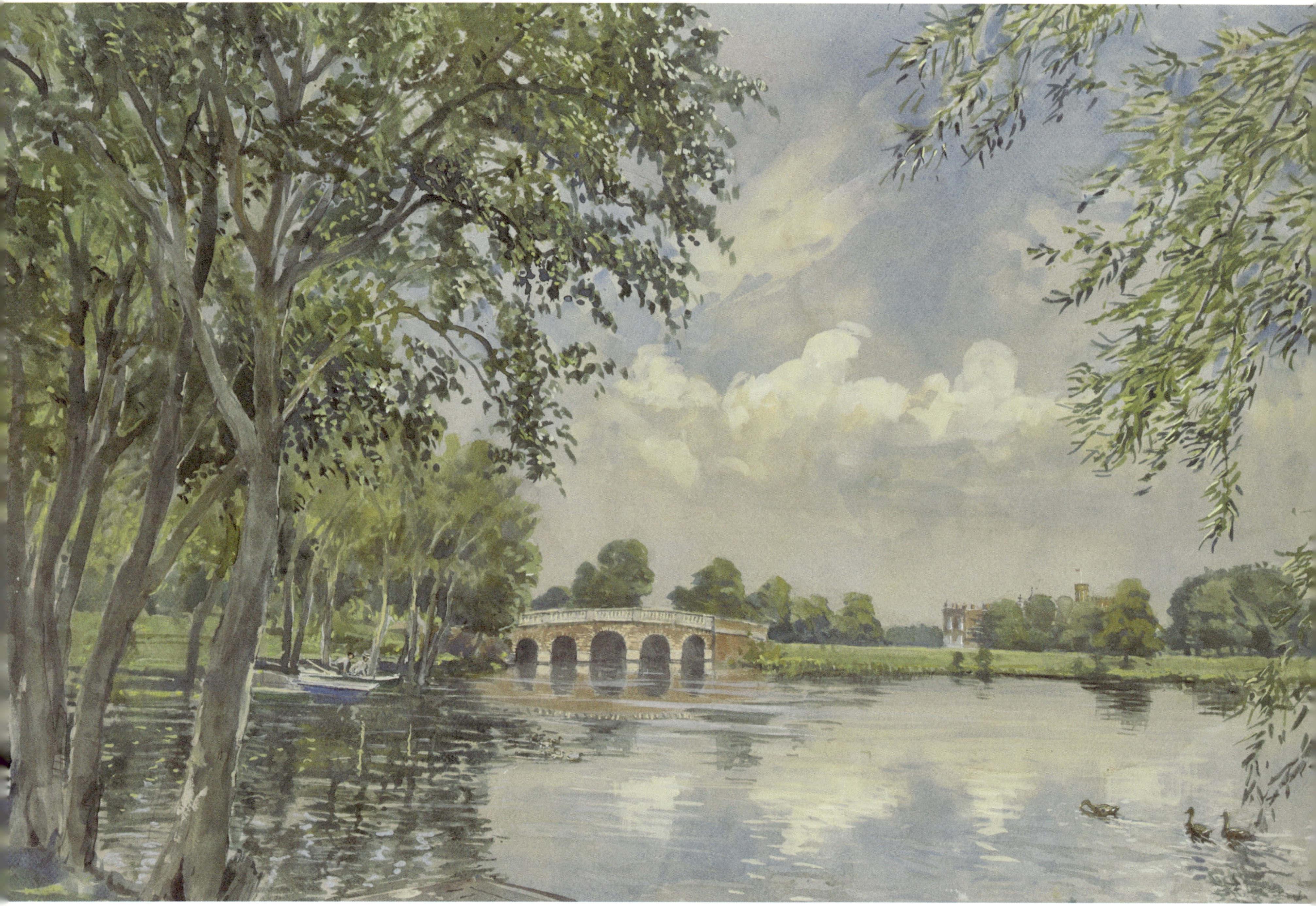

*Burton Constable Hall. Like the Elizabethan hall, Brown built the bridge of brick as there was no local stone (watercolour).*

# BURTON CONSTABLE HALL

## Yorkshire 1772

I ALMOST halted in mid-stride with astonishment and wonder at my first glimpse of this noble Elizabethan house. Tall, built of mellow brick, it stands proud ten miles from Hull in the billiard table flatness of Humberside – an island of woods and park in a bare corn-growing landscape with big skies.

The Constables acquired the estate in the thirteenth century, and indeed still own it today, over seven centuries later. Its incumbent in the mid-eighteenth century was William Constable, who had inherited the house in 1747 when he was twenty-six. Constable prided himself on his connoisseurship. Having acquired a considerable collection of books, paintings, sculpture and antiquities on the Grand Tour, he returned to Yorkshire determined to create a landscape worthy of his great house and its contents. Having previously engaged Thomas White, who had helped Lancelot in other schemes, he finally engaged the great Brown himself to realise his ambitions. By this time William Constable was finding mobility difficult and readily used wheelchairs, an example of which is now on display in the house, whilst a hoist was used to raise him to the saddle.

When Lancelot arrived in 1772 he found the park and gardens badly neglected, and the avenues broken up. Wherever possible, he skillfully kept any established trees to form clumps or leave as individual specimens. He was not beyond attempting the moving of large trees from one place to another, for which he developed a special contraption. Apart from the park planting, he extended the existing lake, dividing it in two by erecting a stone and brick bridge, which hid a dam controlling the water level.

The bridge was intended for the new main drive. This has now been discontinued and an extensive area of small holiday chalets has been developed on the other side of the lake to the house. With a painting it matters not where you look from, but it is crucial where you look to – and this was the case here. To my back stood the ranks of chalets and caravans with all their amusing idiosyncrasies. Before me lay the lake, bridge and Brown's sublime park with the mellow brick of the hall looking strikingly red among the complementary green trees.

The extensive scene with the sky, threatening thunder on this muggy day, somehow suggested to me a large sheet of grey paper and the use of gouache and watercolour. Turner favoured this type of paper, since when it has always been known as Turner grey. The mid-tone ground gives an overall unity, darker areas being blocked in with watercolour washes and light being painted in later with gouache. It is an effective and easy way to create an impression quickly, but always lacks the verve and freshness of a pure watercolour. Many watercolourists despise this method, but I say if it's good enough for Turner it's good enough for me.

Travelling to various Brown landscapes has given me the opportunity to see other unconnected things. My visit to Burton Constable encouraged me to realise a long cherished ambition to travel across the Humber Bridge. I believe that this and other great twentieth century engineering feats will in future generations be considered the great sculptural art forms of our time, as today we view the noble Gothic cathedrals.

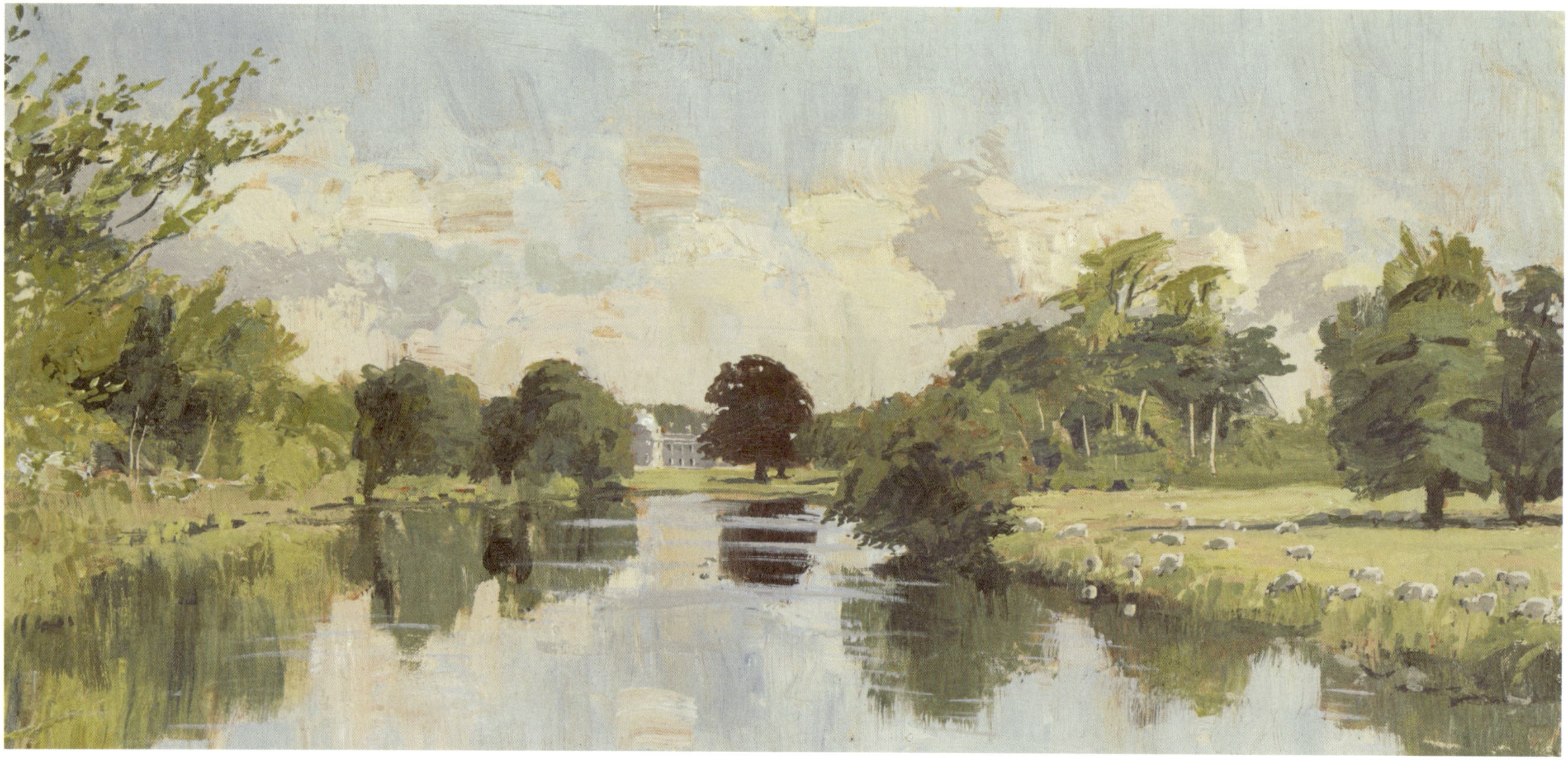

*Scampston Hall, the lake from the road bridge (oil).*

# SCAMPSTON HALL

## Yorkshire 1772

'Capability' Brown visited Scampston Hall in the autumn of 1772 and subsequently drew up plans which the owner, Sir William St Quintin, put into effect using his own labour force, obviously with mutual agreement. A year later he wrote to Brown saying, 'I have also made an island where the water was too broad, and have widened it to ye North of the Bridge according to your plan, which answers prodigiously well, for which I return you many thanks. I shall be in London some time next month, and will certainly wait on you. I beg your acceptance of some Yorkshire Hams.'

Theirs was obviously a successful working relationship, freeing Brown from the reponsibility for supervising a commission far away from his Hampton Court home. Both Sir William, and the owner of nearby Sledmere (Sir Christopher Sykes), were keen amateur gardeners and architects who were only too happy to take control of the schemes, once the plans had been drawn up.

This is a flat well-watered area of Yorkshire near Malton, but in the distance you see the Howardian Hills and what is lacking in picturesque undulations and valleys is made up by the fine tall stands of trees which thrive in this rich alluvial plain. The long serpentine lake is the major feature of Brown's plan; at either end are two bridges, one Palladian near the hall and the other, a road bridge which now manfully copes with the A64 traffic. It was here that I tried to ignore the thundering lorries and paint the sublime view of trees, water and sky with the hall and its distinctive dome in the distance lit by the early morning sun.

The Palladian bridge is ingenious, since it is part pavilion and to the rear there is a secret cascade. About thirty years ago I came to Scampston to paint the various prominent monuments in the park, including this bridge. I did these on a very small scale and interestingly they have been framed in two sets of five pictures each.

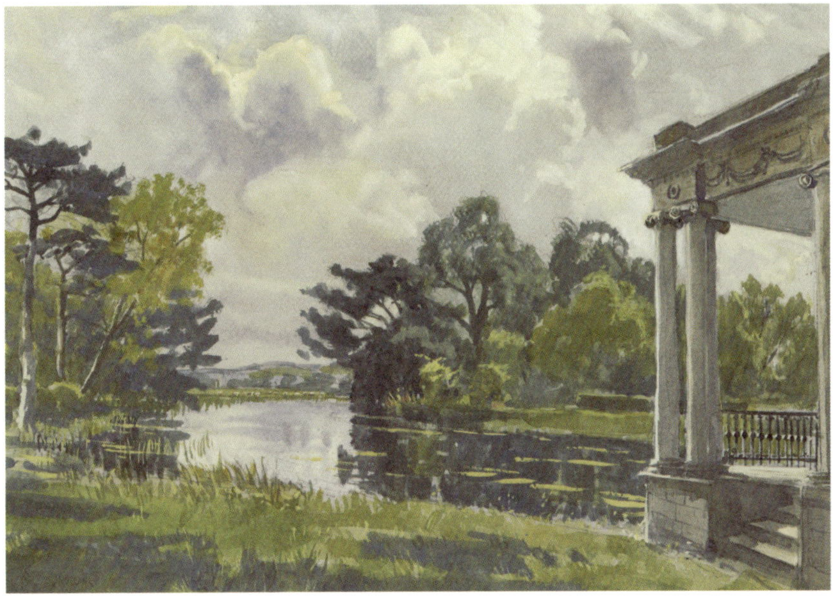

*Scampston Hall. The Palladian bridge which disguises a dam (watercolour).*

William Marlow painted the estate in the early eighteenth century, capturing its landscape at a defined moment in time. Much has changed, sometimes beyond recognition. My own sets of pictures have also seen changes, even in thirty years. A prominent elm is no longer and the old glasshouses have been renewed.

As a topographical painter, I look upon myself not only as an artist but as a recorder of a specific view at a particular time. I therefore have to balance the artistic with the honest interpretation of the subject. Some things I do alter; perhaps the odd intrusive pylon or motorcar might be removed. I therefore spend a lot of time moving about so that an honest rendering of the landscape composes itself pleasingly. This might include standing/sitting/lying on the ground to get the right perspective.

The greatest change at Scampston since I first went there has been the ambitious creation of new gardens within the former walled garden. These were initiated by Charles and Caroline Legard with the help of the international Dutch garden designer, Piet Oudolf. Using drifts of grasses and herbaceous perennials they have made one of the most varied and interesting contemporary gardens, which because they are confined by the walls do not intrude on the 'Capability' Brown landscape beyond.

# WARDOUR CASTLE

## Wiltshire 1773

So much is conjecture; did Brown do work at Wardour Castle or was it Richard Wood? Perhaps each made a contribution. Brown certainly drew a plan on the instructions of Henry, 8th Lord Arundell, who in a letter to Lancelot hoped that Wardour would 'be worthy of your attention'. I like to speculate that Brown had a hand in the magnificent Gothic banqueting hall at Old Wardour Castle. This remains intact, unlike so much of the park that was subsequently swept away for arable land. Nearby, James Paine's vast mansion, built between 1770 and 1776, sits proudly on a hill crowned with oaks and great cedars of Lebanon. Brown was commissioned to produce a landscape plan for the new house, but little was carried out.

Old Wardour Castle stands ruined, having been blown up by Cromwellian forces during the Civil War. The then Lady Arundell defended valiantly with just a few servants against overwhelming odds, her husband being away fighting for the Royalist cause. She only capitulated when the castle was undermined and explosives laid. She was allowed to leave with honour.

Latterly New Wardour Castle (*see page 19*) became Cranborne Chase School for girls. More recently it has been divided up into a number of stylish apartments.

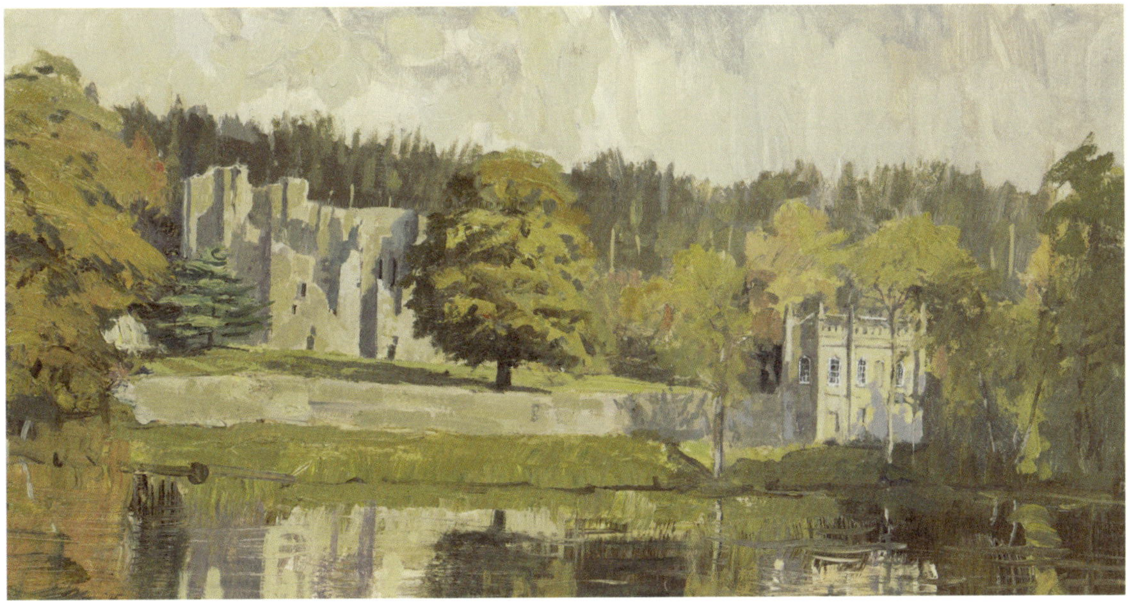

*Wardour Old Castle with the banqueting hall, perhaps designed by Brown (oil).*

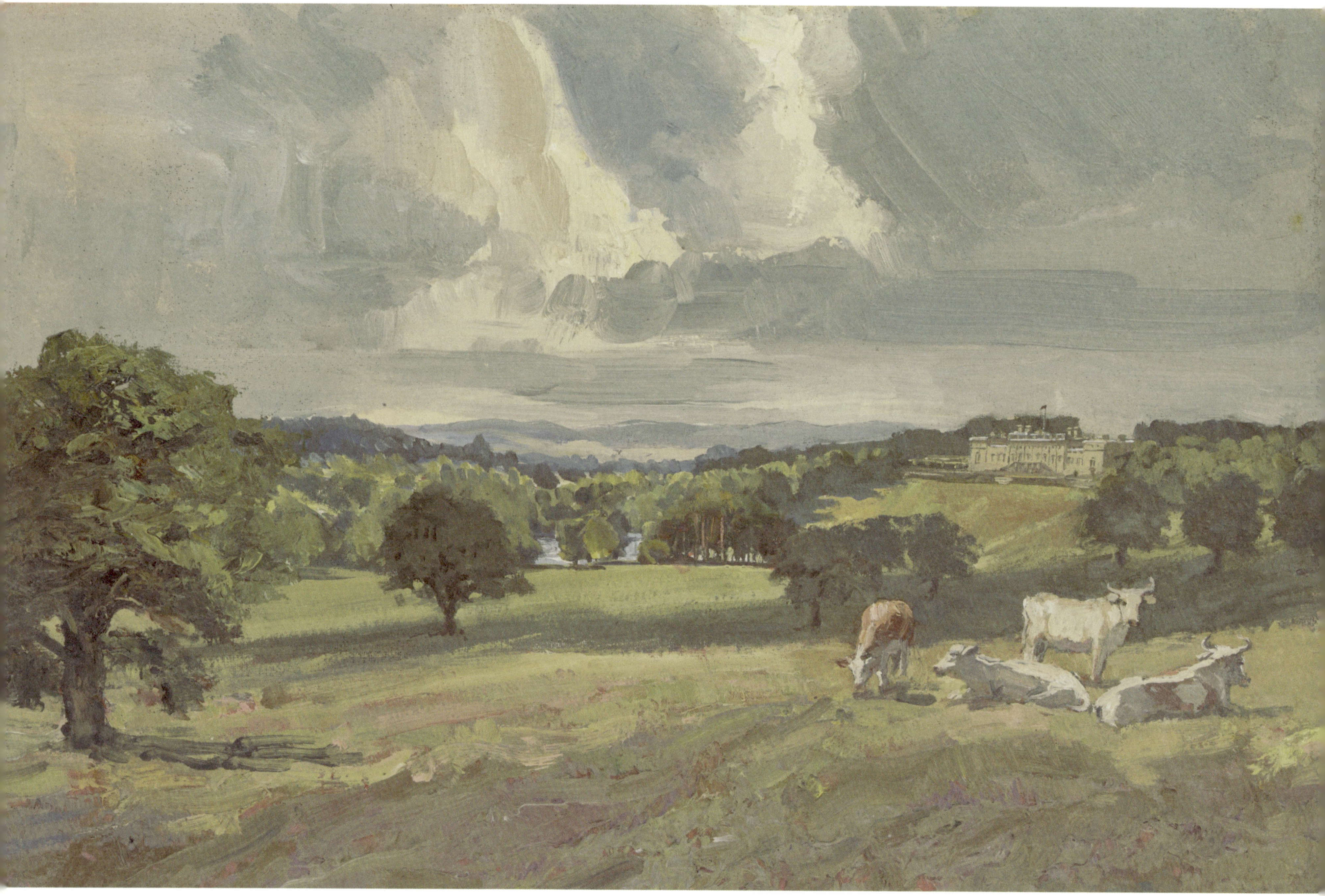

# HAREWOOD HOUSE

## Yorkshire 1774

MANY OF the great industrial northern cities give way within a few miles to remote and uncluttered countryside. Leeds practically bounds Harewood, but its formidable walls isolates the realm of the Lascelles, Earls of Harewood, and its 'Capability' Brown park. Clumps of trees and rolling fields dip down to the lake in the valley, and the large mansion looks out across the scene from the opposite hillside. What a challenge for an artist; here Reynolds, Turner, Girtin, John Varley and Thomas Malton painted. George Richmond, staying to do a portrait, dashed off a picture while changing for dinner as 'a sudden reaction to Brown's wonderful vista'. Harewood House is a treasure trove of these and many other pictures, hung magnificently in Robert Adams' serene rooms. Sadly, externally the eighteenth century John Carr classical front was 'improved' by Barry in the nineteenth century, and now looks like a grand railway station.

Things did not always go smoothly for Brown, as a curmudgeonly letter from Edwin Lascelles indicates: 'Mr Brown was with me the other day to desire I would give him a draft for the remaining £400, parts of the £900 which he was not to desire until the whole was certified and allowed to be done according to contract. I have always said and did insist upon it that the ground was Scandalous Lay'd and beggarly sown, and several other parts were slovenly run over and badly finished, particularly by the island. Mr Brown assures me that he will be at Harewood House, on purpose to meet me and give me satisfaction the week before Easter.'

Lascelles must have been appeased because further payments were made for other work, and when the plantings had matured the grounds were considered one of the great landscapes of Yorkshire.

I thoughtlessly pitched-up unannounced and was told to put my request to paint in writing. Not to be put off I found a convenient right-of-way with fine views over the house and park. The hazard of landscape painting is also its exhilarating excitement, principally caused by the fickle character of the British weather. This was a day of dramatic Yorkshire skies, with the landscape a patchwork of light and shade and the blue Pennines in the distance. A few cows of mixed pedigree grazed nearby and conveniently posed.

OPPOSITE *Harewood House. The park and lake (oil).*

# ROCHE ABBEY

## Yorkshire 1774

Coal, the black gold, sustained many a fine country property, and the contrast between the sprawling mining towns and the often sublime beauty of the nearby country estate could not be more sudden or extreme. Renishaw, made legendary by Sacheverell, Edith and Osbert Sitwell, lies within Sheffield's grasp. Maltby is a grimy red brick sprawl with worked-out coal mines; yet within a mile or so I was driving down a cobbled road through a wooded cleft in the landscape and came to a place of magic and peace. An ancient ruined gatehouse stood hard up against a limestone cliff, and a path down a damp valley beside a little stream concealed by meadowsweet, kingcup and cow parsley led me to the romantic abbey ruins.

Brown drew up plans for the Earl of Scarborough at nearby Sandbeck Park in 1774. Although Roche Abbey is separated from the park by a hill and road, it was decided to develop the picturesque site of the ruined Cistercian abbey as part of the overall landscape plan. His instructions were to 'To finish all the Valley of Roach Abbey in all its Parts, according to the Ideas fixed on with Lord Scarborough (with Poets feeling and with Painters Eye).'

A small lake was created by damming the beck and making a cascade for the outfall. The land around the abbey was raised, which resulted in its low walls and other surviving fragments being grassed over, forming an even sward around the two north and south transepts of the abbey remains. Brown's landscaping may have pleased 'the Painter's eye', but it covered perhaps the most complete ground plan of all the great medieval monasteries. In the 1920s archaeologists began excavating the site, and it is now in the care of English Heritage.

Gilpin wrote, perhaps with a tinge of criticism, that Brown had 'formed a very beautiful scene. But I fear that it is too magnificent. It is possible that this lake may in some future time become its situation; when the marks of the spade and the pickaxe are removed, when osier flourish, and its naked banks become fringed and covered with wood.' Gilpin was right: the lake is overgrown and quite hidden from the abbey. Life in the country is a continual battle against blasted nature!

I happen to rather like nature. An eighteenth century painting of Roche, after its 'capabilities' had been realised, shows the ruins covered in ivy and surrounded by trees. Modern conservation and the romantic view are not happy bedfellows, and the site is now too sanitised for my taste.

I however did find a view which Lancelot might have approved from the overgrown lake near the cascade. There was a glimpse of the abbey through the trees and the competitive spring flowers vying for light were growing up at my feet. It is difficult not to be inspired by the watercolours of Turner, de Wint and especially Thomas Girtin when painting such a scene, so why not grasp it and try and equal their vision?

The limestone, which was quarried on the site, has a luminous quality in sunshine, best captured by progressively darkening the shaded areas in the painting until the light shines out in comparison. It is a delicate balance with pure watercolour to create these dark

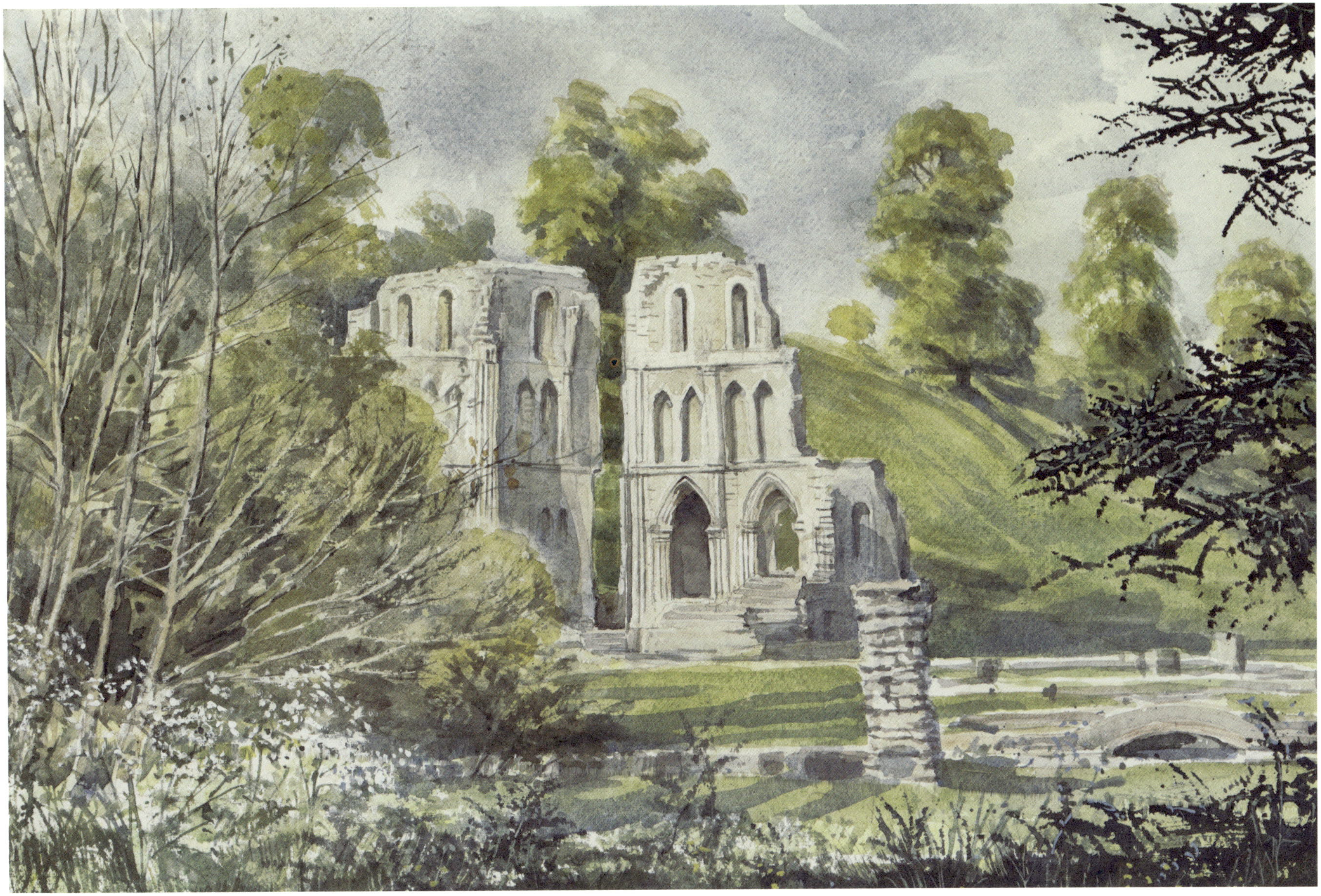

*Roche Abbey showing the re-excavation after Brown had turfed over the foundations of the old abbey (watercolour).*

areas without making the picture appear opaque and heavy. At one stage I made the abbey walls in part too dark, denying them the brightness I sought, so I resorted to the sponge and lifted most of the pigment out, returning to the white paper. This has to be done with care. There is a danger of removing the size from the paper until it becomes like blotting paper. However the Khadi paper I was using was resilient enough to sustain this.

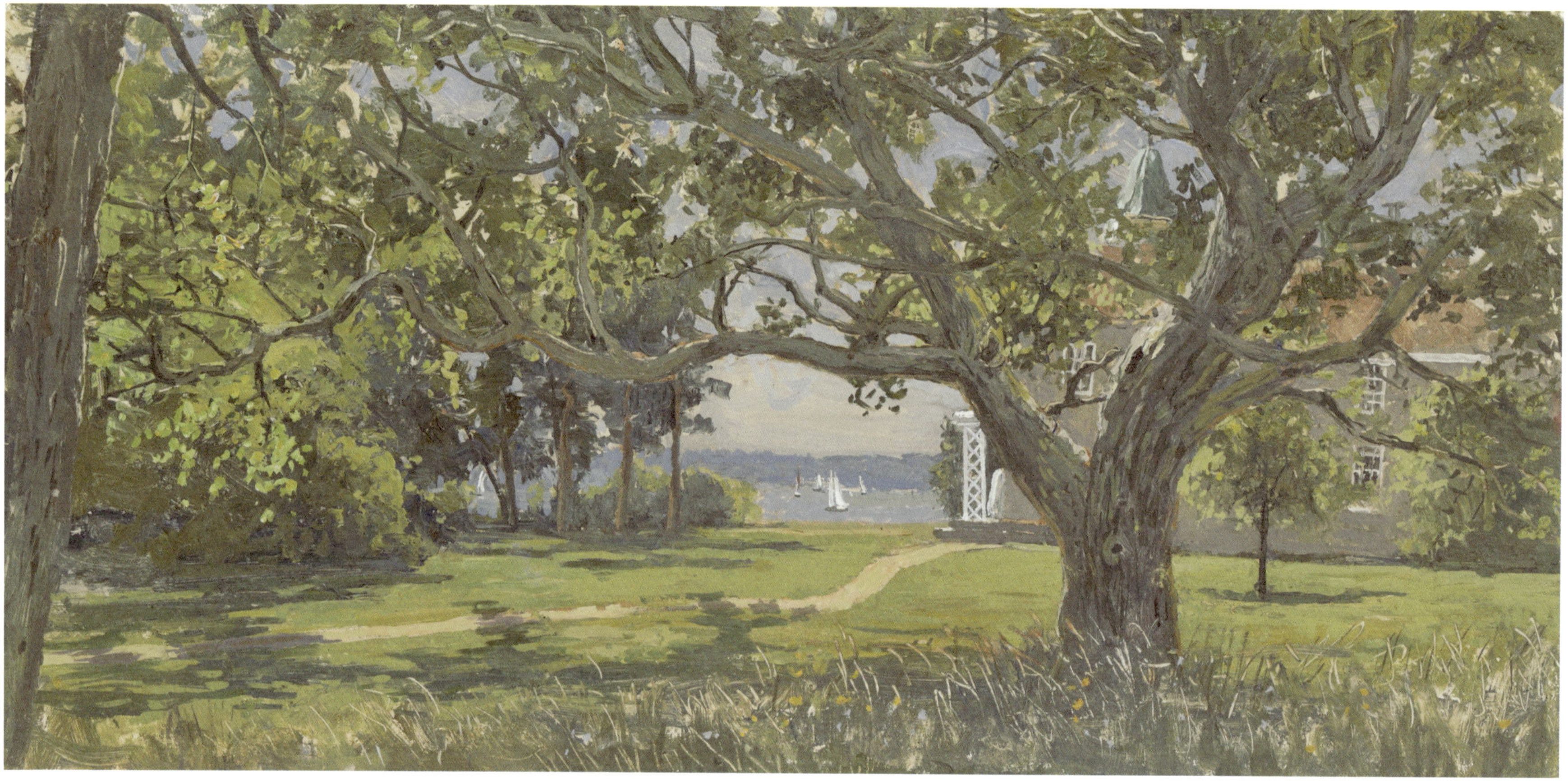

*Cadland House. The gardens conform basically to Brown's original plan but the cottage orneé has been replaced by a substantial house (oil).*

# CADLAND HOUSE

## Hampshire 1774

DRUMMONDS was Lancelot Brown's bank for most of his working career. He opened his account at its offices at Angell Court, near Charing Cross, in the wake of signing the contracts for his work at Petworth in 1753. The bank had been founded thirty years earlier by an Edinburgh goldsmith, Andrew Drummond, for whom Brown did occasional work, as he was to do for other members of the family over the years.

The Hon Robert Drummond had moved south after the Jacobite Rebellion of 1746, in which his father had been killed fighting for Bonnie Prince Charlie. By 1775 he was a respectable and wealthy partner in the bank and owner of an estate on Southampton Water. Inevitably, he turned to 'Capability' Brown to design a new house and create a landscape on the site, which was a slight knoll with views over the estuary.

Responsibility for the house was handed over by Brown to his son-in-law, Henry Holland. The result was a square classical villa in pale yellow brick which glowed in the evening sunlight by the water. The writer about the picturesque, William Gilpin, was a great admirer: 'Tho quite plain, it is one of the most elegant and seems to me one of the most comfortable houses in the country. Abundance of old timber gives the house, tho' lately built, so much the air and dignity of an ancient mansion that Mr Brown, the ingenious improver of it, used to say, it was the oldest new place he knew in England.'

Sadly, in 1947 the house was compulsorily purchased and demolished, and the massive Fawley oil refinery is now on its site.

A few miles away, on the coast overlooking the Solent, Brown designed an octagonal cottage orneé and laid out a circular walk through shrubberies with glimpses of the sea. This was used in the eighteenth century for boating and fishing expeditions, where guests could enjoy themselves informally away from the grand house. The cottage has been replaced by a substantial neo-classical house, but the grounds exist as originally designed.

It is the only existing 'Capability' Brown garden by the sea and Aldred Drummond, descendant of the original owner, kindly showed me Brown's plans: it was a thrilling moment to handle plans which the great man had created! The walks exist just as they were drawn 250 years ago and the view I chose to paint obscurely shows the new house. In the foreground an ancient oak, perhaps once a sapling planted by Brown, frames the picture and the sea looks very blue through the dark reddish Scots pine near the foreshore. It suggests a Mediterranean-like atmosphere on a sunny day, when the blue sky is reflected in the Solent.

The sea can be considered like a vast fractured mirror. Even when winds and currents break up the surface the overall colours of the sky are taken up and reflected back. When the sky is blue there is a great deal of blue in the water, a grey day makes a grey sea, whilst at sunset the light of the sun, broken up, bounces across the waves directly towards you.

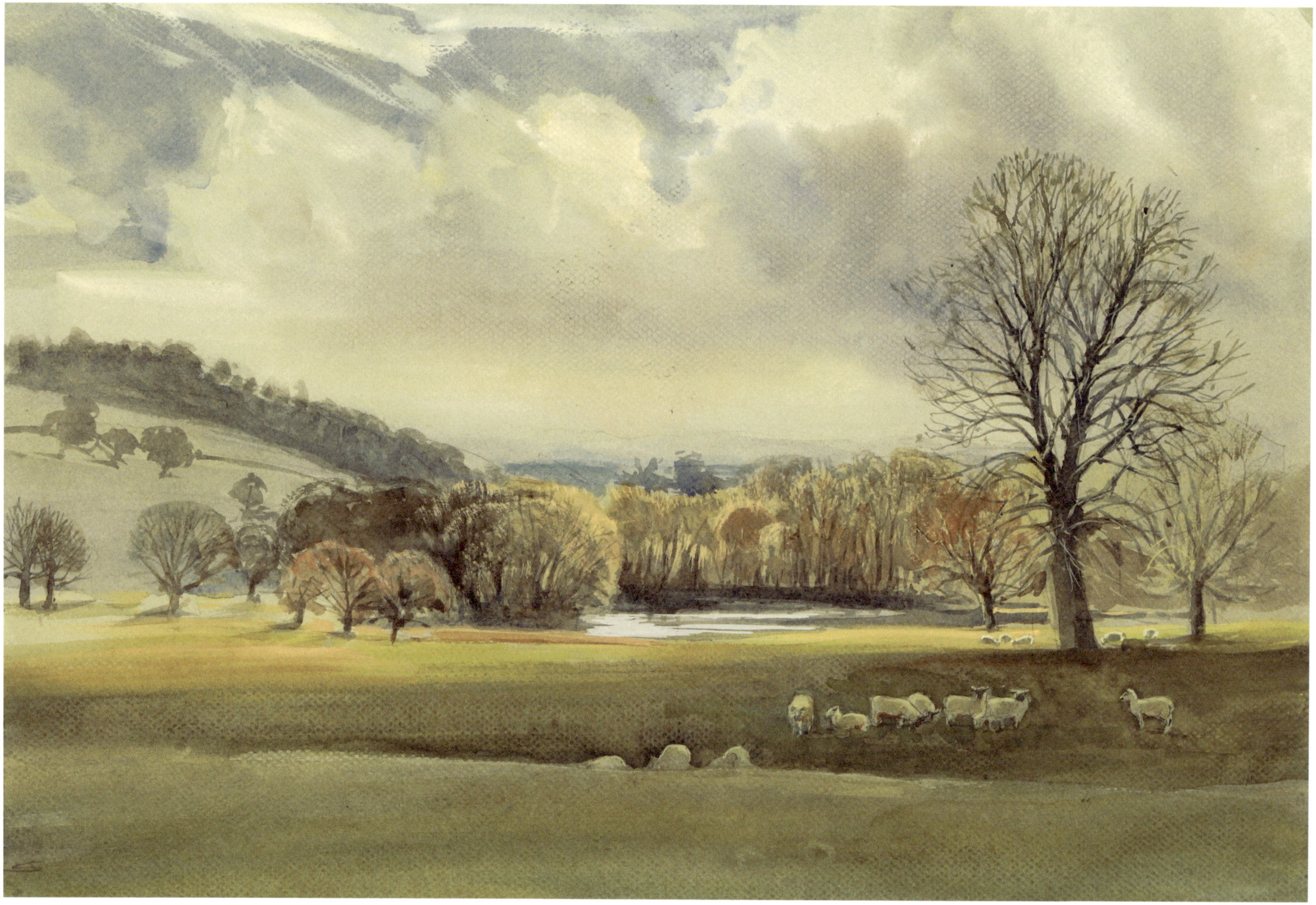

*Berrington Hall. The prospect from the south-facing portico of the Hall (watercolour).*

# BERRINGTON HALL

## Herefordshire 1776

In 1776 the Hon Thomas Harley, after making a fortune in the City, was elected member of parliament for Herefordshire, a county where the Harleys had been large landowners for generations. He bought the Berrington estate near Leominster soon afterwards, and 'Capability' Brown was consulted and agreed to do the landscaping with his son-in-law, Henry Holland, building the house. Brown had no difficulty in choosing a fine commanding site on which to build. I suspect Lancelot was relieved not to be concerned with the myriad problems connected with building a new country house, and his successful collaboration with Holland had long been established, initially in their joint venture at Claremont.

Holland was a pioneer in introducing the plain French neo-classical style, which sought to portray 'the masculine, simple, and majestic manner of the ancient architects of Greece'. The lodge at Berrington is in the form of an un-ornamented triumphal arch and the main house is a square block with an impressive pedimented portico dominating the west front. From here there are magnificent views over the park and lake, and beyond to the Black Mountains in Wales.

The delight of the house to me is the delicious pink stone, which was quarried nearby on Shuttocks Hill and conveyed to the site by a specially constructed railway line. In front of the house there is a curving ha-ha, so that from the portico you are unaware of any interruption in the landscape.

The rolling and well-wooded Herefordshire landscape was the perfect backdrop for Lancelot Brown: all it required was minor improvements. An existing stream was dammed to create a 14 acre lake and the spoil was then turned into a large island. Clumps of trees were planted and the wonderful natural views completed the picture.

I painted at Berrington on a freezing January day of dramatic weather; a blizzard moments later became bright sunshine and vice versa. The hills around were covered in snow and there was a biting north wind, but fortunately I found two views where I could sit in my car and dry the stubbornly wet paper of my watercolour with the fan of the car heater. One of the skills with watercolour painting is judging when to add more paint into a damp or drying colour-wash. A basic rule is either wet into wet or let the paper dry before applying more paint. If a wet wash is introduced to a previous wash before it is totally dry it can cause nasty irregularities, commonly known as 'cauliflowers', on the painting surface.

OVERLEAF *Berrington Hall, detail (oil).*

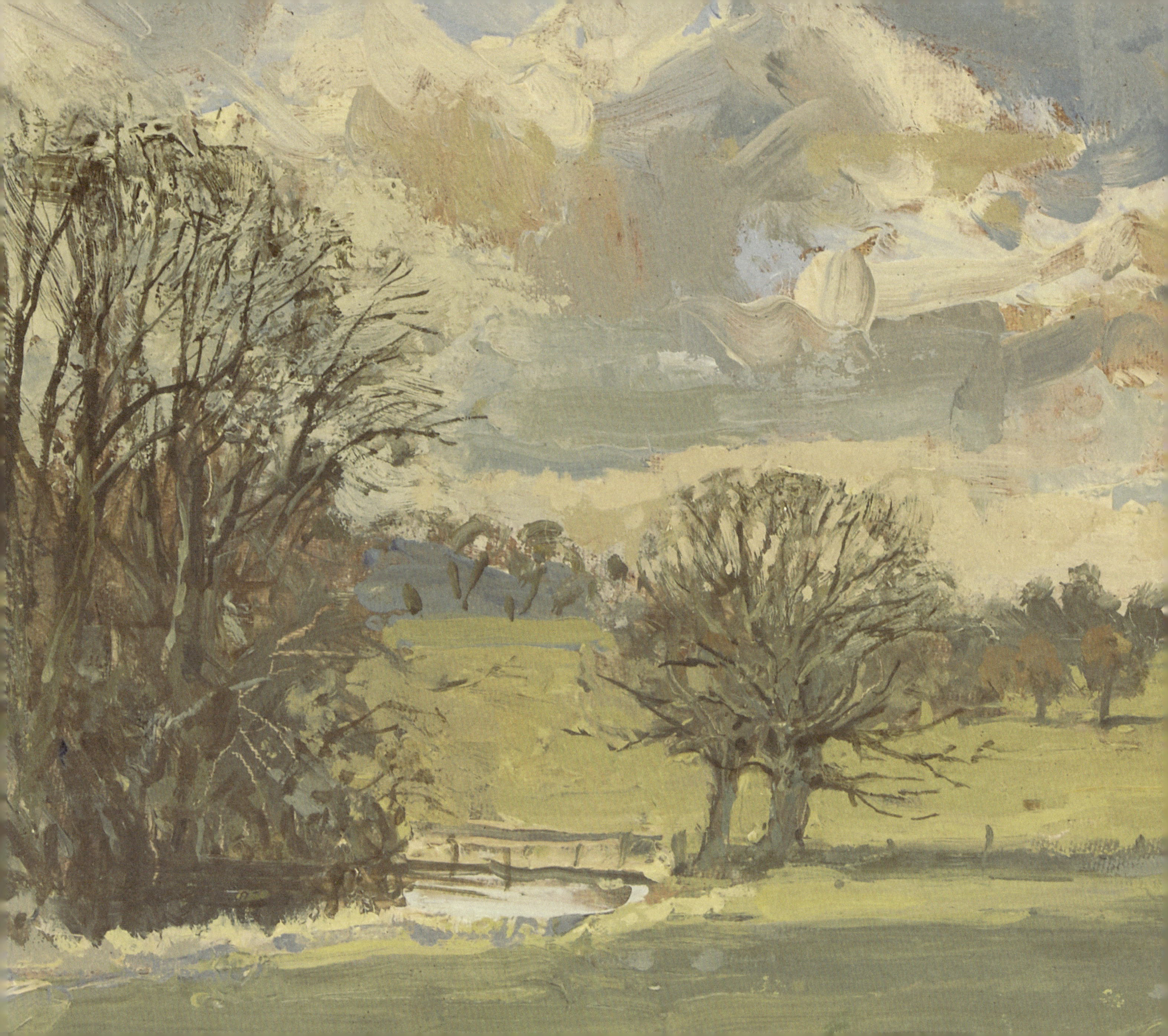

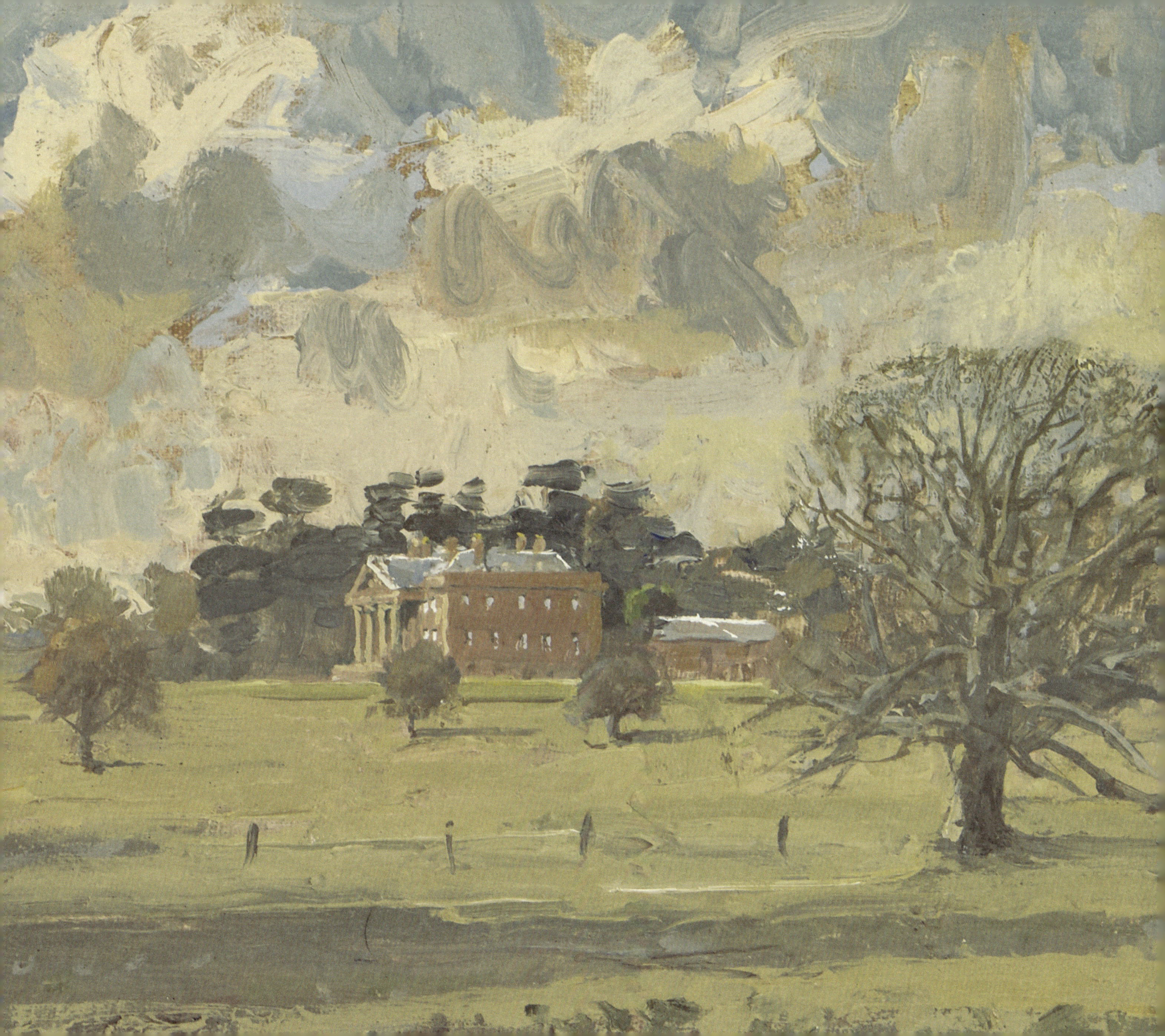

# SOUTHILL PARK

## Bedfordshire 1777

It is a strange trait of many a man to continue to spend extravagantly when his finances would be better governed by prudence. George Byng, 4th Viscount Torrington, was an example. In 1777 'Capability' Brown came to Southill to advise on landscape improvements, making a number of visits. Unfortunately, they coincided with Torrington being declared bankrupt and the work came to a premature halt.

A number of plants and trees were taken from Southill and replanted at nearby Wrest Park for Brown's old client and friend, the Marchioness Grey. These were not plundered but fully paid for. This however did not help the poor Viscount, who eventually sold the estate to Samuel Whitbread in 1795. A new broom and the money made by the brewery that bore Whitbread's name led to a renewal of the house.

After Brown's death Whitbread engaged Henry Holland to undertake considerable alterations, encasing the old brick house in stone and reorientating the main rooms so they faced south, with the entrance in the north. The overall effect is 'solid virtue preferred to outward show in tune with puritan Whitbread tradition'. The stonework caused considerable damp problems over the years and extensive dry rot was found some twenty years ago, leading to extensive refurbishment.

In this case I must admit that Brown was an excuse rather than a reason for going to Southill. Sir Samuel Whitbread is a fine watercolourist and he had been on a number of my courses in France. It was when travelling with them in Romania that his wife, Jane, encouraged me to come to Southill to see for myself the Brown legacy. A hill by the house is called Brown Hill and around are many old cedars, surely a trademark; whilst the landscape historian Johnny Phibbs has found a sunken walkway running through the park, which is again typical of Brown.

Another reason I wanted to visit was that Charles Whitbread, Samuel's eldest son, who now lives in the big house, is an eminent conservationist. His management of the substantial Southill estate is largely geared to sustainability and is farmed organically. The cattle are Old English White and generally the estate is an island of natural wealth in a surrounding agrarian monoculture devoid of life. With my wife Tricia we have farmed organically at home in Wiltshire for about twenty years on a much smaller scale and have found an amazing natural resurgence. Our garden buzzes with many species of bees and our woodlands echo to the song of the birds, so dependent on the insects they feed on.

I painted the old cedars which must have dated from Brown's time and the house that his son-in-law Henry Holland redeveloped, but I needed the cattle, which were grazing elsewhere, so having completed the landscape I moved my base to introduce a bovine theme in my picture. The advantage of painting in tempera or gouache is that pictures can be adapted and altered in the same way as when painting in oil. This is a great help when for instance cattle are always moving and one is not constricted by the frightening prospect of an incorrect brushstroke, as would be the case in a pure watercolour.

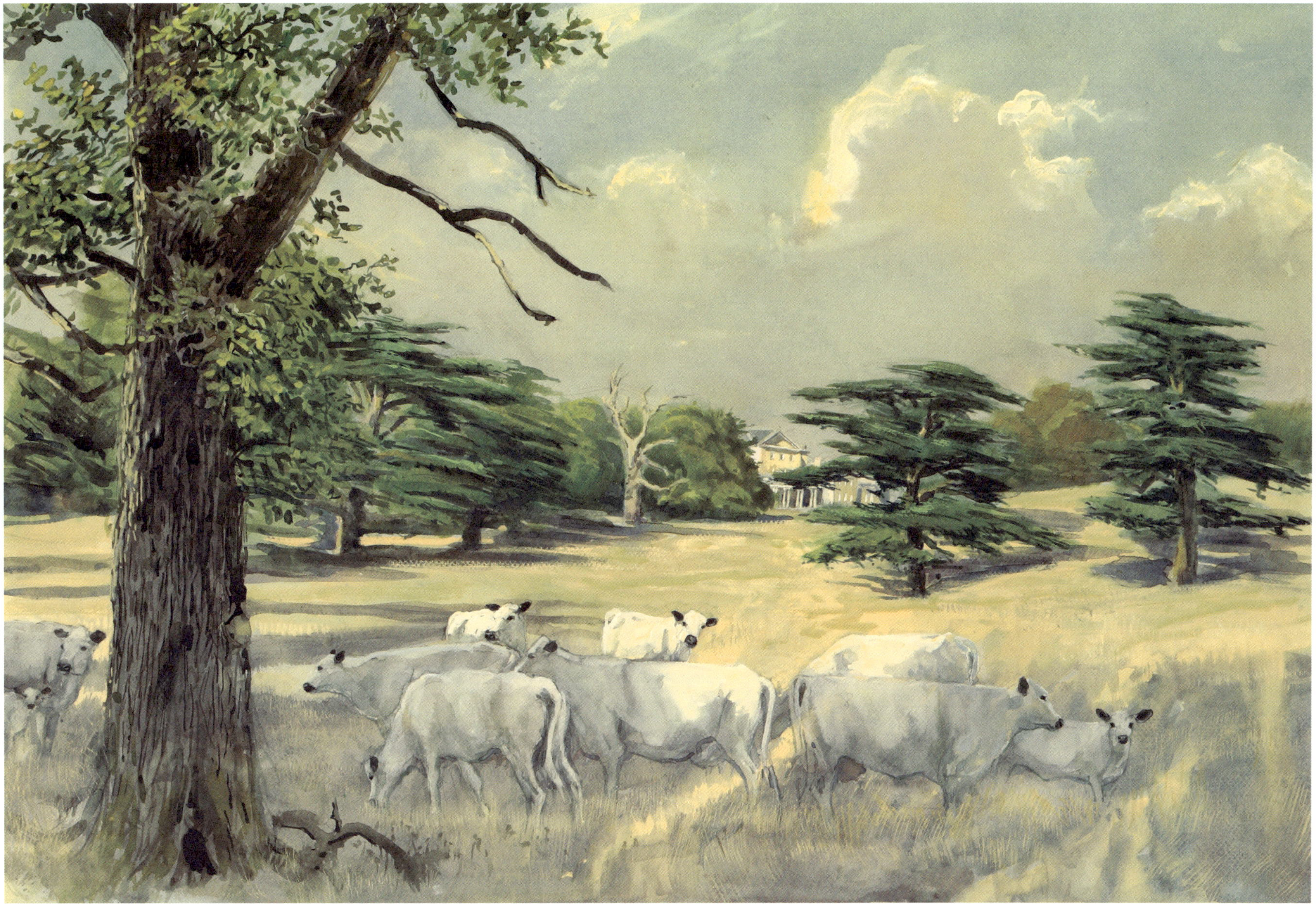

*Southill Park. The hill by the house known as Brown Hill is to the right and the cattle are Old English White (watercolour/gouache).*

# SLEDMERE HOUSE

## Yorkshire 1777

SLEDMERE is near Driffield in the Yorkshire Wolds. Its name means a 'pond in a marsh' but this belies the well-treed and drained park. I arrived to paint on a sultry day in July with a morning temperature already in the high 80s. The foundation stone for the present house was laid in 1751 by Richard Sykes, whose wealth stemmed from shipping and banking in Hull, and who also rebuilt much of the village and church.

Sledmere was inherited by his nephew Sir Christopher Sykes, who married well, and was young and ambitious. A knowledgeable horticulturalist and talented architect, he took an active interest in land improvement, landscape gardening and building. In the 1770s he commissioned plans, firstly from the designer Thomas White and then 'Capability' Brown ( which still exist), but Sir Christopher oversaw the work himself with some skilfull adaptations. He also undertook further improvements to the house with plans and advice from John Carr of York and Samuel Wyatt; and importantly he built up a close relationship with Joseph Rose, the foremost English plasterer of his day. Tragically in 1911 a fire broke out at Sledmere which lasted almost 18 hours and totally destroyed everything but the exterior walls. Fortunately most of the contents were saved by staff and villagers, including the drawings for the decorative plaster-work by Rose. Amazingly during the First World War, when manpower was at a premium, the house was restored to its former condition, and to my eye there is no clue that all is not original.

At the time of the fire the house belonged to Sir Tatton Sykes, one of a long line of colourful eccentrics. He wore eight coats at a

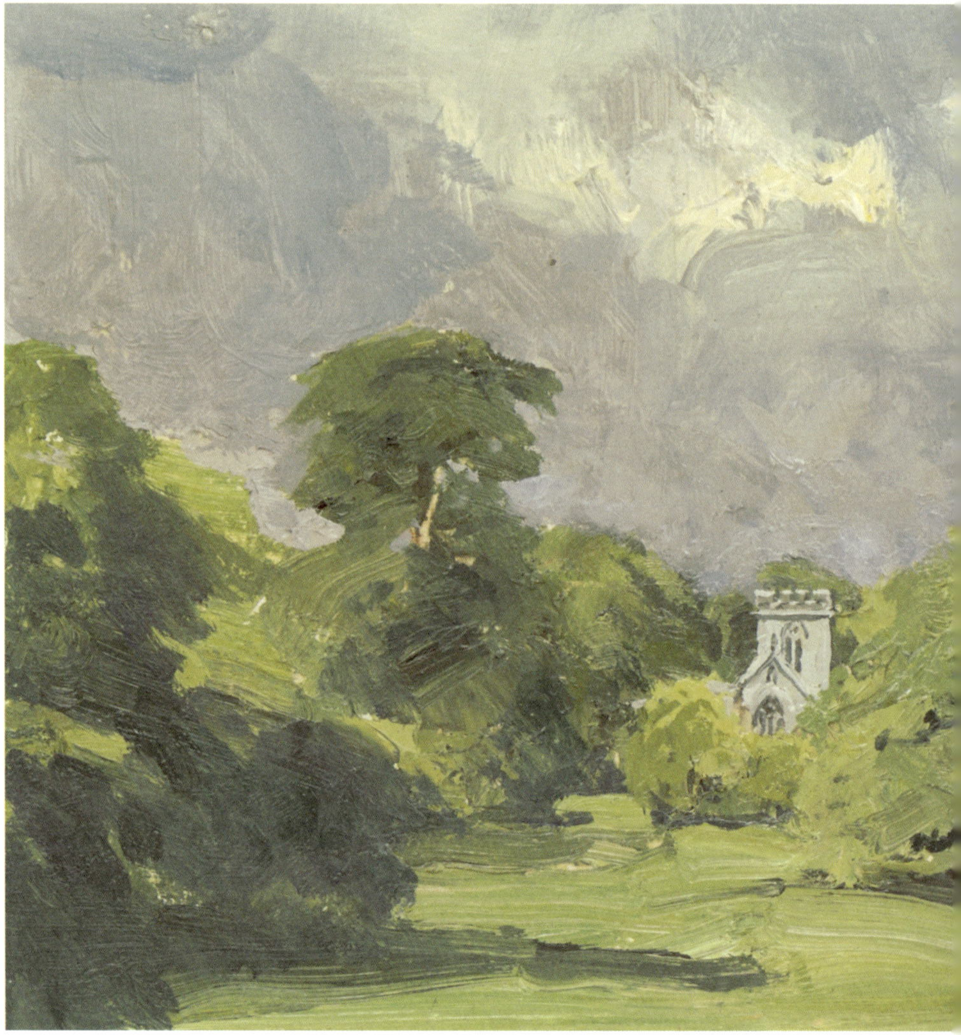

time, successively shedding them during the course of the day so to keep his body temperature constant. He married late and married badly. His bride was the eighteen-year-old Jessie Cavendish-Bentinck, known as Lady Satin Tights and thirty years his junior, whose massive debts and penchant for a string of lovers all but bankrupted the family.

Happily, no sign of her waywardness endures today under the caring ownership of the present Sir Tatton Sykes. I was shown to the elegant first-floor library by his secretary, to delve through great sheeves of estate plans and maps. However my quest was not academic but pictorial and the day was by far too good not to be outside. I was soon in deep shade painting a typical Brownian scene with a winding drive leading through the park trees to the house. Partly revealing itself above the trees was the church tower, the only medieval part, the remainder having been replaced in the eighteenth century by Sir Christopher Sykes.

BELOW *Sledmere House, the park. A detail can be seen on page 18 (oil).*

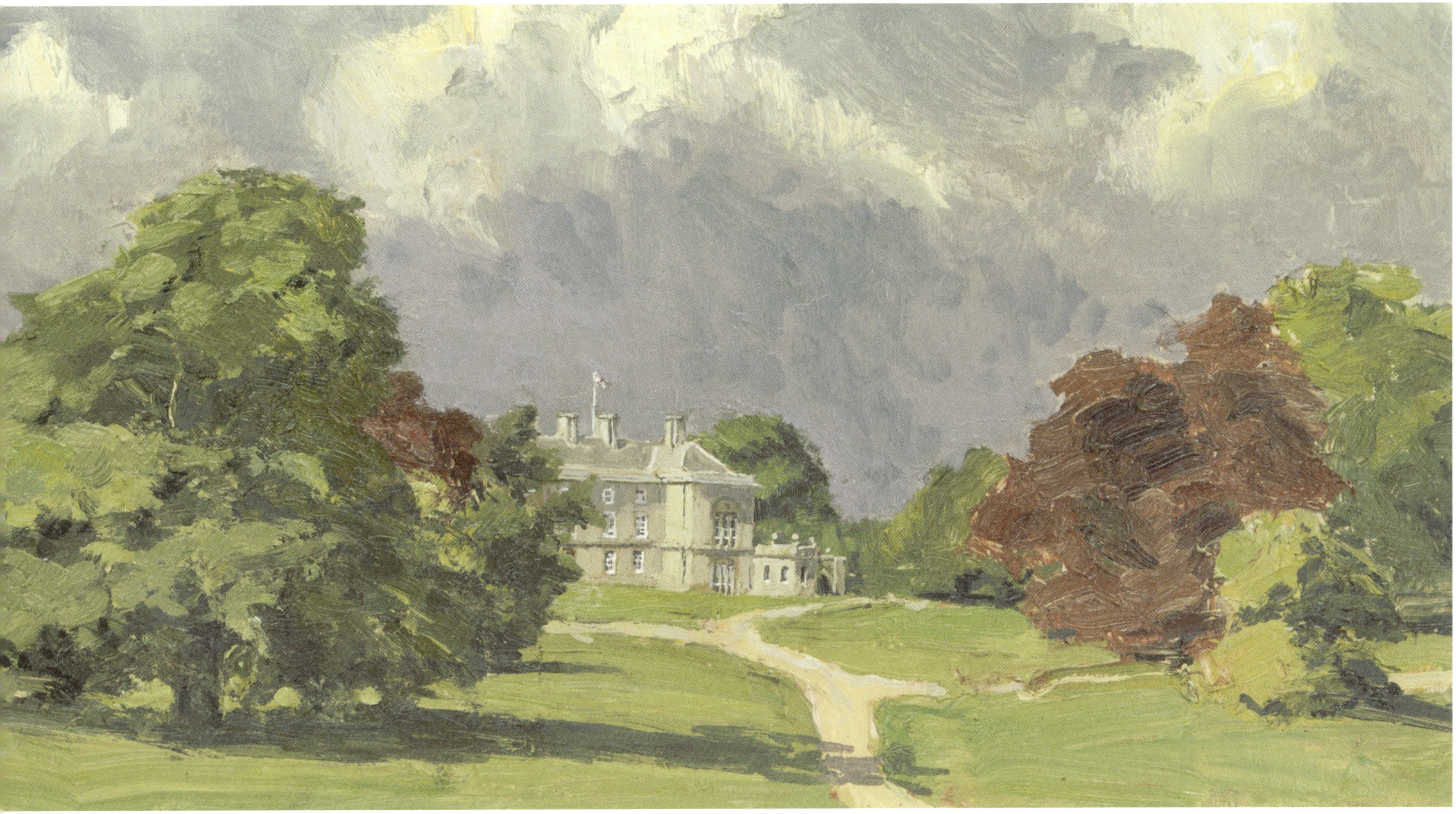

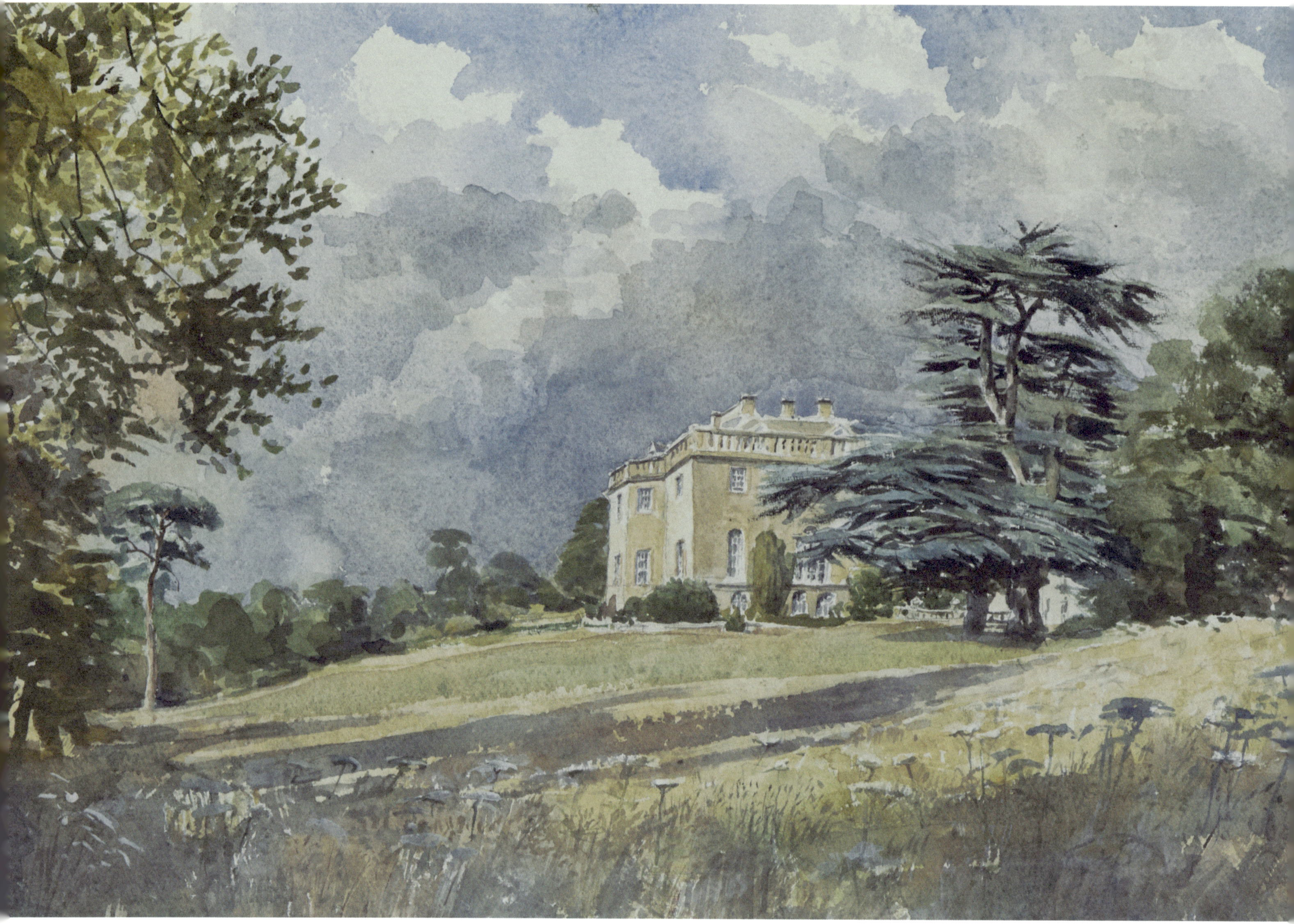

*Nuneham House was substantially altered by Brown with the help of Henry Holland (watercolour).*

# NUNEHAM HOUSE

## Oxfordshire 1778

Although the Oxfordshire estate at Newnham (note the original spelling) was purchased by the Harcourt family in 1722 it was not until 1755 that the 1st Earl of Harcourt decided to build what he described as a villa on the site. The operations included removal of the ancient village and church, both of which were rebuilt elsewhere. The gardens and some work on the grounds had already been undertaken and the situation might well have remained unchanged but for the Earl's tragic death trying to save a dog from a well.

The 2nd Earl, who until inheriting had been imbued with the reactionary ideas of his 'divine philosopher', Jean Jacques Rousseau, revised his views with his earldom and was drawn into Court circles.

Brown was summoned in 1778 and found that the alterations to the estate did not cause any major problems. The ground was well-drained and only needed minor contouring to achieve its 'capability.' Moreover the River Thames wound gently in the valley below, naturally creating a similar effect to the many serpentine lakes he had built elsewhere.

Brown also made extensive alterations to the house in collaboration with Henry Holland, including new servants' quarters and library, as well as the addition of a third storey and a central lantern to light the interior. Other alterations were subsequently done by Robert Smirke for Archbishop Harcourt half a century later.

The estate was requisitioned during the Second World War, handed back to the Harcourt family in the 1950s, who then sold it to Oxford University. It is now occupied by the Brahma Kumaris World Spiritual Centre.

There are fine trees near the house but the park below has been ploughed for arable farming. The views of the Thames are overgrown, so that what I suspect were delightful glimpses of the magnificent river are no longer to be seen. Rarely does a fine landscape survive the breaking up of a country estate. Here the eighteenth century house remains, with it's fine cedars of Lebanon, and there is a picturesque walk through woods to the south designed by Brown. What is encouraging is the management of what remains. Lawns give way to areas of grassland rich in wildflowers and the remaining old trees are obviously being nurtured for their own sake and for that of wildlife.

I painted at Nuneham in August, when the hogweed was just going over and the uncut grass was full of seed heads. This gave me a useful foreground, where a well tended lawn would have been bland and boring. I also made use of a dark sky to make the house glow in the evening light. That same light cast long raking shadows, which with other distinct forms such as wild flowers (as in this picture), hedgerows or lines of trees give the artist an opportunity to go from a light area to a dark and so on through the view. Otherwise, in wider landscapes, shadows cast by clouds can give the same banding. Claude Lorrain put this to good effect in his great classical views, with ranges of misty mountains in mauves and blues interspersed with lighter passages, where the sun lights up a strip of country with perhaps a classical ruin well sited in the middle ground. This could almost be a description of a Brown landscape!

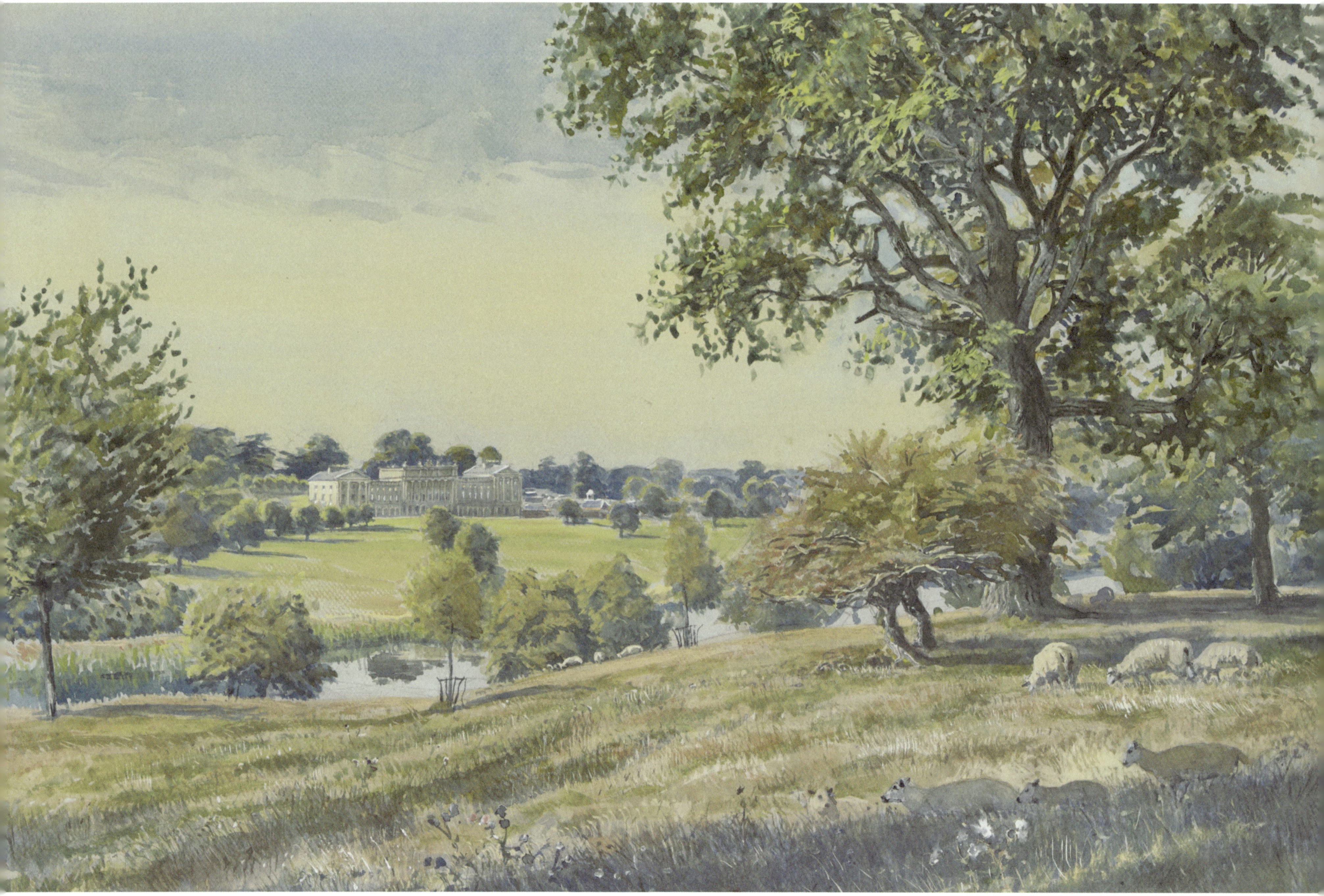

*Heveningham Hall. The park and recently dredged lakes. A detail of the sheep is shown on page 17 (watercolour).*

# HEVENINGHAM HALL

## Suffolk 1781

FOR ONE of Lancelot's last commissions he drew up two plans for landscaping the park surrounding Dutch merchant Sir Gerard Vanneck's new house in the glorious Blyth Valley in Suffolk. The elegant house was designed by Sir Robert Taylor with interiors by James Wyatt, and much of the work was done after Brown's death in 1783.

Heveningham (pronounced Henningham) shared the fate of so many houses in the twentieth century. Sold by the Vannecks to the government in lieu of death duties in 1970, it was later bought by an Arab who did some restoration work. Wyatt's great reception rooms were damaged by fire in 1984 and finally the property with 300 acres was bought in 1994 by Jon Hunt, the founder of the estate agents Foxton's. Since then enormous restoration work has been undertaken and some 5000 acres of surrounding land have been reacquired. 'Capability' Brown's original park is being restored in a magnificent manner. The once silted-up and overgrown lakes are now a ribbon of water running down the valley, with a new classical bridge in ashlar stone spanning their western end. Extensive areas of planting have been undertaken and fine park fencing lines the roads.

I am always drawn to walled gardens and here Arabella Lennox-Boyd has created an intricate and interesting garden, more reminiscent of the baroque of Wise and London than the naturalistic of Kent and Brown. The vegetables are contained in closely clipped box hedges, perhaps a mistake in that the box takes fertility and light from vegetables, which I regard as beautiful in their own right. The walled garden was originally shown on Brown's plan, but without the serpentine crinkle-crankle wall in mellow eighteenth-century brick, a feature not typical of Brown.

Another area of partly woodland garden has been designed by Tom Stuart-Smith. The result is a stimulating contrast in informality, the flowers in the dappled shade of the great old trees giving a much more natural effect. The winding path takes you through a North American garden dominated by golden rod to the orangery, now totally restored and looking out on another part of the park. To the south of the house the ground rises up in a great amphitheatre, where Tim Wilkie has designed a minimalist series of terraces curved in a semicircle above a long rectangular pool. This is reminiscent of a similar feature in the gardens at Claremont, designed by Charles Bridgeman in 1720, which, some fifty years after, was planted with trees by Brown to disguise it!

The stables are also shown on Brown's original plan. They are particularly attractive, built again in warm brick of faded red which seems to almost radiate heat around an oval yard, with a pretty white cupola on the roof.

I first visited Heveningham in 1974 when the house was in a neglected state and all around lay unloved land, either deserted or intensively farmed. The state rooms were empty and its fate then was uncertain. A university friend, Norman Hudson, who subsequently gained his reputation by advising The Historic Houses Association and publishing the annual Hudson's *Historic Houses and Gardens* guides to houses open to the public, showed us around. He was then working for Suffolk County Council, on whom responsibility for this white elephant had been foisted. It seems difficult to believe how times have changed. In the thirty years since the 1980s great fortunes have been made and now houses like Heveningham are treasured and their dignity restored. For the first time since 1914 a prosperous future can be envisaged for the great houses of England.

The problem often on a country estate is not what to paint but how to limit the choice to one or two pictures. There is just so much that I want to do! Apart from the greater landscape with its lakes and clumps of trees, other specific features at Heveningham – such as the ice house, the walled garden, stable yard and the fine new classical bridge – all have Brown characteristics. In the view I chose I found a group of ancient oaks on a mound, the lake below and the house on the high ground beyond with other clumps of trees, some old and some replanted, a view that almost breathed the classical landscape foreseen in the plans drawn up by 'Capability' Brown.

# ACKNOWLEDGEMENTS

Ask a busy person if you want something done. I am indebted to HRH The Prince of Wales for his scholarly foreword.

My first introduction to Lancelot Brown was through John and Kitty Anderson of Kirkharle and since then they have been unstintingly supportive of my endeavours.

Jane Brown through her book *Lancelot 'Capability' Brown, The Omninipotent Magician* gave me the an atmospheric background and the facts for my writings. She has also been generous in advice. Can I also make a posthumous acknowledgement to the other great author on Brown, Dorothy Stroud.

Ceryl Evans at the Landscape Institute has helped me enormously with contacts at various properties.

The National Trust is an important player in the Tercentenary celebrations and have been more than helpful in giving me access to their properties. Might I choose Alison Dalby, Katie Bond and Phil Sharp for special mention.

This year and next will be busy times for those landowners who own a Brown landscape. Indeed their fortune might appear a misfortune when all the academics have finished pouring over every aspect of his work. I suspect they will all feel thoroughly mauled. I however found at the properties I was fortunate enough to visit a great deal of courtesy and kindness in not only showing me around but making available archivists and other experts at their disposal. I would like to thank them all for making this whole project of mine possible.

Jeremy Musson, John Phibbs, Judith Christie, Karen Wiseman, Susan Campbell, Sarah Greenwood and Norman Hudson all played a part in various ways in helping me in my journey of discovery in writing this book.

Beth Walker and Graham Shackleton both helped with Photography.

My children, Emily, Polly, Chloe and Julian and my grandson, Hugo, were all roped in to help with IT and showed great patience. Rosemary McDonald and Liz Leckie both proof read and constructively criticised.

I however would not have succeeded at all but for the enthusiasm and patient editing undertaken by my long-suffering publisher, David Burnett, of Dovecote Press.

I am lucky to have as one of my oldest friends, Humphrey Stone, who is among our pre-eminent book designers. He knew how inefficient I would be in presenting the book but still with the greatest goodwill put into beautiful order my random daubings and scribbles.

Finally the greatest support came from my wife, Tricia, who nurtured me physically and mentally through this whole project and was always there to pick up the pieces at difficult moments.

# INDEX

# THE SUBSCRIBERS

The publisher would like to thank all those listed below, as well as those who chose to omit their names.
Their support helped make this book possible.

Robert and Clare Adams
Katherine Alker
Rosamond W. Allen and Paul E. Landry
Katherine Astor
Philip Astley-Jones
Caroline and Edward Armitstead

Joe Barclay
Alice Berkeley
Val Birrell
Richard and Julie Bonham-Carter
Rupert and Anna Bradstock
Jill de Bretton-Gordon
Charles Buckston
Susan Burlingham

John Carroll
Bernard and Caroline Cazenove
Judith A. Chrisite
Fiona A. Clare
Ginnie Clotworthy
Christine Cogram
Guy Collinssplatt
Deborah Condon
Jennifer Coombs
Edmund and Angelica Cotterell

Paul Dallyn
C. D. Daukes
Louis Deliss
Gerard Downes

Lord Eden
Pamela Edwards
Robert Elkington

Nigel W. Fawkes
Mr and Mrs Richard Firth
The Lady Flight
Claire Fitzalan Howard
Sarah and Peter Fitzgerald
F. Fitzherbert-Brockholes
Richard Foster
Simon Fowler

The Garden Tour Ladies
Anthony and Annie Garnett
Dodie Garnier
Sarah and Simon Garnier
C. A. G. Gibson
Philip C. Godsal
Nigel Goodman
William Gueterbock
Mr Carol Gurney
Gareth Gwilt

Ursula von Hake
Paul Hardy
Friedrich-Wilhelm and Laetitia Haniel
Barbara Harland
S.M.C. Henderson
Peter Hickling
Will and Janine Hillary
Michael and Veronica Hodges
Norman Hudson OBE
Pepi Hughes
Alexander Hunter

Anne and Robert Iliffe

Mrs Michael Jaffé
Rachel James

Fiona Langdale
Suzie Leon
Michael Jodrell
John Langham CBE
Susanna Lyell
Karen Lynch

Charles and Annmarie Mackay
Carina and Bill Maitland
Carola Mangnall
Michael and Caroline Mann
Mark Mansell
Virginia Mayhew
Michael McAvoy
Colin McCorquodale
Rowan and Janet McFerran
Robin McLaren
John and Sarah Middleton
P. D. Miles
Roger and Jane Millard
Robert and Caroline Miller
Therese Minton
Jonathan and Dee Montagu-Pollock
Duncan Montgomery
Stephen and Benetta Morant
Brigid Moreton
Mr and Mrs Robert Myers

Alec I. Nicholson

Margaret Oborne
Jane Onslow
Paddy and Jane O'Riordan

Henry Page
David Panter
Christina Parker
Neil Pattenden
Isobel de Pelet
Penrhyn and Jane Pockney
Luke and Nicky Ponsonby
Michael and Penny Portman
Roger and Fiona Potter
Dr W. J. P. Price
Julian Prideaux

Robert Race
Jane and John Robins
Chloe Robson
Jamie Robson
Natasha Robson

Scilla
M. J. Scott Bolton
Sonya Scott Graham
Gabrielle Selson
William Shand
Susan Simpson
Madeleine Stanley
Julian Stinton
Richard Stirling-Aird
Mr and Mrs P. L. B. Stoddart
Michael and Chantal Stokely
John and Sheila Stoller
Leslie A. A. Stratford

Peter Thorp
Hugh Thwaites
John and Heather Tylor

Francesco di Valmarana
The Earl and Countess of Verulam
Amanda Vesey

Netta Wace
Danena Jane Walmsley
Justin Weir
Sir Samuel Whitbread KCVO
Peter and Diana Williams
Richard Wills
Major Tom Wills
Sylvia and Stephen Wingfield Digby
Mrs Karen Wiseman
Sir George and Lady Wombwell

Isobel Wood
John Wood
Lucy Wood
Min Wood

Avril Young